More Praise for *Islam without Extremes: A Muslim Case for Liberty*

"Akyol is doing important work that should have an impact well beyond his native Turkey." —*American Spectator*

"In this important book, Akyol balances a playfully dispassionate manner with an impassioned defence of the Muslim rationalist tradition, creating an even tone of reasoned principle—a tone that disarms the unwary as it creeps up in ambush."
—David Gardner, *Financial Times*

"Even-handed scholarly work. . . . [An] indispensable book."
—*Publishers Weekly*

"[*Islam without Extremes*] is highly recommended for anyone who wants to answer the question of whether or not Islam is an 'extreme' or viable option when examining issues of liberty, freedom and justice."—Elise Hilton, Acton Institute Power blog

"With grace and style . . . [Akyol] lifts the veil on the beautiful truths and harsh realities of a faith at war with itself."
—*Kirkus Reviews*, starred review

"Eminently readable." —*Booklist*

"Mustafa Akyol's timely book challenges the Muslim stereotypes formed in Western minds after Sept. 11."
—Fethi Keleş, TurkishReview.org

"Akyol presents several convincing explanations for the stagnation of Islam and the authoritarianism that is taking place in the name of Islam." —Sarah Wagner, InsightTurkey.com

"In a touching and deftly woven personal narrative, Mustafa Akyol illuminates one of the central challenges of East-West relations today: Islam's adaptation to modernity. He traces a direct line from the enlightened Islamic scholars of the Middle Ages to their counterparts in the contemporary world, underscoring the differences between progressive Islamism and the more controversial strains of political Islam. Throughout this fine book, he incorporates lessons from Turkey—both Ottoman and Kemalist—for other Muslim societies and even the West."
—Parag Khanna, author of *The Second World*

"Mustafa Akyol traces the often forgotten history of liberalism in Islam and provides an intellectual path for liberalization to flourish today. His case is compelling, coming as it does from someone who is both a faithful Muslim and a committed liberal. This book is a must-read for Americans and others of all religious commitments."   —Kris Alan Mauren, executive director, Acton Institute for the Study of Religion and Liberty

"Akyol is not afraid to tackle the most difficult issues facing Muslim leaders today, i.e. freedom of apostasy and freedom of blasphemy. . . . If you have any serious interest in Islam and its future, do make sure you read this." —Nidhal Guessoum, *Irtiqa*

"Whether or not you agree, Akyol deserves to be more widely read."   —Haroon Moghul, *Religion Dispatches*

"*Islam without Extremes* is undoubtedly an interesting and sincere call for reform in the Muslim world."   —*Sugar Street Review*

Islam without Extremes

Islam
without
Extremes

A Muslim Case
for Liberty

Mustafa Akyol, *1972 -*

W. W. Norton & Company

New York ✦ *London*

Epigraphs for part I and chapter 5 reprinted with permission of Cambridge University Press from *The Cambridge History of Islam*, vol. 2B. Copyright © 1970 by Cambridge University Press. Epigraph for chapter 1 reprinted with permission of the Acton Institute, from *Toward a Free and Virtuous Society* by Robert A. Sirico. Copyright © 1997 by the Acton Institute. Epigraph for chapter 2 reprinted with permission of Oxford University Press, from *What Went Wrong? Western Impact and Middle Eastern Response* by Bernard Lewis. Copyright © 1992 by Bernard Lewis. Epigraphs for chapters 3 and 8 reprinted with permission of the University of Chicago Press, from *Islamic Liberalism: A Critique of Development Ideologies* by Leonard Binder. Copyright © 1988 by the University of Chicago Press. All rights reserved. Epigraph for chapter 7 reprinted with permission of Benjamin R. Barber, from a paper presented at the Istanbul Seminars, organized by *Reset Dialogues on Civilization*. Copyright © 2008 by Benjamin R. Barber. Epigraph for part III reprinted with permission of Michael Novak, from *The Universal Hunger for Liberty: Why the Clash of Civilizations Is Not Inevitable* by Michael Novak. Copyright © 1994 by Michael Novak. Epigraph for chapter 9 reprinted with permission of Vincent Cornell, from his paper entitled "Islam: Theological Hostility and the Problem of Difference." Copyright © 1993 by Vincent Cornell.

For information about permission to reproduce selections from this book,
write to Permissions, W. W. Norton & Company, Inc.,
500 Fifth Avenue, New York, NY 10110

For information about special discounts for bulk purchases, please contact
W. W. Norton Special Sales at specialsales@wwnorton.com or 800-233-4830

Manufacturing by Courier Westford
Book design by Marysarah Quinn
Production manager: Julia Druskin

Library of Congress Cataloging-in-Publication Data

Akyol, Mustafa, 1972–
 Islam without extremes : a Muslim case for liberty / Mustafa Akyol. — 1st ed.
    p. cm.
Includes bibliographical references and index.
ISBN 978-0-393-07086-6 (hardcover)
1. Islam and state. 2. Secularism—Islamic countries.
3. Liberty—Relgious aspects—Islam. 4. Liberalism—Islamic countries.
I. Title.
BP173.6.A4297 2011
297.2'72—dc22

                          2011014936

ISBN 978-0-393-34724-1 pbk.

W. W. Norton & Company, Inc.
500 Fifth Avenue, New York, N.Y. 10110
www.wwnorton.com

W. W. Norton & Company Ltd.
Castle House, 75/76 Wells Street, London W1T 3QT

3 4 5 6 7 8 9 0

To my beloved parents, Tülin and Taha Akyol,
to whom I owe more than I could ever say

Being created free by God, man is naturally
obliged to benefit from this divine gift.

[Thus] state authority should be realized
in the way which will least limit the freedom
of the individual. . . .

The right of the sultan in our country
is to govern on the basis of the will of the
people and the principles of freedom.

His title is "one charged with kingship"
[after all], not "owner of kingship."

—Ottoman Muslim intellectual Namık Kemal,
in his journal *Hürriyet* (Liberty), July 20, 1868

Contents

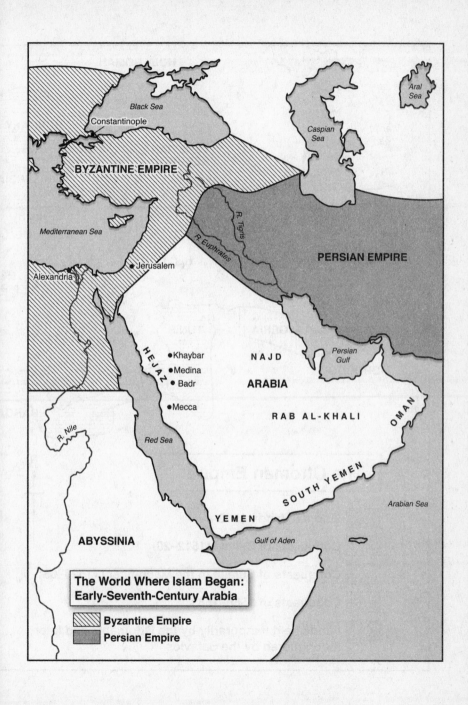

The World Where Islam Began:
Early-Seventh-Century Arabia

Byzantine Empire
Persian Empire

Black Sea
Constantinople
BYZANTINE EMPIRE
Mediterranean Sea
Jerusalem
Alexandria
Aral Sea
Caspian Sea
R. Tigris
R. Euphrates
PERSIAN EMPIRE
Persian Gulf
HEJAZ
Khaybar
Medina
Badr
Mecca
NAJD
ARABIA
RAB AL-KHALI
OMAN
R. Nile
Red Sea
SOUTH YEMEN
Arabian Sea
ABYSSINIA
YEMEN
Gulf of Aden

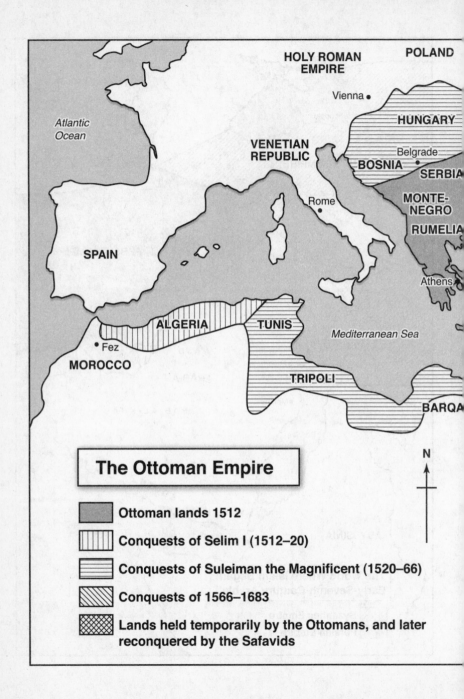

HOLY ROMAN
EMPIRE

POLAND

Vienna •

Atlantic
Ocean

HUNGARY

VENETIAN
REPUBLIC

Belgrade •

BOSNIA

SERBIA

MONTE-
NEGRO

Rome •

RUMELIA

SPAIN

Athens •

ALGERIA

TUNIS

Mediterranean Sea

• Fez

MOROCCO

TRIPOLI

BARQA

N

The Ottoman Empire

Ottoman lands 1512

Conquests of Selim I (1512–20)

Conquests of Suleiman the Magnificent (1520–66)

Conquests of 1566–1683

Lands held temporarily by the Ottomans, and later
reconquered by the Safavids

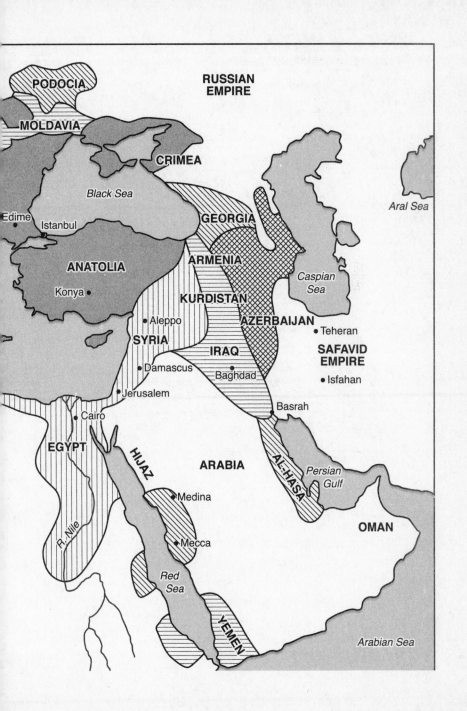

Glossary

Abbasid. Islamic dynasty that held the seat of the caliphate from 750 to 1258; its capital was Baghdad.

Abode of Islam (*dar al-Islam*). Lands ruled by Muslims according to the Shariah (Islamic law).

Abode of Treaty (*dar al-ahd* or *dar al-sulh*). Lands ruled by non-Muslims who negotiated treaties with a Muslim state.

Abode of Trial (*dar al-ibtila*). A term used by medieval Muslim scholars to define the world as a testing ground for humans to use their free will.

Abode of War (*dar al-harb*). Lands ruled by non-Muslims that are considered enemy territory.

Allah. The Arabic word for God, used by Muslims and Arabic-speaking Christians.

al-Maturidi. The tenth-century founder of a school of theology open to reason and free will; an alternative to Asharism.

Almohavids. A rigid Berber Muslim dynasty that conquered much of northern Africa and southern Spain in the twelfth century.

Anatolia. The westernmost point of Asia, also known as Asia Minor. It also has been used to refer to less privileged parts of Turkey vis-à-vis major cities such as Istanbul.

Anatolian Tigers. Successful Anatolia-based companies

that have emerged since the 1980s; similar to such other terms as the Celtic Tiger, Asian Tigers.

Asharism. School of theology, created by al-Ashari, that is skeptical of reason and free will.

ayatollah. "Token of God," the highest rank among Shiite clerics.

Banu Qurayza. An ancient Jewish tribe that lived in northern Arabia until its conflict with the Prophet Muhammad.

Basij. A paramilitary volunteer militia in the Islamic Republic of Iran, active in "morality" policing and suppression of dissidents.

Battle of Badr (624). The first military encounter between the Muslims of Medina and the pagans of Mecca.

Battle of Siffin (657). A part of the first Muslim civil war, fought on the banks of the Euphrates between the supporters of Ali and the supporters of Muawiyah.

Battle of the Trench (627). An unsuccessful siege of Medina by the pagans of Mecca.

Battle of Uhud (625). The second military encounter between the Muslims of Medina and the pagans of Mecca.

Bedouin. A predominantly desert-dwelling, nomadic, Arab ethnic group.

bey. An honorific Turkish title for men.

bid'a. "Innovation"; an unacceptable departure from the alleged tradition of the Prophet Muhammad.

burqa. An all-enveloping garment worn by some Muslim women.

caliph. A "successor" to the Prophet Muhammad and thus the leader of the Muslim community for Sunnis. The first four successors were the Rightly Guided Caliphs. The institution itself is called the caliphate.

Committee of Union and Progress (CUP or *İttihat ve*

***Terakki Cemiyeti*)**. A revolutionary group founded by a branch of the Young Turk movement in 1889; it took total control of the Ottoman Empire after 1913.

Coptic Christians. A major ethnoreligious group in Egypt.

dhimmi. Non-Muslims—typically, Jews and Christians—who received "protected" status in Islamic lands.

Directorate of Religious Affairs (*Diyanet İşleri Başkanlığı*). The official religious body formed by the Republic of Turkey in 1924 to replace the Ottoman religious institutions. Based on the Hanafi school.

Ecumenical Patriarch. The Greek patriarch of Constantinople, first among equals in the Eastern Orthodox communion.

efendi. An honorific title for men in the Ottoman Empire.

fatwa. A legal opinion issued by a Muslim religious scholar.

fez. A red cap worn by Ottoman men before the 1925 Hat Reform in Turkey.

fiqh. Islamic jurisprudence as developed by jurists. Shariah is the ideal, *fiqh* (*fıkıh* in Turkish) is the actual practice.

Franks (or sometimes **Francs)**. Western Europeans in the Islamic Middle East, often associated with crusading armies.

Garpçılar. "Westernists"; a particularly secularist group among the Young Turks of the late Ottoman Empire.

Hadiths. "Reports, news, sayings"; a collection of literature that claims to communicate the Sunna (tradition) of the Prophet Muhammad.

Halakha. The legal side of Judaism, as distinct from Haggadah, the nonlegal material.

Hanafi. Major Sunni Islamic law school, often the most flexible and lenient.

Hanbali. Major Sunni Islamic law school, often the most rigid. Its modern form is Wahhabism, practiced primarily in Saudi Arabia.

Hejaz. The west-central region of the Arabian Peninsula, where Mecca and Medina are located.

Herod. The name of successive kings who ruled the Holy Land before and during the time of Jesus.

Herodian. A Jewish political faction, the partisans of Herod.

hijra. The "migration" of the Prophet Muhammad from Mecca to Medina in 622.

hodja (or *hoca*). "Teacher"; Turkish term for learned men, often religious but also secular.

hurriyah. "Freedom" or "liberty" (*hürriyet* in Turkish).

ijtihad. "Striving, truth-seeking"; independent reasoning in the interpretation of Islamic law.

imam. Prayer leader in Sunni Islam, often one in an official or governmental post. He plays a more prominent role in Shiism as a successor to the Prophet.

Independence Tribunals. Arbitrary courts that Turkey's Kemalist regime established to eliminate political opponents.

intellectualism (or **rationalism**). In theology, the idea that God is rational and that His principles can be understood (at least partly) by the human intellect.

iqta. Land grant from a ruler in return for military or administrative services by a client.

Islahat Edict (*Islahat Hatt-ı Hümayunu*). The Ottoman "Reform" declaration of 1856, which established full legal equality for citizens of all religions.

Islamic Party of Malaysia (PAS). A political party that aims to establish Malaysia as a country based on Islamic law.

Islamism. A modern political ideology devising an "Islamic state" by borrowing from Islam as a religion but also from other ideologies such as socialism and nationalism.

istihsan. "Legal preference" for the sake of the common good; a tool used in Islamic jurisprudence.

Jabriyyah. "Proponents of enforcement"; early Islamic school that denied free will and promoted predestination.

Jadidism. From the word *jadid* (new), an Islamic renewal movement in late-nineteenth- and early-twentieth-century Russia, in contrast to the conservative Qadimism.

jahiliyah. "Ignorance"; a Muslim term describing the pre-Islamic period in Arabia.

Jahmiya. An early and little-known Islamic sect with views similar to those of the Mutazilites.

Jamaat-e-Islami. An Islamist political party in Pakistan founded in 1941.

jihad. "Struggle" for God; not necessarily but often a military effort for the defense or the advancement of Islam and the Muslim community.

jihadism. Extremist Islamist movement that focuses on military *jihad*, often by way of terrorism.

Ka'ba. Literally, "cube"; the cube-shaped main Muslim sanctuary in Mecca, believed to have been built by Abraham and his son Ishmael as the world's first monotheist temple.

kadi (or *qadi*). Religious judge or municipal commissioner (*kadı* in Turkish) in Muslim lands.

kanun. Sultanic law in the Ottoman Empire used to complement and at times replace Islamic law.

Karaite. A Jewish sect that accepts only the Torah as religious law and repudiates the Talmud.

Kemalism. Political ideology—devised by Mustafa Kemal Atatürk and his followers—that focused on nationalism, secularism, and "statism."

Kemalist Revolution. The political and cultural revolution in Turkey between 1925 and 1950 under the rule of Mustafa Kemal Atatürk and his followers.

Kharijites. "Dissenters"; a militant sect in early Islam that denounced all other Muslims and waged war on them. Only a moderate form has survived to date, and it is very marginal.

Khilafat Movement. A political campaign by Muslims in India to influence the British government and to protect the Ottoman caliphate in the aftermath of World War I.

kufr. "Blasphemy" or "disbelief." One who is in *kufr* is a *kafir*, an infidel. The term literally means "to hide by covering," so a *kafir* is one who "hides" the truth even though he has seen it.

laiklik. The self-styled official secularism of Republican Turkey; adopted from the French word *laïcité*.

madrasa. "School" in Arabic; more commonly, a place for Muslim learning.

Mahdi. Muslim messianic figure expected to return in the "end times." More important in Shiite theology than in Sunni doctrine.

Maliki. One of the four schools of law in Sunni Islam.

Mecca. Islam's holiest city, where the Ka'ba, the object of Muslim pilgrimage, is located.

Mecelle (*Mecelle-i Ahkâm-ı Adliye*). The civil code of the Ottoman Empire in the late nineteenth and early twentieth centuries. It was based on the Hanafi legal tradition but also included many adaptations.

Medina. Islam's second-holiest city, where the tomb of the Prophet Muhammad is located.

mihna. "Trial"; specifically, the inquisition established by the Abbasid caliph al-Ma'mun in the early ninth century.

Milli Görüş. "National Outlook," Turkey's main political Islamist movement founded in the late 1960s; it has morphed into various political parties.

mufti. A specialist in Islamic law who is eligible to deliver a *fatwa*, or legal opinion.

Muhammad. The Prophet of Islam who received the revelations of the Qur'an. Unlike Jesus in Christianity, Muhammad had no superhuman qualities, according to the Qur'an, although Muslim tradition later attributed to him some superhuman aspects.

mujahid. One who engages in *jihad*, the holy struggle for God.

mullah. A Muslim cleric educated in Islamic theology and sacred law.

Murjiites. "Postponers"; a school of theology in early Islam that promoted pluralism by saying that theological disputes should be "postponed" to the afterlife to be settled by God.

MÜSİAD. The Independent Industrialists' and Businessmen's Association of Turkey, founded in 1990 by conservative Muslim businessmen.

Muslim. "One who submits" and becomes an adherent of Islam by testifying, "There is no god but God, and Muhammad is His messenger."

Muslim Brotherhood (*Ikhwan al-Muslimun*). The world's oldest and largest Islamist political group, founded in 1928 in Egypt by schoolteacher Hasan al-Banna.

Mutawwa'in. "Volunteers" (sing.: *Mutawwa*); a casual term for the government-sanctioned religious police in Saudi Arabia.

Mutazilites. Followers of a school of theology in early Islam that defended free will and emphasized the legitimate role of reason as well as revelation in the pursuit of truth. Their membership declined after the third century of Islam, but traces of their philosophy survived, most notably, in the Hanafi and Maturidi schools.

Naqshbandis. Members of a major spiritual order (*tarikat*) in Sufism.

National Action League. A Syria-based pan-Arab movement active between 1932 and 1940.

Nizam-ı Cedid. "New Order"; a series of Ottoman reforms under Sultan Selim III in the late eighteenth century.

Nizamiye courts. Secular "regulation" courts initiated by the Ottoman Empire in 1869.

Nur movement. Popular civil Islamic movement in twentieth-century Turkey inspired by the writings of Said Nursi. Its members are known as Nurcus.

Organization of the Islamic Conference (OIC). An international organization founded in 1969 to safeguard the rights of Muslims worldwide. Fifty-seven Muslim-majority states are members.

Orientalist. A Western scholar who studies the societies and cultures of the Orient—i.e., the "near" and "far" East.

Ottomanism. The nineteenth-century Ottoman policy of establishing equality by creating an "Ottoman" identity, regardless of religion or ethnicity.

pan-Islam. The idea that all of the world's Muslims should be unified in a political structure.

paşa. A military commander or distinguished statesman in the Ottoman Empire.

patriarch. The spiritual and political leader in Eastern Christian denominations.

patrimonialism. A form of governance in which all power flows directly from an autocratic leader.

People of Reason (*ahl al-ray*). The early Islamic juristic and theological school that relied on reason as the second source after the Qur'an and suspected the authenticity of the Hadiths. They opposed the People of Tradition.

People of the Book (*ahl al-Kitab*). Qur'anic term for

non-Muslim religious groups with a revealed scripture; typically refers to Christians and Jews.

People of Tradition (*ahl al-hadith***)**. The early Islamic juristic school that upheld the Hadiths of the Prophet as an alternative to reason. They opposed the People of Reason.

Pharisees. Conservative Jews during the time of Jesus who preached a strict adherence to Jewish law and rejection of Hellenism.

Progressive Republican Party (PRP or *Terakkiperver Cumhuriyet Fırkası***)**. A liberal political party founded in Republican Turkey in 1924 and closed down by the regime six months later.

Qadarites (or **Qadaris)**. One of Islam's earliest schools of theology, whose members defended free will and opposed the political tyranny of the ruling Umayyad dynasty. They were the precursors of the Mutazilites.

Qadimism. From the word *qadim* (old), a movement that promoted Islamic traditionalism in late-nineteenth- and early-twentieth-century Russia, especially in contrast to the reformist Jadidism.

qiyas. "Analogical reasoning," a tool used in Islamic jurisprudence.

Qur'an. Literally, "recitation"; Muslim scripture revealed to the Prophet Muhammad in segments over a period of twenty-three years.

Rabbanite. The medieval Jewish tradition that respected the authority of oral law (Talmud), as opposed to the Karaites, who only valued the scripture (Torah).

Ramadan. The holy month of the Islamic lunar calendar during which Muslims fast between dawn and sunset.

Republican People's Party (RPP or **CHP,** *Cumhuriyet*

Halk Fırkası). The political party, founded in 1923 by Mustafa Kemal Atatürk, that established a "single-party regime" by eliminating all political opposition.

riba. "Excess, increase," a financial action denounced in the Qur'an. There is consensus that this refers to usury; whether it also refers to the charging of interest continues to be debated.

Rightly Guided Caliphs. A term used by Sunni Muslims for the first four successors of the Prophet. Shiites only revere the fourth caliph, Ali.

Sadducees. A party of elitist Jews during the time of Jesus who were willing to cooperate with Rome and incorporate Hellenism into their lives.

sahih. Literally, "sound"; Hadiths that are considered to be authentic reports from the Prophet Muhammad.

Salafi. A Muslim individual or movement desirous of returning to the ways of the *salaf*, the pious forebears or the earliest generations of Islam. While some nineteenth-century Salafis were modernists, the movement increasingly turned fundamentalist.

Saracens. European term used during the time of the Crusades to refer to Arabs and even all Muslims.

Saudi. "Of Saud," a dynasty that has founded and ruled successive states in central Arabia since the mid-eighteenth century.

Şeyh-ül İslam. The highest cleric in the Ottoman state, responsible for guiding the executive according to the Shariah.

Shafi. A major Sunni Islamic law school, often more conservative than Hanafi.

Shariah. Islamic law developed by scholars; based on the Qur'an and the Hadiths.

sharif. "Noble, exalted"; honorary title given to descendants of the Prophet Muhammad.

Shiites. "Followers" of Ali, regarding him as the true successor of the Prophet Muhammad and believing in the divinely inspired wisdom of his bloodline. About 15 percent of all Muslims are Shiites.

shura. The Qur'anic principle of "mutual consultation."

Sicarii. "Daggermen"; an extremist splinter group of the Jewish Zealots, who assassinated Roman officials and their collaborators using concealed daggers called *sicae*.

Sola Scriptura. "By scripture alone"; the Protestant doctrine that the scripture contains all knowledge necessary for salvation.

Sufism. The inner mystical dimension of Islam, aiming at raising the God-consciousness of individual Muslims.

Sunna. The Prophet Muhammad's example for Muslims as recorded in the Hadiths.

Sunni. The main branch of Islam, which puts great emphasis on the Sunna (tradition) of the Prophet as a source of belief, along with the Qur'an. About 85 percent of all Muslims are Sunnis.

Taliban. Literally, "students"; a radical Sunni Islamist political movement that governed Afghanistan from 1996 to 2001.

Tanzimat Edict (*Gülhane Hatt-ı Şerifi*). The Ottoman "Reorganization" declaration of 1839, which initiated an era of extensive modernization.

tarikat. Literally, "way, path"; an Islamic religious order within the Sufi tradition.

ta'wil. Allegorical interpretation of the Qur'an and other religious texts, as opposed to literalism.

TÜSİAD. The Turkish Industrialists' and Businessmen's Association, the top business association in Turkey, founded in 1971; similar to the Business Roundtable in the United States.

Ulama. "Scholars"; traditionally used to refer to Islamic jurists and theologians (*ulema* in Turkish).

Umayyad. The first hereditary Islamic caliphate; a dynasty that ruled from Damascus from 661 to 750, when overthrown by the Abbasids.

umma. The worldwide Muslim community of believers.

urf. Local customs in any given society, which both the Qur'an and Islamic jurisprudence recognize.

vizier. A high-ranking official in the Ottoman Empire (*vezir* in Turkish); equivalent to a minister.

voluntarism. In theology, the idea that God should be defined as an absolute power whose actions cannot and should not be explained through reason; the opposite of intellectualism.

Wahhabi. Adherent of a strict and literalist interpretation of Islam based on the teachings of Muhammad Abd-al-Wahhab; a revived form of the Hanbali school.

waqf. Muslim religious foundation (*vakıf* in Turkish) whose profits are used for charitable purposes.

Young Ottomans. A group of Ottoman intellectuals who emerged in the 1860s and advocated a liberal agenda compatible with Islamic norms.

Young Turks. An intellectual and political movement that emerged toward the end of the nineteenth century and gradually dominated the Ottoman Empire. They were secularist and nationalist (especially when compared to the Young Ottomans).

zakat. "Purification"; almsgiving of some portion of a Muslim's wealth. One of the five pillars of Islam.

Zealots. A political movement in first-century Judaism that sought to incite the Jews to rebel against the Roman Empire.

Introduction

> Nothing is what it seems.
> —AL PACINO, in *The Recruit* (2003)

I GREW UP IN ANKARA, Turkey's capital, as (then) the only child of a middle-class family. My father was a newspaper columnist—a career I would also pursue—and my mother was a primary-school teacher. They were both Muslim believers but too busy with daily life to find time to teach me about religion. Therefore, when my grandfather, a very devout Muslim, suggested that he could help me become better acquainted with God, my parents happily supported the idea. At the time, I was about eight, not doing much during the summer holiday besides playing with other kids on the street; my grandfather lived, with my equally pious and bighearted grandmother, just a few blocks from our apartment. So we all agreed that I would visit my grandparents in the mornings and, after enjoying their delicious breakfasts, receive a crash course in Islam.

In the next couple of weeks, my grandfather spent a few hours every day showing me how to perform the regular Muslim prayers, took me to the neighborhood mosque, and taught me to form Arabic letters and words with colorful beads. My first big achievement was to write the pillar of the Muslim faith: *La Ilahe Illallah*, or, "There is no god but God." My grandfather also told me stories about prophets such as Yusuf (Joseph) or Musa (Moses), while I listened with juvenile curiosity and novice religiosity. I truly enjoyed learning about God and the religion He had revealed.

One day, in my grandfather's library, I came across a prayer book with three quotes on its back cover. The first two quotes were from the Qur'an, and they were about how and why God created humanity. One was the verse: "He it is Who made for you the ears and the eyes and the hearts; little is it that you give thanks."[1] I was deeply touched by this message. For the first time, I realized that my sight, hearing, and feelings are "given" to me by God. Surely, I said to myself, I should thank Him more.

But the third quote on the book's cover, which was from another source called Hadiths (sayings), was not moving but disturbing. "If your children do not start praying at the age of ten," it said, "then beat them up."

I was horrified. I knew that my grandfather—a kind, compassionate man—would never even talk rudely to me, let alone beat me. But here I was, eight years old, discovering that my religion—the religion I was so enjoying learning about—instructed parents and grandparents to hurt their children. I was shaken up.

When I brought this quote to the attention of my grandfather, he comforted me with a smile, reassuring me that the "beating" suggestion was for ill-behaved children, not nice ones like me. And such punishment was, he added, for their own good.

Although relieved by my grandfather's words, I was not fully satisfied. Why, I asked myself, would God ask parents to beat their children to force them into prayer? It seemed not only cruel but also unreasonable. Forcing a child—or any person—into a religious practice could never produce a sincere religiosity. Wouldn't a prayer be meaningless, I thought, if you were saying it not because you wanted to connect with God but because you wished to avoid a slap in your face?

THE LANDS OF THE UNFREE

Three decades have passed since those summer days in my grandparents' house, but my gnawing suspicion about the if-they-don't-pray-then-beat-them-up strategy has stayed with me. The more I studied Islamic literature and Muslim societies, the more I found examples of that oppressive mindset. And I continued to ask: Is this really what Islam enjoins?

Today, the same question haunts the minds of millions of my coreligionists—and millions of others. Is Islam a religion of coercion and repression? Or is it compatible with the idea of liberty— that individuals have full control over their lives and are free to be religious, irreligious, or whatever they wish to be?

There are many good reasons to ask these questions. Islamic societies in the contemporary world are really not the beacons of freedom. In extreme cases, such as Saudi Arabia, there is the weird phenomenon called the *Mutawwa'in*, the religious police, who monitor people on the streets and "correct" behaviors that they find "un-Islamic." If prayer time approaches and you are not preparing for worship, the *Mutawwa'in*, with sticks in their hands, may come by to ensure that you head to the mosque. They also force Saudi women to cover their entire bodies, and disallow even a friendly chat with the opposite sex. The Saudi kingdom also closely monitors its borders and bans "un-Islamic" products and publications. Other faiths such as Christianity are not allowed to proselytize—or even to exist within the kingdom's borders.

The Islamic Republic of Iran presents somewhat softer examples of oppression. There, women are granted better status than in Saudi Arabia, there is some public space for free discussion, and there are a few relatively democratic institutions, such as a parliament. But Iranian society is still very far from being free. Women are still forced to obey the perceived Islamic dress code. Families must remove satellite dishes from their rooftops so they won't be exposed to Western television. Political dissidents are crushed. And the final word in governance belongs to a group of mullahs, or clerics, who supposedly are guided by God—a claim that perhaps is possible to trust but impossible to verify.

Afghanistan, under Taliban rule from 1996 to 2001, was the worst case in the Islamic world, for it brutally suppressed even the slightest freedoms. Not only were women forced to wear the all-encompassing *burqa*, they also were completely excluded from public life. All sorts of "non-Islamic joys"—such as listening to music, playing chess, or even flying a kite—were banned by the Taliban regime. And those who broke these strident laws were punished in the harshest ways. The Taliban banned all other faiths and destroyed their ancient shrines and symbols, such as two 1,500-year-old statues of the Buddha in Bamiyan.

Saudi Arabia, Iran, and Afghanistan are extreme cases; most Muslim countries are not as repressive. Yet every Muslim country still suffers from a deficit of freedom, in varying degrees. According to the "freedom index" of Freedom House, a Washington-based institute, not a single Muslim-majority country can be defined as "fully free." Most nations don't have religious police, but they do still have serious deterrents to liberty. Apostasy—the abandonment of Islam for another faith—can bring strong social reaction or even legal persecution. Even in the West, some Muslims have proved to be oppressive by reacting violently against those who satirize or even criticize Islam— as experienced firsthand by writer Salman Rushdie, filmmaker Theo van Gogh, and the *Jyllands-Posten*, the Danish newspaper that published satirical cartoons of the Prophet Muhammad.

Given this seemingly rich evidence, many people in the West have concluded that Islam as a faith is incompatible with liberty. In the eyes of many Westerners, it is an intolerant, suppressive, and even violent religion. Why else, the reasoning goes, would Islamic societies be so unfree?

Before anyone rushes to that conclusion, let me relate a story.

UNDERSTANDING "JUST HOW BRUTAL ISLAM IS"

In November 2006, terrifying news about Khalid Adem, a Muslim Ethiopian immigrant living in Atlanta, shocked Americans. The man was found guilty of aggravated battery and cruelty to his own daughter. What he did, reportedly, was to use a pair of kitchen scissors to remove the clitoris of the two-year-old girl. At Adem's trial, his wife sadly explained her husband's logic: "He said he wanted to preserve her virginity. He said it was the will of God."[2]

About a year later, Warner Todd Huston, an American pundit, wrote about the incident on a popular website and denounced "this common Muslim practice of the mutilation of a little girl's private parts." He also made a broader inference. "We need to understand," he told his readers, "just how brutal Islam is in how it treats its most vulnerable members: girls and women."[3]

There was certainly an inexcusable brutality to this situation, and both the Muslim Adem and the non-Muslim Huston believed that it was the decree of Islam. Yet both were wrong. For what Adem did to his daughter is a practice—known as "female genital mutilation"—that comes not from the scripture of Islam but from a millennia-old tradition in Africa. It is based on an age-old assumption that women might be "immoral" if they enjoy sexual intercourse. Artifacts from Egypt indicate that the practice predates Islam, Christianity, and even recorded history.[4] Unfortunately, it is still widely practiced in Egypt, Sudan, and other parts of Africa—among not just Muslims but also other faith communities. In Ethiopia, whose population is 63 percent Christian, nearly four out of five women still were genitally mutilated just a few decades ago.[5] Besides the nature-worshipping animists, even a Jewish tribe in northeastern Africa maintains the terrible custom.[6]

So, on closer inspection, what seems at first glance a problem with Islam turns out to be a problem with some local tradition—something that passes from generation to generation without much questioning.

Should we take a hint?

Could other problems present in the Islamic societies of today stem not from religion but from the preexisting customs, attitudes, and mindsets of those societies?

And is it possible that even some Muslims themselves—Muslims like Khalid Adem, who wrongfully believed that mutilating his baby girl was "the will of God"—might not be aware of this discrepancy?

THE WORD OF GOD IN THE HISTORY OF MEN

My own "aha!" moment with the above question came at the age of seventeen, when I first read the entire Qur'an, in translation—something few Muslims I know ever do. To my surprise, almost none of the extremely detailed rules and prohibitions about daily life that I had seen in some ultraconservative "Islamic books" were there. The Qur'an was also noticeably silent on the issues of stoning adulterers, punishing drinkers, or killing those who abandon or "insult" Islam. Nor was there mention of an "Islamic state," a "global caliphate," or the "religious police." Many things that I see in the Muslim world and don't find terribly pleasant, I realized, are simply not in Islam's scripture.

This, in a sense, is not unusual. Every religion has a "core," often a text that is believed to be of some divine origin. Then this core unfolds into history—to be understood, interpreted, and misinterpreted by men. As Islam's divine core, the Qur'an, entered into human societies, many additional doctrines, rules, practices, and attitudes were added to the words of scripture. At certain fateful junctures in Islamic history (which I examine in this book), some particular interpretations of the Qur'an prevailed over others—not because they were necessarily more valid, but because they were politically or culturally more convenient.

Thus, the Islam of today carries the weight of fourteen centuries of tradition. Far worse, it even carries the weight of the political crises and traumas endured by Muslims in the past two centuries.

The better news is that not only is it possible to reinterpret Islam in newer, fresher ways, there also are signs that these new interpretations are likely to thrive. One key example is modern-day Turkey, where, as we shall see, there is an ongoing, silent, Islamic reformation.

Before rushing into Turkey, though, I need to relate another story.

Understanding How Brutal
"Non-Islam" Can Be

On a very cold and snowy morning in January 1981—just several months after my "summer school" at my grandparents' house—my mother woke me very early. Normally, she would prepare me for school, but she and I had other plans for that day. After a quick breakfast, we left home and took two separate buses to go to Mamak, a destitute neighborhood in the suburbs of Ankara. Our destination was not a park, not a mall, but a scary place: the military prison.

This was a huge facility with many barracks, all surrounded by electrified barbed wire. There were many soldiers holding machine guns, some looking down sinisterly from ugly watchtowers. Honestly, the whole scene looked very much like a gulag.

After we stood for about an hour at the prison entrance, the soldiers took us, along with a dozen other mothers and a few children, to a courtyard that was divided in half by a yard-wide fence of barbed wire. "Line behind the fence," one soldier yelled. "You have only ten minutes." Then I saw a group of inmates marching toward us in military fashion. The soldiers were yelling at them as well: "March! Left, right, left!" A few seconds later, the group was also ordered to chant the slogan "How happy is the one who says I am a Turk"—the famous motto of Mustafa Kemal Atatürk, Turkey's secularist founder. And then, as the inmates lined up on the other side of the barbed-wire fence, I came face to face with him—my father.

He was much thinner than four months earlier, the last time I had seen him, and his head was shaved. Yet he had the same big smile on his face, and he greeted us happily. As I remember vaguely, he told me that he was very comfortable at the prison and that he would be home soon. But he and my mother were hiding some bitter facts from me: There was systematic torture at Mamak Prison, and most inmates, including my father, were on trial for capital crimes.

For what? Well, for nothing but being a public intellectual. As I said, my father was a columnist, one with a particular political line: he was a member of the Nationalist Action Party (MHP) and the associated "nationalist" movement, which was mainly a reaction to a growing tide of Communism in Turkey. So my father wrote books refuting the Marxist-Leninist ideology and criticizing "Soviet imperialism." In *Violence in Politics,* he condemned all authoritarian regimes, focusing on the French, Bolshevik, and Iranian Revolutions and their similarities. He also opposed the militant tendencies in his own political camp. Hence, even some of the leftists respected him as a voice of reason on the right.

But the coup launched by the Turkish military on September 12, 1980, recognized no such nuances. The generals ordered the arrest of all politicians and activists from all camps, whose number, in the next three years, would amount to a staggering six hundred thousand people. Some of these detainees were held without trial for many months, only to be released later without any conviction. (My father's share was fourteen months in prison.) Thousands were subjected to brutal torture, during which 175 died, and many others were left disabled. Fifty people were sent to the gallows. The whole process, in the words of a Turkish liberal, was "an orgy of violence."[7]

The generals argued that they had launched the coup to "end the era of anarchy and terror" that beset Turkey in the late 1970s as a result of armed clashes between Marxist and nationalist militants. That was not untrue, but the terror the junta unleashed proved to be far greater. Besides, it sowed the seeds of future violence. The Kurdish inmates, who suffered the worst forms of torture in the infamous military prison in Diyarbakır, craved revenge after their release, and some of them, under the banner of the armed Kurdistan Workers Party (PKK), launched a terrorist campaign that would hit Turkey in the decades to come.

Notably, all this cruelty took place in Turkey, a Muslim-majority country, but it had almost nothing to do with Islam. The Marxists were against Islam, and while the nationalists respected it, their main motivation was patriotism. (These two opposing camps regarded the Islamic-minded youth, who remained paci-fist, as sissies.) And the most brutal of all camps, the military, followed the doctrine of none other than Atatürk—one of the most secularist leaders the Muslim world has ever seen.

In other words, on that cold winter day at Mamak Prison, I, as a Muslim kid, faced tyranny not in the name of Islam—as some Westerners would have readily expected these days—but in the name of a secular state. As I grew up, I observed even more examples of the same trouble. Instead of "religious police" forcing women to cover their heads, for example, I saw "secular-ism police" forcing women to uncover their heads.[8]

That's why, I think, when I saw "Islamic" dictatorships in other countries—such as Iran, Sudan, and Afghanistan—I did not assume an inherent connection between Islam and authori-tarianism. Rather, I realized that the authoritarian Muslims in the Middle East and the authoritarian secularists in Turkey shared a similar mindset, and that this illiberal mindset, rather than religion or secularity as such, is the problem. I also found it quite telling that the same problem has haunted non-Muslim countries in Asia, such as Russia and China.

So, I asked myself, could the authoritarian regimes in the Muslim world stem not from Islam but from the deep-seated political cultures and social structures in this part of the world, on which Islam is just a topping?

In other words, could authoritarian Muslims be just authoritarians who happen to be Muslim?

FROM MECCA TO ISTANBUL

Those are some of the questions that I will explore in this book, while presenting a more liberal-minded understanding of Islam—in a long argument divided into three main parts.

In Part I, I will go to the very genesis of this religion and show how its core message of monotheism—with implications such as the individual's responsibility before God—transformed the Arabs and then the whole Middle East in remarkable ways. We will see how rationalist and even liberal ideas emerged in those earliest centuries of Islam, and why they failed to become definitive in the long run. We will also examine the distinction between the eternal message of the Qur'an and its temporal implications, even including some of the political and military acts of the Prophet Muhammad.

Part II deals with more recent history. First, there is a chapter on the Ottoman Empire, the Muslim superpower from the sixteenth to the twentieth century. I will particularly focus on how the Ottoman elite imported liberal ideas and institutions from the West and, most important, reconciled them with Islam. This is a story largely forgotten both in the West and the East, but also a very important one for both.

Then we will examine the anomaly of the twentieth century, which gave us oppression, militancy, and even terrorism in the name of Islam: Islamism. As we shall see, this modern ideology, which is different from the fourteen-century-old religion to which it refers, is quite misguided in itself but also very much mishandled by its foes, including the West.

The last chapter of Part II focuses on Islam in modern-day Turkey. The reason for this is not only that I am a part of that story, and thus know it well. It is also that the exceptional story of Turkey, which is largely unnoticed in the West, represents a growing synthesis of Islam and liberalism. The Ottoman legacy certainly plays a role here, along with the lessons Turkey's Muslims have learned from their interaction with the country's secular forces. In addition, Turkey has recently become the stage for an experiment unprecedented in the history of "Islamdom": the rise of a Muslim middle class that has begun to reinterpret religion with a more modern mindset. For centuries, Islam has been mainly a religion of peasants, landlords, soldiers, and bureaucrats, but in Turkey, since the "free-market revolution" of the 1980s, it has also become the religion of urban entrepreneurs and professionals. These emerging "Islamic Calvinists," as a Western think tank referred to them—alluding to sociologist Max Weber's famous thesis on the "spirit of capitalism"—strongly support democracy and the free-market economy.[9] Furthermore, they are far more individualistic than their forefathers. Consequently, as a Turkish observer recently put it, they want to hear about "the Qur'an and freedom," rather than "the Qur'an and obedience."[10]

Yet these more modern-minded Muslims, and the millions of their co-religionists throughout the world who are concerned about the authoritarian elements within their tradition, still need an accessible synthesis of the liberal ideas they find appealing and the faith they uphold—which, despite all the appearances to the contrary, might actually be compatible.

They need, in other words, a genuinely Muslim case for liberty—something Part III provides, with religious arguments for "freedom from the state," "freedom to sin," and "freedom from Islam."

THIS IS THE BRIEF STORY of why and how this book came to be. It is the fruit of an intellectual and spiritual journey that began in my grandfather's house thirty years ago and has continued uninterrupted to date. I went to modern, English-language schools, which taught me a great deal about the liberal tradition of the West, but meanwhile I retained my passion to learn, discover, and experience more about my religion. Hence, since the early 1990s, I have engaged with various Islamic groups and have seen firsthand their virtues as well as their flaws. In the end, I decided to subscribe to none of those groups, but I have learned from the ways of each of them.

One trait I have developed over the years is an instinctive aversion to tyranny. I had seen it first as the eight-year-old kid behind barbed wire, looking down the barrel of secular guns. But as I studied the Middle East, first in college and then in my job as a journalist, I came to realize that the barrels of Islamic guns are no better. Despots acting in the name of "the nation" or "the state" obviously were terrible—and so were despots acting in the name of God.

Ultimately, I have become convinced that a fundamental need for the contemporary Muslim world is to embrace liberty— the liberty of individuals and communities, Muslim and non-Muslims, believers and unbelievers, women and men, ideas and opinions, markets and entrepreneurs. Only by doing so can Muslim societies create and advance their own modernity, while also laying the groundwork for the flourishing of God-centered religiosity.

To explain why this is not as impossible as it might seem to some, I first need to go back fourteen centuries to explore how Islam unfolded in history—and, in the meantime, what happened to liberty.

PART I

The Beginnings

The period in which formative developments took place in Islam, and at the end of which Muslim orthodoxy crystallized and emerged, roughly covered a period of two centuries and a half.

—FAZLUR RAHMAN (1911–1988), Muslim scholar

CHAPTER ONE

A Light unto Tribes

If it is true that each individual has such a
destiny [beyond society], then he cannot be
treated merely as a means to an end, but as an
end in himself.

—ROBERT A. SIRICO, Roman Catholic priest[1]

IN THE YEAR 610 AD, an Arab man from the small town of Mecca
heard an extraordinary voice in a cave. "Recite," the voice commanded him. "Recite in the name of your Lord who created man."

And the world changed forever.

That man was Muhammad, a member of Banu Hashim, a
prominent clan in Mecca. Although raised as an orphan, he lived
a comfortable life, thanks to his prominent relatives. While still
in his teens, he started accompanying his uncle, Abu Talib, on
trading expeditions to Syria, so he could gain experience with
commerce. Soon he would become a merchant himself, a successful and respected one. At the age of twenty-five, he married
Khadija, a rich forty-year-old widow who was even more accom-
plished in business.

Trade was one of the two economic pillars of Mecca. The
other one, related to the first, was polytheism. The cube-shaped

building at the heart of the city, the Ka'ba, was a pantheon for some three hundred idols. Other Arabs visited Mecca every year in order to honor these gods, blessing the city not just with prestige but also with profits.

Years passed and Muhammad reached the age of forty. By all accounts, his marriage was a happy one. He was a highly respected member of society and considered a very moral man. People called him "the Trustworthy One" and asked him to settle disputes. He could have continued to lead a good life, making money and dying comfortably, but Muhammad was destined for more. Throughout his life, he had moral concerns about his society. The ruthless treatment of Mecca's downtrodden—the poor, the slaves, and most women—deeply troubled him. He was also bothered by the core of his native culture: idolatry. How bizarre, he thought, for people to worship objects made by their own hands.

Muslim tradition tells us that Muhammad was illiterate. Some have disagreed, pointing out that, as a merchant, he must have been familiar with documents, but he surely was not a man of letters who would sit down and read literature. Yet he was a thinker, and he often would leave Mecca for a cave on a nearby mountain, seeking peace of mind. He would sit in that cave for hours and contemplate nature, society, and the meaning of life.

During one of these private meditations, he heard the commandment, "Recite." This very first word of the revelation he received—*iqra* in Arabic—hinted at the name of the scripture it would ultimately form: the Qur'an, which means "recitation."

Muhammad found the strange voice in the dark cave not just unexpected but also so terrifying that he climbed down the mountain and ran home. Trembling, he begged his wife: "Cover me, cover me." He feared that evil spirits had possessed him. But Khadija turned out to be more confident. Holding her horrified husband in her arms, she said, as reported later by Muslim sources:

> You are kind and considerate to your kin. You help the poor and forlorn and bear their burdens. You are striving to restore the high moral qualities that your people have lost. You honor the guest and go to the assistance of those in distress. This cannot be, my dear.[2]

Khadija then suggested that they discuss this strange experience with her Christian cousin, Waraqa. Well-versed in theology and scripture, the latter did not hesitate to conclude that the spirit that touched Muhammad was indeed a good one. The voice in the cave, and the message, was quite reminiscent of the experiences of Moses and the Hebrew prophets. Waraqa exuberantly cried to Khadija: "Holy! Holy! Your husband is the prophet of his people!"

That conviction would shape the rest of Muhammad's life. He continued to have doubts for a while but soon became fully persuaded that he was indeed chosen by God, the only one, to save his people from idolatry and moral corruption. "There is no god," his credo declared, "but Allah." That Arabic term was simply a derivative of the word *al-Ilah*, which meant "the God."[3]

The revelations would continue for twenty-three years, until Muhammad's death on June 4, 632. These verses of the Qur'an, as they became known, would guide him and his gradually increasing flock of adherents throughout their astonishing journey. Some revelations would support and encourage Muhammad; others would warn and even admonish him. And, ultimately, they would turn him from a seventh-century Arab merchant to an eternal guide to billions of people.

A MAN WITH A MISSION

What was the source of the revelations that the Prophet Muhammad received? Did he imagine a voice, or was there really a divine source that spoke to his mind? In other words, did the Prophet create the Qur'an or did the Qur'an create the Prophet?

All Muslims (including me) believe the latter. This belief is simply what makes someone a Muslim. It is of course an article of faith, which requires a leap of faith, but, arguably, it is also a credible one. The Qur'an itself, first of all, is very consistent with its claim of divine origin. It is written from the perspective of God and God alone. Verse after verse, chapter after chapter, it hits the reader with its most fundamental character: theocentricity—i.e., God-centeredness. So, unlike the New Testament, which speaks of the life of Jesus, the Qur'an does not speak *about* Muhammad. Rather, it speaks *to* him. Thus, it says almost nothing about his life story, which was written down only a century and a half later by Muslim biographers.

Over the centuries, debate has raged over whether Muhammad, or some other person from his milieu, could have possibly produced the Qur'an. Muslims argue that it is a literary masterpiece, it speaks of scientific facts that people of that era could not have known, and it even makes prophecies that have been confirmed by history.[4] All these claims are debatable, and are being debated, between Muslims and others. But even some non-Muslim students of Islam have accepted Muhammad's sincerity in his belief that he was indeed the messenger of God. "We find a quite original piety, a touching devotion, and a quite characteristic religious poetry in the Qur'an," wrote German Catholic theologian Adam Möhler in 1830. "It is impossible for this to be something artificial and forced . . . [and] to see Muhammad as a mere cheat."[5]

Another argument for Muhammad's sincerity is that if he were an imposter looking for fame and success, he is unlikely to have embarked on such an unpromising enterprise. From hindsight, the early history of Islam proved to be marked by astonishing success, but such an outcome was not foreseeable in the beginning. In fact, during the earliest years of prophecy, an average Meccan would not have gambled on the victory of Muhammad, who seemed like a hopeless lunatic challenging the established culture of generations. "Your nephew has cursed our gods, insulted our religion, mocked our way of life, and accused our forefathers of error," protested the most powerful men in Mecca, to Muhammad's uncle.[6] He was, apparently, doing everything to get himself in trouble.

Little wonder, then, that Muhammad's mission did not bring him peace of mind until his very last years. His first thirteen years in Mecca, in fact, were full of humiliation, threats, and abuses. At some point, the elders of the city asked him to compromise from his unyielding monotheism by refraining from denouncing idolatry. Apparently he gave some consideration to that, but only until he was strongly reprimanded in a revelation.[7] Threatened with hellfire, the repentant Muhammad continued to proclaim the falsity of the gods of his fathers, bringing only more hostility and oppression on him and his fellow believers.

The next phase of his prophetic mission took him to the city of Medina, where he and his followers would continue to face the threat of annihilation. He would be physically injured in the devastating Battle of Uhud. According to the late William Montgomery Watt, the eminent British professor of Islamic studies, all this resilience pointed to a genuine devotion. "Only a profound belief in himself and his mission," he argued, "explains Muhammad's readiness to endure hardship and persecution during the Meccan period when from a secular point of view there was no prospect of success."[8]

But what were the core ideas of the mission in which Muhammad so passionately believed? And how did they transform society?

CREATING THE INDIVIDUAL FROM THE TRIBE

In Muslim terminology, the Arab society before the advent of Islam is called *jahiliyah* (the state of ignorance). From a religious point of view, the most definitive characteristic of that society was idolatry. Yet a sociologist would probably emphasize another trait: tribalism.

Life in the arid Arabian Desert was very harsh, and the only way to survive was to live in a closely-knit group. Therefore the Arabs had created many clans and tribes, and the individual was easily sacrificed for the good of these collective kinships. Because of constant warfare between the tribes, and subsequent attrition, men were considered to be more valuable, and there often was a shortage of them. Moreover, poverty precluded the possibility of raising a large family. Therefore, families might decide to kill some of their newborn females, who were seen as not as useful and honorable as males. What mattered was the interest of the tribe, not the nameless individuals who happened to be a part of it.

Similarly, the penal system recognized the tribe, not the individual. Since it was very easy for an individual to disappear without a trace in the desert, there was no way to punish the criminal who had perpetrated the disappearance. Instead, both the crime and the punishment were handled with a collective vendetta. If someone from tribe A killed a person from tribe B, then the former would be asked to offer one of its members as retribution. It was the classic idea: eye for an eye—but any eye.

This collectivism was necessitated by geography, to be sure, but also by theology—or the lack thereof. The Arabs believed in multiple gods, but not one of these deities was perceived as a judge who could hold men accountable for their deeds. There was no belief in an afterlife, so the individual had no unique eternal destiny. "The only immortality that a man or woman could achieve," as one historian puts it, "was in the tribe and the continuation of its spirit."[9]

But the Qur'an would challenge all these assumptions. First, it defined man as God's "viceroy on earth," elevated above all other creatures, including the angels.[10] From the very beginning, the Qur'an also emphasized the individual's personal responsibility to his Creator. One of the early chapters stipulated that this responsibility would be tested by God in the moral choices that man makes:

> Have We not given man two eyes,
> and a tongue and two lips
> and shown him the two highways?
> But he has not braved the steep ascent.
> What will convey to you what the steep ascent is?
> It is freeing a slave
> or feeding on a day of hunger
> an orphaned relative
> or a poor man in the dust;
> then to be one of those who have faith and urge each other to
> steadfastness, and urge each other to compassion.[11]

In other words, God was expecting humans to perform good works for other humans. And, in the world to come, He would judge every individual according to his works. The righteous would be rewarded in heaven, whereas the unrighteous would be punished in hell. And no one—not his family or his tribe— would be able to save a sinner.[12] "Today you have come to Us as individuals," God would rather tell all people on Judgment Day, "just as We created you in the first place."[13]

This Qur'anic theology would create a religious movement with "an intense concern for attaining personal salvation through righteous behavior."[14] And, according to Hans Küng, the eminent Catholic theologian, this focus on personal salvation would help the individual emerge from the bond of the Arab tribe:

> The consistent monotheism that Muhammad proclaimed was aimed not only at a new community but also at a new individual responsibility. . . . If there is only one God and this God is the Creator, sustainer and judge of human beings, then individuals assume a special dignity; they are no longer playthings in the hands of several rival deities, nor mere objects in an all-determining system of clans and tribes but the creatures of this one God, indeed his "successors," responsible to Him.[15]

The change would be reflected in popular terminology. In the pre-Islamic period of the *jahiliyah*, the key terms *nasab* (lineage) and *hasab* (inherited merit) determined the individual's status in society. The latter referred not to the individual's personal accomplishments but rather the totality of the success attributed to his ancestors, by which his worth was measured. Yet the Qur'an stressed that what really mattered was one's *fadl* (merit), which individuals can only earn as a result of their personal deeds.[16]

Soon the Qur'an would also forbid blood feuds, introduce legally fixed criminal penalties, and order almsgiving to help the poor.[17] According to Marshall G. S. Hodgson, a historian of Islamic civilization, all these injunctions "helped give individuals a status independent of clan associations, and so could foster individualistic culture traits."[18]

Despite being new for the Arabs, these were old ideas— ones that had been proclaimed first by Judaism and later by Christianity—which also laid the groundwork for empowerment of the individual.[19] And that monotheist continuum was precisely what the Qur'an was proudly acknowledging. "We have sent down the book to you with truth," God said in it to Muhammad, "confirming and conserving the previous books."[20] Those "previous books" were the Jewish and Christian scriptures, and the Qur'an was just claiming to continue the same Abrahamic tradition— a statement that is factually true, regardless of whether one sees the Qur'an's origin in divine revelation, as a Muslim would do, or in human compilation, as others would probably prefer.

THE CALL TO REASON

If the Qur'an carved the individual out of the tribe, then what did it ask him to do? Simply to have faith? To have a blind, unquestioning, dogmatic belief?

Not really. The Qur'an instead aims to heighten certitude in the minds of its readers, by presenting rational arguments. Appearing about fifty times in the Muslim scripture is the verb *aqala*, which means "to connect ideas together, to reason, or to understand an intellectual argument." Throughout its pages, the Qur'an repeatedly invites the reader to use these faculties to reflect upon the created universe, and man's own self, as "signs" for finding God. All the wonders of creation, such as the movements of the heavenly bodies, atmospheric phenomena, the capabilities of the human body, the variety of the animal and vegetable life so marvelously designed for men's needs—all of them, according to the Qur'an, translate into "signs for people who use their intellect."[21]

The Qur'anic reasoning is guided by religious dictums, to be sure, and its verses introduce many articles of pure faith, such as the existence of the afterlife, angels, and miracles. But although one needs to go beyond empirical reason to believe in such notions, one does not need to clash with it. In fact, those who clash with reason, according to the Qur'an, are the unbelievers. "They are people," a verse bluntly decrees, "who do not use their intellect."[22] "Muhammad," observed Belgian-born scholar Henri Lammens, "is not far from considering unbelief as an infirmity of the human mind."[23]

In the later chapters, we will see how this Qur'anic emphasis on reason gave rise to the Rationalist school in Islam, which in turn laid the philosophical foundation for individual freedom.

THE RIGHTS GOD GAVE TO MEN—AND WOMEN

The Qur'an also introduced into Arab society the concept that individuals have inalienable rights. Justice was at the core of Muhammad's social message, and justice meant not just punishment for those who commit crimes but also protection from those who could violate others' rights.

This was grounded in the Qur'anic message of protecting the

weak against the strong. "By God," said Muhammad, "an Abyssinian slave who obeys God is better than a Qurayshi chieftain who disobeys Him."[24] For the Quraysh, the most prestigious tribe in Mecca, this bold egalitarianism was simply shocking.

Another reform introduced in the Qur'an strengthened the nuclear family—husband, wife, and children. Inheritance would now be confined primarily within the immediate family, not shared throughout the tribe. The regulations were made piecemeal, "but the tendency was persistently toward asserting individual rights on the basis of equality before God."[25]

Although it may be news to the modern reader, another of the Qur'an's revolutionary innovations was its recognition of rights for women. In the pre-Islamic period, except for rare examples such as Khadija, Muhammad's wife, a woman was typically a slave to men. She did not have the right to own property; she herself was property. A man would pay a "bride-price" to a girl's father. And when he died, the inheritance passed only to his sons—the wife and daughters received no share.

With Islam, all that would change. First, the Qur'an ordered that the bride-price should be paid to the bride herself, and that she should keep it as long as she wished, as a financial safety net. Second, the Qur'an also decreed that females should receive a share of inheritance. It was only half of what their male siblings would get, but in a society in which men were considered to be responsible for care of the whole household, this was a generous amount. The Qur'an also granted women the right to accept or reject a marriage offer, and it established the marital bond on the basis of "love" and "mercy."[26]

What the Qur'an brought was not full equality between the sexes, but, when considered in context, it was a great improvement. "In such a primitive world, what Muhammad achieved for women was extraordinary," says British historian Karen Armstrong. "The very idea that a woman could be a witness or could inherit anything at all in her own right was astonishing."[27] That's why the rights of women in Islamic law—the Shariah—would remain ahead of the West well into modern times. In the Middle Ages, some Christian scholars even criticized Islam for giving too much power to menials such as slaves and women.[28] Even when Great Britain applied its legal system to Muslims in place of the Shariah, as it did in some of its colonies, married women were stripped of the property that Islamic law had always granted them.[29]

The tragedy is that while women's rights peaked in the West in the twentieth century, in Islamdom it stagnated for centuries and even declined to its current reprehensible state. In the upcoming chapters, we will see the reasons for this.

Improvement and evolution, and not total revolution, was often the method of the Qur'an. Slavery was not abolished, for example, but manumission was encouraged, and the position of the slave was improved enormously. The "Arabian slave . . . was now no longer merely a chattel but was also a human being with a certain religious and hence a social status and with certain quasi-legal rights."[30]

Even rights for animals were introduced. Pagan Arabs used to treat them quite cruelly, even to the extent of cutting off lumps of flesh to eat while the poor creatures were still alive. Muhammad banned all such practices as well as animal fights organized for entertainment. Reportedly, he once told a man that he could go to paradise simply for giving water to a thirsty dog.[31]

Yet still, the concept of "rights" would not become a major theme in Islamic law. Mohammad Kamali, professor of Islamic law, points to this problem and notes that while the Qur'an introduced many individual rights—such as rights to life, property, privacy, movement, justice, personal dignity, and equality before the law—classical Islamic literature focused on duties.[32]

In other words, an Islamic theory of rights could have been developed, for it had a basis in the Qur'an, but just as with Christianity, Muslims had to wait until modern times to look at their scripture with a more individualistic perspective. That's why some new books of Islamic jurisprudence have chapters on "the rights and freedoms of the individual," something the classical works lacked.[33]

THE POLITICS OF THE PROPHET

So far, we have focused on the message of the Qur'an. But what about the events that it precipitated? What about, for example, the political order that the Prophet Muhammad founded? Didn't he establish a theocratic state that waged wars and pursued conquests? These are good questions, and the answer is not as simple as it might seem.

In fact, Muhammad did not start his mission as a political leader. The Qur'an told him that he was "only a warner and a bringer of good news."[34] When he was worrying that most pagans did not listen to his preaching, God was telling him to let go. "We did not appoint you over them as their keeper," a verse reminded, "and you are not set over them as their guardian."[35] The Qur'an also recognized the Meccans' right to disbelieve. It threatened unbelievers with hellfire, but it also emphasized that, in this world, they should be free to choose their own path. "It is the truth from your Lord," one verse read, "so let whoever wishes have belief and whoever wishes be an unbeliever."[36]

The first thirteen of the Prophet's twenty-three-year career went on like this—totally apolitical and nonviolent. This attitude partly changed only after he had to flee from Mecca—where he was on the verge of being killed by prominent pagans who were offended by his uncompromising monotheism—to Yathrib, a town that would later be known as Medina (the City). This *hijra*, or migration, would be a turning point in the prophet's mission and would mark the very beginning of the Muslim calendar.

The Muslims in Medina, a recently formed community, welcomed the Prophet with hymns and warmly accepted his Meccan followers. Here they were all brothers in faith, in a community free from oppression. And the Prophet of God was not only a spiritual leader now but also a political one. Yet, interestingly, the Prophet did not establish a theocracy in Medina. Instead of a polity defined solely by Islam, he founded a territorial polity based on religious pluralism.

This is evident in a document called the Charter of Medina, which the Prophet signed with the leaders of the other community in the city: the Jews. Three Jewish tribes had lived in Yathrib for some time. After some negotiations, they signed a pact with Muhammad that recognized him as the head of Medina, but it granted both faith communities the right to live in their autonomous ways. "To the Jews their religion," read one of the clauses, "and to the Muslims their religion." The idea was that the city belonged to both of these groups, and each had to contribute to its defense in the event of an outside threat. "All tribes are one community," the charter declared, "distinct from other people."[37]

The word for community used here, interestingly, was *umma*, which later acquired an exclusively Islamic meaning. Today, Muslims use the term only to mean fellow Muslims. But, in the

Charter of Medina, the *umma* consisted of people from different faiths who had formed a political community with joint interests. What this meant, according to a Western scholar, is that "Muhammad's original Medina 'community' was a purely secular one."[38] The religious pluralism in the charter was probably a result of custom rather than an innovation by the Prophet. However, if the Prophet's political mission will be seen as normative for Muslims, the pluralist and even the "secular" nature of the charter cannot be overlooked.

Unfortunately, the system established by the charter did not last long, mainly due to growing tension between the Muslims and their archenemies, the Meccan pagans, who had killed, tortured, and finally expelled the Muslims from their homeland. "Permission to fight is given to those who are fought against," the Qur'an soon declared. "They are expelled from their homes without any right, merely for saying, 'Our Lord is God.' "[39]

What linked this Meccan threat to Medinan Muslims and the fate of the Jews in the city, according to Muslim sources, was the Jews' decision to collaborate with the enemy. Consequently, two of the three Jewish tribes, which violated the charter by helping the Meccans, were expelled from Medina. The third Jewish tribe, the Banu Qurayza—which negotiated with the Meccan army when the latter besieged Medina to annihilate the whole Muslim community during the critical Battle of the Trench— was less lucky. This treason, as Muslims saw it, would be punished by the most controversial decision that Muhammad ever made: the mass execution of all the tribe's males and the enslavement of the women and children.

The validity of this story has been doubted by some modern Muslim scholars.[40] One of them, Walid N. Arafat, thinks that the story is a later invention. "To kill such a large number is diametrically opposed to the Islamic sense of justice and to the basic principles laid down in the Qur'an," he argues, pointing to the verse: "No soul shall bear another's burden."[41]

Yet even if the mass execution had really happened, as the mainstream view holds, one should note that it took place not as a commandment of the Qur'an but as the result of the customs of the time.[42] "We cannot judge the treatment of the Qurayza by present-day moral standards," notes Norman A. Stillman, professor of Judaic history. "Their fate was a bitter one, but not unusual according to the harsh rules of war during that period." Stillman also reminds us that, in the Old Testament (Deut. 20:13–14), the Israelites were enjoined to do the same thing to their enemies: the slaughter of adult males and the enslavement of women and children, which was, after all, "common practice throughout the ancient world."[43]

And this takes us to a crucial question: Are all things that Muhammad did normative for Muslims? Or do some of them reflect not the everlasting rules and principles of Islam but rather those of the Prophet's time and milieu?

MUHAMMAD THE HUMAN

Some modern Muslim theologians, and even some classical ones, who address the question above have come to the conclusion that the "historical" and the "religious" aspects of Muhammad must be separated.[44] The Prophet brought a message relevant for all ages, in other words, but he lived a life of his own age.

Recognition of this is the key to saving ourselves from falling into one of the two very common and related mistakes. The first, which is made by non-Muslims, is to criticize, and sometimes even condemn, Muhammad according to our modern standards.

The second mistake, which is made by Muslims, is to take the standards of his time as eternally valid and to try to bring them into the modern era.

Take, for example, another of his controversial deeds: his marriage to Aisha, who was, according to our definitions, quite underage.[45] Of course, this is absolutely unacceptable by modern standards, but it was quite normal then, when puberty was commonly regarded as the natural age for marriage. (Arabs in the seventh century also tended to reach adulthood at an earlier age than Westerners do today.)[46]

Other controversial aspects of Muhammad—that he had several wives, owned slaves (whom he treated very benevolently), or ordered acts of violence such as the fate of the Banu Qurayza—became controversial only in the modern era and in the eyes of modern critics. "It is clear that those of Muhammad's actions which are disapproved by the modern West," notes William Montgomery Watt, "were not the object of the moral criticism of his contemporaries."[47]

For the Muslim mind, this "historicity" of the Prophet should not be scandalous. In fact, expecting from Muhammad a perfect universal wisdom, totally unbound from his time and culture, would not be consistent with Qur'anic theology. Unlike the image of Jesus in Christianity—who, as the Word of God, had existed since eternity and entered into history by becoming flesh—Muhammad was just a human. He was not the Word of God; he was a humble man touched by the Word of God. "I am only a human being like yourselves," the Qur'an ordered him to state. "It is only revealed to me that your god is One God."[48]

Interestingly, though, Muslim tradition would later exalt him to a suprahuman figure who, like Jesus, existed before time and universe and performed many miracles on earth. In the next chapter, we will see how this "Prophetology" contributed to the rise of an all-encompassing *Sunna* (prophetic tradition) as a stagnant force in Islam more than a century after the Prophet's death.

THE GREAT MYSTERY IN ISLAM

The final years of the Prophet's life would be ones of victory. After five years of war, he signed a peace treaty with the pagans of Mecca in March 628. The next two years gave the Muslims a good opportunity to evangelize the new faith and gain converts from all over the Arabian Peninsula. Then, after a skirmish between two tribes that were allied with Medina and Mecca, respectively, the peace treaty dissolved. With an overwhelming army of ten thousand men, Muhammad marched toward Mecca. For the elders of the city, the only recourse was to surrender to the man whom they had chased out just six years earlier. They all feared that he would take revenge on his enemies, but instead he issued a general amnesty and forced no one to accept Islam.

Right after his entrance into the city without bloodshed, the victorious Muhammad marched toward the Ka'ba. Arabs believed that this ancient shrine was built by Abraham, their monotheist ancestor, to worship God. Over time, however, it had become a pagan pantheon, and when Muhammad opened its gates, he found it filled with more than three hundred idols. One by one, he shattered the idols with his own hands. "Truth has come," said the verse he recited, "and Falsehood has vanished."[49]

Muslim sources report that among the icons in the Ka'ba, only the frescoes of Jesus and Mary were spared, for they were deeply respected in the Qur'an.[50] This was a sign of the fact that Islam, which abhorred paganism, regarded Christians, as well as Jews, as members of partly misguided yet still valid faiths. Designated by the Qur'an as "People of the Book," these fellow monotheists would be granted the right to live and practice their faiths under the rule of Islam.

In just twenty years, Muhammad had stunning accomplishments. Soon, as other Arab tribes came to accept his message, he became the most powerful man in the Arabian Peninsula. But this was not his personal triumph. "When God's help and victory have arrived and you have seen people entering God's religion in droves," the Qur'an told him, "then glorify your Lord's praise and ask His forgiveness."[51]

This theocentricity would remain as the most fundamental character of Islam. By rejecting any intermediaries between man and God—such as an established church—Islam did not become an "organized religion" in the Western sense, so it continued to empower the individual. The result was not the modern individual with civil liberties that we have today, but it was a clean and progressive break from the tribalism of the age of paganism. "Muhammad could not . . . produce a full-blown individualism to satisfy our present Western liberal ideas," argues Karen Armstrong, "but he had made a start."[52]

Another commentator who touched upon the liberalizing mission of Islam was Rose Wilder Lane (1886–1968), one of the founders of the American libertarian movement. (Most Americans would also recognize her mother, Laura Ingalls Wilder, from her legendary novel *Little House on the Prairie*.) In her 1943 book, *The Discovery of Freedom: Man's Struggle Against Authority*, Mrs. Lane devoted a special chapter to Islam. Her argument was that there had been three great attempts to establish free societies on earth. The first she credited to Abraham, who saved men from "the tyranny of capricious gods." The second attempt was made by Muhammad, whom she defined as "a self-made business man" who "establish[ed] the fact of individual freedom in practical affairs." The third great attempt, Lane argued, was the American Revolution.[53]

Today this might sound a bit counterintuitive to many Americans and other Westerners, who think that the liberal ideas that have flourished in Western civilization do not have many parallels in the Muslim world. And the current state of freedom, or the lack thereof, in the Islamic East seems to justify that point of view.

One scholar who noticed and commented on this paradox is David Forte, an American professor of law:

> There is a great mystery in Islam. Islam should have been the first civilization to have abandoned slavery; it was the last. Islam should have been the first to establish complete religious liberty; today, non-Muslims suffer egregious persecution in Muslim lands. Islam should have been the first to establish social equality for women. Instead, women who stray outside the family's code of behavior are murdered with impunity. Islam should have been the foremost civilization to observe the humanitarian laws of war, but its empires have been no different from others; some claim they have been worse.[54]

But why? What happened? Why did the start that Muhammad made not reach its logical conclusion?

It will take a few more chapters to find an answer—and we will start with what went right.

CHAPTER TWO

The Enlightenment of the Orient

The medieval Islamic world . . . offered vastly more freedom than any of its predecessors, its contemporaries and most of its successors.

—BERNARD LEWIS, historian of the Middle East[1]

IN 632, shortly before his death, the Prophet Muhammad made his final pilgrimage to Mecca, where he delivered his Farewell Sermon, which has had historical significance for all Muslims since then. "O people," he said to a large crowd of Muslims, "your lives and your property are inviolable." He went on to condemn usury, blood vengeance, and murder. "Verily you owe your women their rights," he reminded the men, "and they owe you yours." He also denounced tribal, ethnic, and racial divisions. "All mankind is from Adam and Eve," he said, and added: "An Arab has no superiority over a non-Arab. . . . Also a white person has no superiority over a black person, nor a black person over a white person except through piety and good deeds."[2]

A few months after the Farewell Sermon, the Prophet

became ill and suffered pain and weakness for several days. On June 8, 632, he silently passed away in the arms of his beloved wife Aisha. For the Muslim community that had been following him since the first revelation twenty-three years earlier, this was a challenging moment. Some refused to believe the bad news, others were shocked. But Abu Bakr, one of the Prophet's closest companions, took the lead and addressed the community. "Whoever amongst you worshipped Muhammad, Muhammad is dead," he famously declared. "But whoever worshipped God, God is alive and will never die."

The Prophet had not left behind any institution or heir—a curious matter to which we will return. At this point in time, the Muslim community had to decide what to do next. After some discussion, they decided to choose the most trusted among them, Abu Bakr, as the "caliph" (the "successor" of Muhammad). Abu Bakr's "caliphate" would be followed by those of Umar, Uthman, and Ali—other prominent companions of Muhammad. Sunnis regard these four as the "Rightly Guided Caliphs" of Islam, whereas the Shiites only revere Ali and consider the other three to have been usurpers of the authority that Ali deserved.

The most notable work of the Rightly Guided Caliphs was territorial expansion. When the Prophet died, Muslims were dominant only in the Arabian Peninsula. In just three decades, they formed an empire stretching from Libya to Afghanistan. These conquests would continue under the Umayyad dynasty, which followed the Rightly Guided Caliphs, and the Islamic Empire would extend as far as Spain in the West and India in the East. Later on, parts of Africa, Asia Minor, the Balkans, the Caucasus, and Southeast Asia were also Islamized. Although military conquests continued to play an important role in Islam's expansion, in some areas, such as East Africa, India, China, and Indonesia, Islam spread via peaceful merchants and preachers.

This vast Muslim-dominated part of the world—Islamdom—would be the stage for Islam's experience in history. And its saga would be shaped by two separate dynamics: On one hand, the message of Islam would inform and transform the peoples of Islamdom; on the other hand, the preexisting and long-established cultures of these peoples would affect, and sometimes overshadow, Islam's message.

A RELIGION OF THE SWORD?

If Islamdom owes its expansion mostly to military conquests that were carried out under the banner of *jihad* (struggle), should we then conclude that Islam is "a religion of the sword"?

Not exactly. The conquests expanded the political rule of Muslims, to be sure, but the conquered peoples were not forced to convert to Islam, and many of them retained their religions. The Qur'an had announced, "There is no compulsion in religion," and, with the exception of a few cases—such as the fanatic Almohavids in North Africa—forced conversion remained anathema in Islamdom.[3]

Why, then, did the Muslims decide to conquer the world?

One major goal was to "spread the Word of God," to ensure that it would become known to all. The Arabic word used for the conquests was *fath,* meaning "opening." So a land conquered by Muslims would be "opened" to Islam, while non-Muslims could continue to live there. The object of *jihad*, in other words, was not to convert by force but "to remove obstacles to conversion."[4] (Similar views were expressed by St. Thomas and St. Bernard with regard to the Christian crusade.)[5] A second purpose of conquests was to spread what the Muslims believed to be a just political order. A third motivation, especially after the era of the Rightly Guided Caliphs, would simply be the lust for wealth and power.

The non-Muslim peoples in the conquered lands received *dhimma* (protection) by Muslims. In return for the safeguarding of life and property and the right to worship freely, the *dhimmis* (the protected) paid a special tax and had to accept certain social limitations that implied their capitulation to Muslim rule. (Over time, these limitations expanded, and the status of non-Muslims became less favorable, as Muslims adopted the preexisting attitudes of the Orient toward religious minorities.)[6] Christians and Jews were the first groups to be given *dhimma,* but as the rule of Islam spread, Zoroastrians, Hindus, Buddhists, and others were also included by way of *ijtihad* (independent reasoning).

When compared with the modern notion of equal citizenship rights, the unequal *dhimma* of course would be unacceptable. But according to the norms of that era, it was quite advanced. The earliest non-Muslims who found the *dhimma* a lifesaver were the Christians of Syria and North Africa, who were persecuted by the dominant Christian power of the time, the Byzantine Empire, because of differences in theology. The Byzantines believed in the Chalcedonian Creed, which held that Jesus Christ had two natures, divine and human. Most Christians in Egypt and Syria were Monophysites, who believed in one divine nature. This theological dispute imposed not just religious suppression but also heavy taxes on the Monophysites. Thus, when Muslim armies appeared at the gates of their cities, with insouciance to intra-Christian theological disputes and leniency on taxes, most Middle Eastern Christians welcomed the conquerors, regarding "their Arab fellow Semites as deliverers from Greek tax-gatherers and orthodox persecutors."[7]

At times, these local Christians even actively helped the Muslim conquests. When Byzantine-ruled Damascus was besieged by the Arab army in 634, the city's Monophysite bishop secretly informed the Muslim commander, Khalid, that the east gate of the city was weakly defended, and he supplied the Muslim troops with ladders for scaling the wall. After the conquest, the city's Cathedral of St. John was divided into two: one half was used as a church, the other half became a mosque.[8] In most conquered territories, early Muslim rule not only allowed the survival of Christian churches, it also permitted the building of new ones, as the archaeological record indicates.[9]

Jews, too, found their position improved under Arab Muslim rule. In an apocalyptic Jewish work of the time, God was praised, for "He has only brought the Kingdom of Ishmael," that of the Arabs, in order to save Jews from the "wickedness" of Byzantium.[10] Until modern times, many Jews considered life under Islamic rule preferable to that of medieval Europe, and often they found safe haven in Muslim lands after being persecuted in Christian ones.[11]

THE RULE OF LAW, NOT THE RULER

The *dhimma* system was just one of the many implications of a basic idea that the Qur'an introduced: Humans have rights ordained by God, and no other human can violate these rights. This idea would allow Muslims to create a civilization based on the rule of law.

Here we should stop to consider what "rule of law" means. The lack of law, and an authority that imposes it, can easily lead to anarchy and chaos, under which it would be impossible to protect the rights and freedoms of human beings. But the mere existence of law, and an imposing authority, is not necessarily a blessing, because the law can also be unjust and tyrannical. The "rule of law" under Stalin, for example, was horrendous. In that case, the purpose of the law was to protect not the rights and freedoms of individuals but the ideologies and interests of the Communist Party. Whenever a ruler or oligarchy makes laws to protect its own interests, the "rule of law" will be unjust and unfree.

What is needed, then, is a rule of law whose purpose is to protect not the ruler or a privileged class but the rights of each individual. This was, notably, what law meant in Islamdom. And the key concept was what has recently become a dirty word: the Shariah. Strictly speaking, *Shariah* translates to "the way" or "the path," but the historic meaning it acquired is "Islamic law," as developed by Muslim scholars in reference to the Qur'an and the tradition of the Prophet.

This definition of the Shariah is common knowledge, but the key point that it underlines often goes without notice: the fact that the Shariah was developed (or, more precisely, "discovered") by scholars means that it was not dictated by the state. If it had been dictated by the state, it probably would be like Roman law, which began by noting, "The prince is not bound by law."[12] But in Islamdom, all rulers were deeply bound by the law, for the law existed before, and stood above, their reign. That is why immunity from prosecution—which is enjoyed to this day by monarchs, heads of state, members of legislatures, and diplomats in other legal systems—is totally absent in the Shariah. Under the latter, no one is immune, and everyone is equal.[13]

As a result, right from the genesis of Islam, the Shariah acted as a constraint on arbitrary rule and became the guardian of justice. After the initial thirty years under the Rightly Guided Caliphs, the political leadership of the *umma* passed to dynasties, whose members often ruled not with the highest morals but with what St. Augustine called *libido dominandi,* lust for power. It was the Shariah, and the scholars who upheld it, that would stand against their tyranny and defend the rights of the people. (For that reason, most Muslim societies have a deep-seated respect for the Shariah—a respect that often puzzles Westerners.) Some liberal theorists have seen a parallelism between this function of Islamic law and the "natural law" tradition of Europe, on which the liberal political tradition rested.[14]

In reality, the theory did not always work. There were occasions when scholars gave in to the demands of temporal authorities and lent them support for their ambitions.[15] But there were other times when they acted as a firm check on despotism. When Ala-ud-din Khilji, a fourteenth-century Muslim ruler in India, wanted to overtax his wealthy Hindu subjects, he was dissuaded by his top scholar because doing so would violate the property rights recognized by Islam. "Whenever I want to consolidate my rule," Khilji complained, "someone tells me that this is against the Shariah."[16]

Similarly, in the Ottoman Empire, between the fourteenth and the early twentieth centuries, the Shariah served "not [as] a tool of the upper class," in the words of Israeli historian Haim Gerber, but as "a means for people of the lower classes to defend themselves against possible encroachments by the elite."[17] Gerber, who studied seventeenth- and eighteenth-century Ottoman court decisions, points to examples of Ottoman *muftis* (official jurists) who, despite being paid by the government, "did not hesitate to speak out against the government when [they] came face to face with an injustice."[18]

An interesting case was a reply given by an Ottoman mufti of the seventeenth century to a local governor in Palestine who wanted to force immigrants in the town of Lydd (today's Lod) to return to their villages. The mufti's *fatwa* (religious opinion) read:

> It is not permissible to force them to emigrate from a town they have taken to be their home, and to which they have become accustomed . . . for the believer is the lord of his soul; he may live in whichever country he sees fit and in whichever town he chooses. In no nation or religious community is it permissible to harass them and force them to go out.[19]

According to Gerber, the Shariah principle here was unmistakably individualist: "The rights of the state are depicted as opposed to the rights of the individual, and the latter are found to be superior."[20]

That's why, throughout the Ottoman centuries, when the sultan or local governors dared to violate the rights of their subjects, crowds would start protests by chanting, "We want Shariah!" They were simply asking for justice.

Stones, Lashes, and Swords

Most contemporary Westerners who hear anything positive about the Shariah immediately tend to ask, "But isn't the Shariah a very brutal legal system that orders lashings, the severing of hands, or even the stoning of criminals?" They would be right to raise that objection, because most contemporary Muslims who claim to implement the Shariah cling to its medieval forms, which include corporal punishments that are indeed brutal by modern standards.

But in the Middle Ages, the standards were much different and Islamic law was in fact offering "the most liberal and humane legal principles available anywhere in the world," according to Noah Feldman, a professor at Harvard Law School.[21] Feldman also notes that the harsh corporal punishments of the Shariah required very high standards of proof and were designed for a specific context:

> Before the modern era, no society had what we would today call a fully developed police department, and the classical Islamic constitutional order typically had just a handful of officers responsible for enforcement of ordinary laws. Extreme and visible punishments serve as salient reminders to the public to follow the law. More important, if the odds of being caught and punished for wrongdoing are low, as they typically will be in a society without a police force, then the punishment must be set high to produce something approximating the right amount of deterrence. The corporal punishments of the shari'a were clearly designed originally for such a world of very limited enforcement—much like the English common law that punished every felony with death.[22]

"From a pre-modern view," concurs historian Marshall Hodgson, the Shariah was actually "mild." In an age when torture was the standard procedure for dealing with suspects, Islamic law even "seemed dangerously soft on criminals."[23]

It is also important to note that enacting corporal punishment in lieu of prison terms was the only viable solution in the milieu into which Islam was born. In the Arabian Desert, imprisonment was a highly impractical, almost impossible, procedure: "It could be more burdensome to those who applied it than to those subjected to it."[24]

Today, the problem is that most contemporary proponents of the Shariah overlook these historical circumstances and insist on a literal implementation that does not pay attention to its purposes. Imam al-Shatibi in the fourteenth century had sorted out the purposes, or "higher objectives," of the Shariah, listing them simply as the protection of five fundamental values: life, religion, property, progeny, and the intellect.[25] Modern theologians such as the late Fazlur Rahman, the Pakistani-born scholar of Islamic law, have long been arguing that Muslims today need to reform the Shariah by taking these "higher objectives" as the unchanging norm, not the actual practices through which these objectives were realized a millennium ago.[26]

Other problems in the Shariah, such as misogyny, come from the fact that Islamic law incorporated a great many medieval attitudes, customs, and traditions during its formative centuries. Stoning, which has no basis in the Qur'an, probably came from Judaism.[27] In the upcoming chapters, we will see how this post-Qur'anic hardening of Islamic law occurred.

THE RULES OF ENGAGEMENT

Another common concern nowadays in the West about Islam, and especially about Shariah-minded Muslims, is terrorism. Yet, in the Middle Ages, the Shariah was in fact a bulwark against what we would now call "terrorism": the intentional targeting of enemy noncombatants. Islamic scholars had worked out a detailed theory of "just war," which took great pains to honor and protect civilian lives. Bernard Lewis, the eminent historian of the Middle East, notes the following:

> Fighters in a jihad are enjoined not to kill women, children, and the aged unless they attack first, not to torture or mutilate prisoners, to give fair warning of the resumption of hostilities after a truce, and to honor agreements. The medieval jurists and theologians discuss at some length the rules of warfare, including questions such as which weapons are permitted and which are not. There is even some discussion in medieval texts of the lawfulness of missile and chemical warfare, the one relating to mangonels [missile throwers] and catapults, the other to poison-tipped arrows and the poisoning of enemy water supplies. . . . Some jurists permit, some restrict, some disapprove of the use of these weapons. The stated reason for concern is the indiscriminate casualties that they inflict.[28]

"At no point do the basic texts of Islam enjoin terrorism and murder," Lewis adds. "At no point . . . do they even consider the random slaughter of uninvolved bystanders."[29]

Islamic scholars had unambiguously opposed the intentional killing of noncombatants, because the Qur'an ordered: "Fight in the Way of God against those who fight you, but do not go beyond the limits."[30] And the Prophet was on record for having ordered his troops: "Do not kill the very old, the infant, the child, or the woman."[31] Thence came the Islamic rules of war, something today's Islamist terrorists are working hard to ignore or bypass.[32]

The medieval Islamic concern for moral warfare is most apparent when contrasted with the wanton killing practiced by some of the Muslims' enemies, such as the Mongol invaders and the Crusaders. When the Crusaders sacked Jerusalem in 1099, they slaughtered the local population indiscriminately. "They killed all the Saracens and the Turks they found," wrote a contemporary historian. "They killed everyone whether male or female."[33] Similar atrocities continued under later Crusaders, such as Richard the Lionheart, who ordered that some 2,700 Muslims, including women and children, be put to the sword one by one at the Castle of Acre.

In return, Muslim forces led by Saladin (in Arabic, *Salahaddin*, "the Righteousness of Religion") not only spared noncombatants but also released many prisoners of war. When Saladin reconquered Jerusalem in 1187, the city was unharmed, and only the "Franks," the Christians from Europe, were expelled, whereas Eastern Christians were allowed to stay. A modest ransom was assessed, but those who could not afford it were excused. Saladin even paid for the ransom of some of the Franks, as his personal almsgiving. The Christians were so positively impressed by this humaneness that legends flourished in Europe that Saladin had been baptized a Christian and had been dubbed a Christian knight.[34]

He was, in fact, simply a Muslim ruler who abided by the Shariah.

THE ISLAMIC FREE MARKET—AND ITS INVENTIONS

Another blessing of the Shariah was the protection of property rights. Should a ruler be tempted to usurp property, he was blocked by "the shari'a's acknowledgment of the sanctity of private property and its corresponding prohibition of theft."[35] To further consolidate the protection of law, the scholars had developed a version of the legal doctrine of trusts. This allowed the transmission of wealth across generations through the creation of the charitable foundation, the *waqf*, which was legally immune from governmental interference.[36]

The result was "a vigorous and robust civil society," including charities, hospitals, and schools—all supported by the private foundations that were under the Shariah's protection.[37]

Islam not only guaranteed the protection of wealth but also encouraged its creation through economic activity. The Qur'an promoted work and trade and defined commercial profit as "God's bounty."[38] The Prophet, himself a merchant, is on the record with such sayings as: "He who makes money pleases God."[39] He is also known to have rejected calls for price-fixing, noting that only God governs the market.[40] "Muhammad," as French historian Maxime Rodinson succinctly put it, "was not a socialist."[41]

With that encouragement, Islamdom in its earliest centuries integrated Middle Eastern merchants into "a vast free-trade zone"[42] and established "financial and commercial capitalism."[43] Muslim scholars developed some economic practices and techniques that soon made their way into Europe. The method of charging interest without going against the religious ban on usury, *muhkatara*, soon became *mohatra* in Latin. The Arabic term *mudaraba*, which referred to a business partnership, is most likely the origin of the Italian *commenda*, the precursor of the modern "limited company."[44]

The journey of the Arabic term *sakk*, which means "written document" and referred to the papers that medieval Muslim merchants used instead of currency, is more clear: It is the origin of the French word *checque* and the English word *check*.[45]

These are just a few examples. "Anything in western capitalism of imported origin," notes Fernand Braudel, the great French historian, "undoubtedly came from Islam."[46] It was no accident that Maimonides, the great Jewish scholar and philosopher of twelfth-century Spain, complained of Jewish traders doing business in an "Islamic manner."[47]

The extent of "what the West owes to Islam" is debated frequently among historians. There is, for example, an interesting theory on the possible Islamic origins of the British common law, which clearly resembles the Shariah in its "judge-made" nature—different from the state-imposed Roman law tradition of continental Europe.[48] But obvious exports from Islamdom to the West can easily be traced today in English words with Arabic roots. A short list would include algebra, alchemy, alkali, almanac, amalgam, alembic, admiral, alcove, mask, muslin, nadir, zenith, tariff, sugar, syrup, checkmate, lute, and guitar.[49] And, of course, there are the Arabic numerals.

An Easygoing Religion

The West was importing from Islamdom for a reason. From the eighth to the thirteenth century, the latter was "the richest, most powerful, most creative, most enlightened region in the world."[50] Muslim scientists had made groundbreaking discoveries in the fields of physics, chemistry, biology, medicine, astronomy, and optics.[51] "Had there been Nobel Prizes in 1000," argues an American historian, "they would have gone almost exclusively to Moslems."[52] Islam's theologians anticipated many of the complex issues their Christian counterparts would address much later.[53] Islamic cities were much cleaner and more polished than European ones. That explains why a nun in the tenth century was so impressed with Cordoba, a city in then–Muslim-ruled Spain, that she called it "the ornament of the world."[54]

The freedom Islam offered to the peoples of the Orient, and the way it stimulated the individual, was critical to this grandeur. This was "an unusually flexible social order, which gave anyone who became a Muslim an opportunity to develop his talents on a scale that was relatively unfettered by pre-modern standards."[55] An outcome of this flexibility was rapid urbanization. Thanks to its individualism, Islam had "opened the way for the rise of the recognizably modern city, in which unrelated, ethnically diverse citizens interact with one another under accepted codes of legal and personal conduct."[56] No wonder that by the year 800, "the Middle East had thirteen cities with populations of over fifty thousand, while Europe had only one—Rome."[57]

In the face of this success, there came both admiration and bitterness from Europe. Christian priest Paul Alvarus in the ninth century voiced the latter when he wrote, with annoyance:

> Christians love to read the poems and romance of the Arabs. They study Arab theologians and philosophers, not to refute them but to form a correct and elegant Arabic. Where is the layman who now reads the Latin commentaries on the Holy Scriptures, or who studies the Gospels, prophets or apostles? Alas! All the talented young Christians read and study with enthusiasm the Arab books.[58]

The Christians who were fascinated by Muslim culture were soon dubbed by their more conservative co-religionists as

Mozarab—a term that literally meant "Arab wannabe."[59] There were understandable reasons for this. The library in Cordoba, during the reign of Caliph al-Hakam II in the tenth century, is said to have 400,000 manuscripts, whereas the library of Charles V of France, "Charles the Wise," who lived four centuries later, had only 900.[60]

Another appeal of Islam for medieval Christians was that it seemed to be a more easygoing religion. "The chief attraction of Islam was that it was practical; it did not demand seemingly superhuman efforts," argues Orthodox theologian Nicolas Zernov:

> The Christian East on the eve of the Islamic conquest had forgotten the limitations of human nature. Many members of the Church desired to imitate the angels; hence the mass movements towards the sexless life of monks and nuns; hence the exodus from towns and villages into the desert; hence the feats of self-mortification which showed the extent to which men could subdue their bodies at the dictates of the spirit. Some of these Eastern ascetics slept only in a standing position, others immured themselves in dark cells or lived on pillars, or ate only herbs, and even those not more than once a week.
>
> Islam stopped all these excesses. It swept away the exaggerated fear of sex, discarded asceticism, banished the fear of hell for those who failed to reach perfection, quenched theological enquiry.[61]

The Christians' "exaggerated fear of sex" continued until modern times, whereas Islamdom remained more sex-friendly until, again, modern times. Even the more conservative scholars of the Shariah had written about "women's right to sexual pleasure."[62] Attitudes toward intimacy, too, were remarkably different in premodern Islamdom and the West. Whereas Westerners in premodern times viewed the sexual act as a "battleground" where the male exerts his supremacy over the female, Muslims saw it as "a tender, shared pleasure." Sexual satisfaction, Muslims also believed, "leads to a harmonious social order and a flourishing civilization."[63]

These contrasts between Islamic and Christian cultures in the Middle Ages are all the more striking when one considers how completely the tables have turned since then. Today, it is Muslim clerics who complain about the fascination of their youth with the attractive Western culture. It is Islam that is seen as an extremely strict, disciplined, and sometimes even self-torturing religion. And it is Islamic societies that often appear sexophobic.

Today, it is the West that is free, easygoing, and wealthy. And it is Islamdom that clearly is not.

But why? What happened? If Islam enlightened the Orient so remarkably, what went wrong?

CHAPTER THREE

The Medieval War of Ideas (I)

Liberal politics are incompatible with . . . a
[religious] community, unless it is further
believed that the individual members of the
community have been endowed with reason
and free will by their Creator and that they
have no certain knowledge of what were/are
the Creator's intentions.

—LEONARD BINDER, *Islamic Liberalism*[1]

IT WAS A SEARING JULY DAY in the year 657, and the banks of
the Euphrates River were impossibly dry. At a site called Siffin, a breathtaking scene: Two Muslim armies—both compris-
ing thousands of men bearing swords and lances—faced each
other. One was led by the Ali, the fourth caliph and the cousin
and son-in-law of the Prophet Muhammad. The other army was
led by Muawiyah, the governor of the newly conquered province of Syria, a vast territory that included modern-day Syria,
Israel/Palestine, and Jordan. The dispute had begun a year earlier when Uthman, Ali's predecessor as the third caliph, was

assassinated by a gang of Muslim rebels. Ali had replaced Uthman, but Muawiyah, who was from the same tribe as Uthman, blamed Ali for failing to punish the murderers. He also declared his own caliphate—initiating the first *fitna* (civil war) in Islam.

The two armies had encamped at Siffin (in present-day Syria) for almost three months, waiting for their leaders to come to an agreement. Unable to do so, Ali finally ordered a full attack, which he joined personally with his legendary bravado. The Battle of Siffin lasted three days, the death toll spiraled, and the supporters of Ali seemed to be winning.

Muawiyah, who opted to watch the fighting from a pavilion, became increasingly pessimistic. But he had one final ploy. Inspired by a suggestion from one of his advisers, he told his bodyguards to put pages from the Qur'an on the points of their lances and shout, "The law of the Lord! That shall decide between us!" This chant meant that the two sides should cease fighting and settle matters by peaceful arbitration. Most of Ali's soldiers could not resist that call. So the swords dropped and talks resumed.

But this strategy also failed. The arbitration, set for several months after the battle, ended indecisively, and the two sides remained hostile. The de facto solution would be to keep the status quo: Muawiyah would rule over Syria, whereas Ali would rule the rest of the Muslim territories—Arabia, Iraq, and Persia.

Over time, Ali's followers would become known as "the supporters of Ali," or Shi'atu Ali, or, simply, the Shiites. Muawiyah, who would outlive Ali, established the Umayyad dynasty, which ruled Islamdom for the next ninety years. The mainstream Islamic current formed under this empire would become known as the Sunnis.

A third Muslim faction started with a group of soldiers who

broke away from Ali's army when he accepted arbitration with Muawiyah. Such a "human intervention" in a matter that should belong only to God, they said, was heresy. Soon this faction declared Ali and Muawiyah to be infidels and vowed to fight against both. They were labeled Kharijites, or "the Dissenters." Four years after the Battle of Siffin, a Dissenter assassinated Ali with a poison-coated sword.

Only a quarter of a century after the Prophet's time—"the age of happiness," as Muslims called it—fellow Muslims were spilling each other's blood. What happened to the idea that all believers were brothers in faith?

The Curse of Political Power

The answer lay not in faith but in another factor that created trouble for Islam from the very beginning: political power. No theological dispute made enemies out of Ali and Muawiyah—or, in a previous dispute, out of Ali and Aisha, the Prophet's widow. Rather, they disagreed over a somewhat mundane question: Who had the authority to rule? Interestingly, the disagreement in politics would gradually create schisms in theology as well. Shiites soon developed a doctrine holding that the only legitimate heirs of the Prophet were descendants of Ali. Sunnis argued that no matter who the ruler was, he should be obeyed for the sake of order and stability. The fanatic Dissenters—who were, in the words of a Muslim commentator, "the first terrorist movement in Islamic history"—swore to convert or kill all other Muslims.[2]

This splintering was inevitable, because it is in the nature of political power to create rivalries. In Islam, the only exception to this rule was the era of the Prophet Muhammad, whose authority was accepted by all Muslims. His mandate, after all, came from above. But after his death, the mandate came down to earth and became complicated by all things human—differing perceptions, contradictory interests, clashing loyalties. The first caliph, Abu Bakr, did his best by establishing an honest principle. "Obey me so long as I obey God and His Messenger," he proclaimed. "In case I disobey God and His Messenger, I have no right to obedience from you."[3] But who would decide whether he and his successors really obeyed God and His Messenger? Who would decide who was righteous? It took only a decade for that question to breed tension, and two decades to create a civil war.

At this point, a modern commentator might suggest a live-and-let-live pluralism, or even the separation of religion and political power. That modern commentator might also add that pluralism and secularity are modern concepts and that it is unfortunate that Islam never had the chance to discover them. But, alas, Islam *did* have the potential to establish pluralism and secularity. One school of thought, at the very least, had developed the perfect theology for it.

A GOD-CENTERED PLURALISM

In the midst of the who-is-right-and-who-is-wrong dispute between Ali and Muawiyah, a group of Muslims came up with a reconciliatory idea. They argued that it was simply impossible to solve a dispute over righteousness. Only God would have the ultimate knowledge, they insisted, so humans should refrain from decisive judgments about each other. "Had God willed, He would have made you a single community," a verse of the Qur'an declared, quite tellingly. "Every one of you will return to God and He will inform you regarding the things about which you differed."[4] With this verse in hand, these Muslims decided to "postpone" to the afterlife questions of who-is-right-and-who-is-wrong. Hence, they soon became known as the Murjiites (Postponers).

Notably, the theological argument that these seventh-century Muslims found for religious tolerance—that ultimate decisions should be left to God—was the exact argument that John Locke would put forward a millennium later in *A Letter Concerning Toleration*.[5]

The Postponers strongly opposed the Dissenters and their tendency to judge people's faith by looking at their outward religious practice. For the former, faith was not a form of action that a Muslim had to display through his works, but rather a consciousness that he would feel in his heart. To be a Muslim, they said, was to internalize "the knowledge of, submission to, and love of God."[6] Once a person had faith, he would be saved despite the sins he had committed. (Some have argued that they had developed an almost "Pauline" theology.)[7] The Postponers were so ecumenical that they even said that acceptance of most unorthodox doctrines, such as "tritheism"—the Christian doctrine of the Trinity as it is often understood by Muslims—would not necessarily imply infidelity.[8]

Besides opening the way to religious pluralism, the Postponers' theology also invalidated the idea of theocracy or theologically based political opposition. Since God alone could determine the sincerity of the faith of rulers, they argued, political authority should not be justified or questioned on theological grounds.[9] That's why, unlike the fanatic Dissenters who labeled anyone with whom they disagreed an "infidel," the Postponers were able to dissociate themselves from the mutually despising factions without condemning any of them.[10]

Unfortunately, a separate school of the tolerant Postponers did not last long. Their pluralist theology faded amid the heated conflicts between self-righteous factions. But their stance against fanaticism made sense to other Muslim parties. It especially had a considerable influence on Imam Abu Hanifa, the founder of one of the four—and the most tolerant—Sunni schools: Hanafi.

DOES GOD WILL THE TYRANNY OF THE TYRANTS?

We will come back to Abu Hanifa again and again throughout this book. First, however, we need to see how the very force that the Postponers tried to push away from religion—i.e., political power—played a role in the first serious theological controversy in Islamdom: the dispute between the defenders of human free will and the proponents of divine predestination.

Before Islam, Arabs were utterly fatalistic. They believed that men were helpless toys of *dahr*, or fate, which was determined by stars and other forces of nature.[11] The Qur'an rejected this mythology by proclaiming that it was God, an authority to whom men could appeal, who decided their fate. Moreover, the Qur'an spoke about humans' responsibility to make moral decisions.[12] But did this also mean that God, the all-powerful, granted men real power to control their lives?

At the turn of the seventh century, a group of Muslim theologians called Qadaris assembled in Syria, the new intellectual center of Islamdom, and answered that question affirmatively. It would have been unjust for God to reward and punish humans, they argued, if He had not given them the right to choose. Accordingly, they developed a doctrine that emphasized personal responsibility, disposition, and human self-determination.

But not everyone was in favor of the Qadarite movement, and

soon an opposing school emerged with the name of Jabriyyah. The term literally meant "proponents of [God's] enforcement," and its champions refused to acknowledge that humans had any free will. Men, they believed, were simply doing what God had "written" for them.

This intellectual controversy soon caught the eye of the political authorities: the Umayyad caliphs. The first of these was Muawiyah, the governor of Syria, who had clashed swords with Ali. When Muawiyah died, the caliphate passed to his son, Yazid, a despot who would soon become hated by both Sunnis and Shiites for killing Hussein, the grandson of the Prophet, during the tragic massacre at Karbala in 680. Not all of Yazid's descendants were as terrible as he was, yet the Umayyads still made a bad name for themselves as corrupt tyrants. Among other things, they were despised for introducing forced labor, which was seen by Muslims as a throwback, "one of the perverted practices of pre-Islamic tyranny."[13]

In other words, the Umayyads had a legitimacy problem. They first tried to fix it by giving themselves a lavish title: "the Caliph of God." This was way too ambitious, because even the highly respected Rightly Guided Caliphs, the closest companions of Muhammad, had called themselves only "the Caliph of the Prophet." The Umayyads were clearly eager to manipulate religion for political power. That's why the debate between the Qadaris and the Jabriyyah interested them: The latter's predestinarian argument, they realized, could be very useful for justifying their rule. If God had determined everything in eternity, they argued, He must have determined the sovereignty of the Umayyad dynasty as well. If God had not willed it, they said, they would not be sitting on the throne.

The theological controversy then turned into a political one between the Qadaris and the Umayyad court. In his *Epistle on Free Will*, the leader of the Qadaris, an ascetic scholar named Hasan al-Basri, openly challenged Umayyad caliph Ibn Marwan.[14] One of al-Basri's followers, Ghaylan al-Dimashqi, went even further. Rulers did not have the right to regard their power as "a gift of God," he argued; they had to be aware of their responsibility for people before God. He even asserted that if all Muslims truly obeyed God and His law, there would be no need for any caliph.[15]

That was too much. The caliph soon had al-Dimashqi arrested and executed, along with two like-minded colleagues. The movement would remain suppressed during the ninety-year reign of the Umayyad dynasty.

Then there is one final and quite telling detail about the Umayyad era. Of the fourteen successive Umayyad caliphs, two of them, Umar II and Yazid III, can be regarded as exceptions to the rule, for they were pious and modest men who tried to reverse the tide of repression and corruption. Yazid III in particular is famous for the inaugural speech he gave in Damascus in 744, when he stressed his accountability to the people and vowed to avoid his predecessors' abuses of power. He promised not to squander money on wives or children, not to transfer wealth from one province to another without reason, and not to overtax the *dhimmis*, the "protected" Christians and Jews. He even assured his audience that he would step down if he failed to fulfill these promises and that he would accept whomever they chose in his stead.[16]

Now, this good caliph did not just come out of the blue; historians think that he was closely connected with the Qadaris.[17] Apparently, the political idea of responsibility to people was closely linked with the theological idea of free will. Regrettably,

Yazid III stayed in power for only six months before he died from natural causes. And then Umayyad rule returned to business as usual.

The Rise of the People of Reason

The controversy between the proponents of free will and pre-destination was an important one, but it was only a prelude to the real war of ideas in the formative centuries of Islam: the clash between the *ahl al-ray* and *ahl al-hadith*, or the People of Reason and the People of Tradition.

This dispute started mainly as a disagreement over the method of the making of the Shariah, whose crucial role for Islamdom we examined in the previous chapter. All Muslims agreed that the Qur'an must be the primal source of the Shariah, but that did not explain much, for the Qur'an is a relatively short book—no longer than the New Testament—and its main focus is purely spiritual issues, such as God's purposes, man's moral duties, and the afterlife. Qur'anic verses about crime and punishment or marriage and inheritance, strictly earthly issues, would barely cover a few pages altogether. The bulk of the Qur'an consists of "broad, general moral directives."[18]

How these general moral directives—such as justice, fairness, and goodness—would be applied to specific rules and regulations was the central question of the Shariah. The Qur'an itself pointed to two other sources: (1) human reason, and (2) the Prophet himself, as an "example" for Muslims to follow. But this example was somewhat limited to Muhammad's own context, so Muslims started to face totally new questions as they left the Arabian Peninsula and moved to more cosmopolitan centers of the Middle East, such as Egypt, Syria, and, especially, Iraq.

Little wonder that Iraq would become the center for the Shariah scholars who used human reason as the second definitive source after the Qur'an. They were, in other words, adherents of *ray*, an Arabic term that means "reason," or "reasoned opinion." The most famed and authoritative scholar to emerge from this school was Abu Hanifa, the sympathizer of the Postponers' school. His thinking was based firmly on the Qur'an and human reason and a little less on the "example" of the Prophet:

> He felt apparently that local conditions differed, and that even if Medina was through force of circumstances the city of Mohammed, yet it was a desert town and therefore you could not possibly expect a desert law to apply to city life, when it came to matters of universal import. . . . [Hence] Abu Hanifa relied on his threefold cord of Koran, *qiyas*, and *Ra'i*, with occasional use for *istihsan*, and scarcely any for *Hadith*.[19]

The Arabic terms used here are important. *Qiyas* means "analogical reasoning," and *istihsan* means "legal preference for the sake of the common good." These two rational tools, along with a third one, *urf*, which refers to local customs in any given society, would be Abu Hanifa's main frames of reference. Hence, his version of the Shariah would be a dynamic and flexible one that would uphold the general principles of the Qur'an in any context, by being able to adapt itself to new realities.

The *Hadiths* consisted of sayings or reported acts attributed to the Prophet Muhammad. And, as we shall see in detail later, these would become the pillar of the opposing school of jurisprudence called *ahl al-hadith*, the People of Tradition.

A GOD WITH PRINCIPLES

Abu Hanifa was the pioneer of the juristic side of the rationalist school. Yet matters of jurisprudence were ultimately linked with those of theology—views on the nature of God, revelation, and man. Hence, in Iraq, a school of theologians known as the Mutazilites tried to address all these issues within a rational perspective. As genuine believers of Islam, and sophisticated intellectuals who knew other traditions, including Greek philosophy, their aim was to demonstrate the compatibility of Muslim faith and reason.

Most Mutazilites were followers of Abu Hanifa (thus, Hanafis) in jurisprudence, others were Shiites.[20] But all of them subscribed to the free-will idea of the Qadaris. For them, this was not just a preferred view—it was a logical outcome of one of God's crucial attributes: justice. Since God was absolutely just, they reasoned, He would not reward or punish His creatures without reason. Thus, humans would receive reward in heaven or punishment in hell as a result of their free choice. Anyone who believes in a just God, the Mutazilites concluded, had to accept that man is "the creator of his deeds."[21]

But what did justice mean? And how could humans know what was just or not? The opponents of the Mutazilites argued that it was wrong to first define what justice is and then expect God to conform to it. Whatever God does, they said, that would be the norm for justice. Even if He put all people in hell for no reason, that would be a very just thing, for justice has no definition beyond whatever He does.

For the Mutazilites, this depiction of an unprincipled God was giving Him not praise, as their opponents thought, but disrespect. For them, it was in the nature of God to be just and good, and He would never go against these principles, although He had the power to do everything He willed. "He cannot torture the innocent, and demand the impossible," Mutazilites insisted, not because He does not have the power to do so, but "simply because He is God."[22]

Here it might be worth noting that these opposing views of God are also present in the Christian tradition. The equivalent of the Mutazilite view is called "rationalism" or "intellectualism," because it argues that God is rational and His ways are, at least partly, comprehensible by humans. The other view, called "voluntarism," defines a God whose ways are simply unknowable and unbound by any principle we know.

One prominent commentator who raised this issue in 2006 was Pope Benedict XVI, who, in his controversial Regensburg (Germany) address, criticized voluntarist views in Islam. He was accurate to warn that such views might "lead to the image of a capricious God, who is not even bound to truth and goodness," but he was not as accurate to assume that that was the only view in Islam. In fact, the Holy Father's argument—that "God does not become more divine when we push him away from us in a sheer, impenetrable voluntarism"—was exactly the view the Mutazilites defended twelve centuries earlier, long before it was passed on to medieval Christendom by a latter-day Mutazilite named Ibn Rushd, known in the West as Averroes.[23]

The rationalism of the Mutazilites also led them to conclude that God, and thus His universe, "operated according to rational laws," a premise that called on scientific inquiry.[24] From this emerged the scientific boom of the medieval Islamic world.

Besides having their own viewpoint on the nature of God, the Mutazilites disagreed with their opponents over the nature of revelation as well. The revelation in question was the Qur'an, and Mutazilites argued that it was "created," whereas opponents insisted that it was "uncreated." Semantics are important here. For the "uncreated Qur'an" adherents, the Muslim scripture had existed with God since eternity—similar to the nature of Jesus as described in the Fourth Gospel of John. For the Mutazilites, the Qur'an was certainly the Word of God, but He spoke it at a certain point in history. Otherwise, they argued, the scripture would be elevated almost to the level of a second deity—something that, they argued, contradicts Islam's uncompromising monotheism.

Although this debate about the nature of the Qur'an was related mainly to theology, it also had interpretative consequences, for "a created Qur'an can be *interpreted*; an uncreated Qur'an can only be *applied*."[25] No wonder the Mutazilite view of the scripture allowed a less literalist reading of it, which they needed especially for explaining the seemingly anthropomorphic verses of the Qur'an—references to God's "hands," "faces," and "throne." The Mutazilites were strongly opposed to anthropomorphism, so they developed a method of allegorical interpretation called *ta'wil*, which soon influenced rationalists from other religious persuasions. Indeed, during the ninth and tenth centuries, Rabbanite and Karaite Jews, Coptic Christians, and Shiite and Sunni theologians used the Mutazilite *ta'wil* to defend the rationality of their own scriptures.[26]

A Medieval Theory of the Land of the Free

The Mutazilites have often been misunderstood and sometimes have been confused with some of the more secular "philosophers" who also sprang from the Rationalist strain in medieval

Islam but then became so enthralled by ancient Greek dogmas that they were almost materialist freethinkers. In fact, the Mutazilites were devout Muslims eager to serve their faith by making it accessible and compelling to educated non-Muslims.[27] They have been described as providing a middle path between "the right" (i.e., the antirational Muslims) and "the left" (i.e., secular or non-Muslim philosophers).[28]

Their contributions were impressive. By defining human beings as free and autonomous agents who have the capacity to understand God and His creation, they laid out some of the basic ideas that we today call "modern" and even "liberal." Their ideas, in the words of an American law professor, indeed "appear to share—indeed to anticipate—many principles associated with Western law," such as "rationality, objectivity, principles of individual liberty and equality."[29]

An interesting example of this was the extension of the free-will doctrine that the Mutazilites and their predecessors, the Qadaris, upheld. This idea led them to conclude that the world must be a free place so that humans would have "the power to choose" (*al-tamakkun wa-l ikhtiyar*). Thus, the whole world, they argued, had to be seen as an Abode of Trial (*dar al-ibtila*), where people are tested on whether they are willing or unwilling to accept the true faith.[30] The Mutazilites also realized that this acceptance of faith could occur only with genuine conviction—with "an action of the heart"—an idea that they also inferred from a Qur'anic verse: "There is no compulsion in religion."[31] Their conclusion was that people deserved the "liberty to make religious choices."[32]

This was, a Western scholar notes, a solid basis for tolerance of disbelief and other "erroneous" attitudes, "not because all options were equally valid, as modern pluralists would claim, but rather because erroneous views were meant as a test of Muslim fortitude and thus had to be withstood rather than removed."[33]

Some political ideas that grew out of this were also remarkable. Al-Farabi, a tenth-century Muslim philosopher who extended the Mutazilite philosophy to sociology and politics, wrote *Kitab as-Siyasah al-Madaniyah*, or *The Book of Civil Politics*. He started by noting that all governments on earth are imperfect, except the one established by the Prophet Muhammad in Medina, for that was governed in direct communion with God. Yet, al-Farabi reminded his readers, such a theocracy became impossible after the Prophet's death, so the rules of a just government had to be established by human reason.

Then he described his own ideal government, which he dubbed "the community state," whose inhabitants would enjoy complete freedom (*hurriyah*). This would be "an egalitarian organization where people are free (*ahrar*) to do whatever they want." Moreover, they would be "willing to recognize the leadership of those who promise to give them more freedom . . . and a greater opportunity to follow their particular inclinations."[34] When such a freedom-promoting government exists, al-Farabi added, "people from outside flock to it," and this leads to a "most desirable kind of racial mixture and cultural diversity," which would guarantee the flourishing of talented individuals such as philosophers and poets.[35]

Sounds a bit like America, doesn't it?

Al-Farabi was foresighted indeed. Franz Rosenthal, the late professor of Arabic studies, said the following about him:

> The modern reader can hardly fail to notice that the Muslim philosopher succeeded in giving a true description of the essentials of democracy. He also captured the

full meaning and significance of the concept of political freedom for the happiness and development of the individual.[36]

The ideas of al-Farabi as well as other Muslim thinkers—such as al-Kindi, Ibn Sina, and Ibn Rushd—were translated into Latin and contributed to the rise of modern Western thought. That's why all of them also have Latinized names: Alpharibus, Alkindus, Avicenna, and Averroes, respectively. Another Muslim thinker, Ibn Khaldun in the fourteenth century, wrote *Introduction to History,* which is, according to the late British historian Arnold Toynbee, "undoubtedly the greatest work of its kind that has ever yet been created by any mind in any time or place."[37] In the book, Ibn Khaldun developed, among other things, a theory of economic liberalism that advised governments to minimize taxes, secure private property, support free markets, and avoid budget deficits.[38] The World Bank has recently referred to him as "the first advocate of privatization."[39]

In short, the idea of freedom—in the theological, political, or economic sense—was not unknown in classical Islamdom, as some have claimed. The People of Reason clearly aspired to it, and they may have been headed toward establishing a genuinely Islamic liberalism.

Yet they were not the only folks around. There also were, as we have seen, despotic caliphs who despised such wayward liberals, and, even more important, an opposing and steadily growing camp called the People of Tradition.

CHAPTER FOUR

The Medieval War of Ideas (II)

The sinners among the People of Tradition
are God's friends. But the pious ones among
the People of Innovation are God's enemies.

—IMAM AHMAD IBN HANBAL,
founder of the Hanbali school of Islam

TWO DECADES into the ninth century, a scholar appeared in Baghdad who would today be called "a radical cleric." A Baghdad native, he had left the city at the age of sixteen to spend time in other parts of Islamdom, and especially the Hejaz region, the western part of the Arabian Peninsula. The scholars there, and particularly those in Medina, believed that the Iraqis had gone too far in their rationalism in matters of religion. Some even thought that giving any role to human reason in religious matters was a dangerous innovation (*bid'a*), a term that would soon become the Muslim equivalent of the Christian heresy.

Soon after his arrival in Baghdad, our "radical cleric," Imam Ahmad ibn Hanbal, quickly became the most zealous champion of this antirationalist view, starting a popular campaign against the People of Reason. The city was accustomed to intellectual debates, but Hanbal and his nascent group of followers were there not to debate but to denounce. In his sermons, Hanbal fiercely condemned all the rationalist schools mentioned in the previous chapter: the pluralist Murjiites, who preferred to "postpone" to the afterlife the who-is-right-and-who-is-wrong discussion; the Qadaris, who defended man's free will and opposed predestination; the Jahmiya, a variant of the Mutazilites; and the Hanafis, the followers of Abu Hanifa, who founded a rationalistic and flexible type of jurisprudence. According to Hanbal, all these people had to be banned and their books had to be buried.[1]

In fact, Hanbal did not even consider these People of Reason to be Muslims, even going so far as to advocate their execution. Anyone who declared that the Qur'an was "created," he said, must be asked to repent; if he refuses, he must be killed.[2] Luckily, Hanbal had no law enforcement under his command to execute his enemies. Yet his followers were able to be intimidating in different ways. Once, an ascetic from Tarsus (Asia Minor) named Ahmad al-Sarrak, a proponent of the "created Qur'an" view, arrived in Baghdad. Hearing about the man's "heresy," Hanbal commanded that no one sit with him. The humiliated al-Sarrak fled to Abadan, but an associate of Hanbal's convinced the ruler there to have a crier announce at all the inns that no one was to sit with him, and the poor man was expelled from that city as well.[3]

Hanbal's own alternative to reason as a source in religion was twofold. In matters of theology, it was a simple and blunt dogmatism. For example, he simply refused to discuss the meanings of some of the ambiguous verses in the Qur'an—such as the ones about God's "face" or "throne." All such mysteries, Hanbal argued, had to be accepted *bila kayf* (without asking how). That term would soon become a theological principle for his followers.

Hanbal's second emphasis, which was the basis for his whole notion of jurisprudence, was the "tradition" (Sunna) of the Prophet Muhammad—which we shall now examine more closely.

SUNNA VERSUS REASON

All Muslims deeply respect Muhammad, the Prophet of Islam, so his tradition is invaluable for all of them. But exactly what his tradition means, and how it should be understood, is disputed. This was, at the very least, a serious bone of contention in the ninth century.

In the eyes of the People of Reason, the Prophet was the most righteous interpreter and practitioner of the Qur'an, but he did not possess any special, suprahuman wisdom. The Qur'an included all the revelation God transmitted to the Prophet, and he, as "the first of the Muslims," followed the scripture just as all other Muslims are supposed to do.[4] Thus, a Muslim would already be following the example of the Prophet if he follows the Qur'an and uses his judgment when faced with new questions. The Qur'an, after all, constantly calls men to *aqala*, to reason.

The People of Tradition disagreed. Since they were unhappy with the "excess of reason," to put it mildly, they had to find some authority that would limit the scope of reason, which they saw as an instrument of temptation and deviation. That's why, in their eyes, the tradition of the Prophet became an all-encompassing source of wisdom that defined everything. Ahmad Hanbal was famous for never having eaten a single watermelon because he could find no precedent for that in the tradition of the Prophet.[5] In another instance, he is reported to have asked his wife Rayhana to stop wearing a certain kind of shoe because "it didn't exist in the Prophet's time."[6]

This new understanding of the Sunna was a radical break from a liberal maxim that earlier scholars of the Shariah, such as Abu Hanifa, subscribed to: "The primary principle is permission."[7] This meant that liberty was to be presumed as the natural human condition and not abridged without reason.[8] But in Hanbal's world, only what could be proven to be in the Sunna was permitted. Some fundamentalist Muslims today, who refuse such "innovations" as democracy by arguing that "the Prophet did not vote," are echoing this very same mindset.[9]

To be fair, not all People of Tradition were as rigid as Hanbal. His teacher, al-Shafi, was a little more flexible, and some have defined al-Shafi's school as "semi-rationalist."[10] Al-Shafi's teacher, Malik, was even a little more adaptable, for he and his Medina-based community subscribed to the "living tradition" of the Prophet, whose scope was more modest than the all-encompassing tradition adhered to by Hanbal and his followers.

These names—Hanbal, al-Shafi, and Malik—are important, for they were the founders of three of the four major Sunni schools of jurisprudence. Among them, al-Shafi's school became the most definitive, for the method that he devised soon became the norm for others. The "Shafi revolution" would be so significant, and rule-setting, that even the students of Abu Hanifa, the standard-bearer for the People of Reason, would have to conform to it and thus withdraw from some of the rationalism espoused by their teacher.

The Rise of the Hadiths

Al-Shafi's impact on Islamic jurisprudence is quite complex, but at its core lies the elevation of the prophetic tradition (Sunna) to the level of the Qur'an. He envisioned the Prophet—who until then had been widely seen as an interpreter and practitioner of God's law—as a second "lawgiver" whose words and deeds were as authoritative as the Qur'an.[11] Hence, it started to matter whether the Prophet really ate watermelons—and how he dressed, ate, brushed his teeth, combed his hair, and grew his beard.

By the time al-Shafi developed his theory, almost two centuries had passed since the death of the Prophet, so figuring out his Sunna was no easy task. There was a "living Sunna" that encapsulated such practices as the way daily prayers should be performed, which had been transmitted from the Prophet's time in an unbroken chain of observance. But in an age when there were no archives, records, or newspapers, how could anyone find out what the Prophet had said or done in a particular situation two centuries earlier?

Al-Shafi, Hanbal, and their adherents found their answers in the Hadiths, or sayings, attributed to the Prophet and allegedly witnessed by his closest companions. (That's why they were called *ahl al-hadith*, the People of Hadith.) These narratives were actually hearsay—what people believed, or claimed to believe, to be accurate reports from the Prophet's era. "One day I saw the Prophet walking toward the mosque," for example, a Hadith would recount from one of the Prophet's companions. Then this would be supported by an account of the six or seven people, on average, who heard the story from one another: "This is what

Al-Imam Tirmithi narrated through Ibn Mahdi from At-Thawri from Waasil and Mansour and Al-A'mash from Abee Wae'l from Amr ibn Shurahbeel from Ibn Mas'oud who said . . ."

Of course—as in "telephone game"—it was highly optimistic to think that the original message could have survived such a long chain of transmitters. The presence of so many embellished stories only intensified the challenge. The Qur'an was written down during the Prophet's lifetime, and canonized right after his death, but the Hadiths were simply oral traditions. That's why it was an open field for anyone who wanted to put some alleged word into the mouth of the Prophet in order to justify a view to which he subscribed, or an interest he wanted to pursue. The very fact that the Hadiths became more authoritative under al-Shafi and other People of Tradition added to the motivation for fabrication.

Hence, at the turn of the second century after the Prophet's death, Islamdom became a Hadith wasteland, with traditions justifying almost every view. Arab nationalists made up narratives showing the Prophet as an Arab supremacist; others soon responded with Hadiths praising the virtues of Persians or Turks.[12] Another motivation was simple self-interest. "Eating flour cookies makes man stronger," one Hadith read, and it was no accident that the man who put this into circulation, Muhammed b. Hajjaj Mahai, was selling—guess what?—flour cookies.[13]

Other forgeries were clearly designed to denounce the schools of thought that the People of Tradition despised. "Two groups in my community were cursed by seventy prophets," one such Hadith declared, allegedly citing the Prophet. "They are the Qadariya and the Murjia."[14] These two groups were, as we have seen, the defenders of free will and the pluralist Postponers. There was an apparent absurdity here, for these groups had emerged several decades after the Prophet's death so he had never known about them. But while the Prophet of the Qur'an was a modest man who said, "I am only a mortal like you,"[15] and "I do not know the unseen,"[16] the Hadiths had already turned him into an omniscient prognosticator who knew everything about the future.

This aggrandized and manipulated Prophet could also comment on the rulers who came after him and say such incredible things as, "God writes down only the good deeds of the ruler and not the evil ones."[17] This was probably a forgery put in circulation during the early eighth century in order to justify the tyranny and corruption of the Umayyad caliphs.

Another very interesting Hadith seems to have been devised specifically to denounce those who did not show enough obedience to the Hadith reports: "Let me find no one of you reclining on his couch," the Prophet allegedly says in it, "who, when confronted with an order of permission or prohibition from me, says: 'I do not know [whether this is obligatory or not]; we will follow only what we find in the Book of God.' "[18]

At the turn of Islam's second century, everyone, including the most dedicated supporters of the Hadiths, knew that there was a staggering number of forged traditions. The People of Tradition just claimed that it was possible to sort out the authentic ones from the forgeries, and that they had the authority to make that evaluation. Thus, beginning with Ahmad Hanbal himself, they started to compile the narratives, work out their chains of transmitters, and create collections of *sahih* (sound) Hadiths. The most prominent of these scholars, al-Bukhari, is said to have chosen 2,602 Hadiths from a pool of more than 300,000. This gives an idea of not only the number of inauthentic Hadiths that were present at the time but also the likelihood that al-Bukhari would have sorted out only the authentic ones.

Yet soon the *Sahih Bukhari* and the Hadith collections of five other scholars became highly respected, and even sanctified, among the People of Tradition. Some even started to argue that these Hadiths were so authoritative that they could abrogate the Qur'an. (This theory of abrogation was among al-Shafi's inventions.)[19]

This ascendance of the tradition (Sunna), which was constructed two centuries after the Prophet it claimed to represent, would lead to the creation of what French historian Maxime Rodinson calls "the post-Qur'anic ideology." And this would be quite different from that of the Qur'an, which "accord[ed] a greater role to reasoning and rationality."[20]

"Toward Strictness and Rigorism"

The ascendance of the People of Tradition marked a turning point in the history of Islamdom. With their introduction of a huge number of Hadiths as authoritative religious injunctions, the scope of rational inquiry was minimized, and the Shariah became a much more rigid set of rules. The whole tendency, notes Joseph Schacht, a leading Western scholar on Islamic law, was "toward strictness and rigorism."[21]

Ironically, while zealously opposing rationality as a dangerous "innovation," the People of Tradition brought their own innovations to the Shariah, such as the stoning of adulterers, the killing of apostates, social limitations on women, bans on art and music, and punishments for wine drinking and other sorts of sinful behavior. None of these are in the Qur'an; all of them are in the Hadiths.

What really brought about this hardening of the Shariah was the projection of the customs and values of the medieval Orient back to the Prophet. The degradation of women's rights was one example. In fact, the Qur'an and thus the Prophet had taken a great leap forward, "endowing them with property and some other rights, and giving them a measure of protection against ill treatment by their husbands. . . . But the position of women remained poor, and worsened when, in this as in so many other respects, the original message of Islam lost its impetus and was modified under the influence of pre-existing attitudes and customs."[22]

These "pre-existing attitudes and customs" crept into the Shariah via Hadiths attributed to the Prophet. The seclusion of women was a case in point. The Qur'an ordered seclusion only for the wives of the Prophet Muhammad, as a sign of their unique status. Yet in the Byzantine and Persian cultures that Muslims gradually adopted, it was customary for upper-class women to be secluded from all men but their own. The egalitarianism of Islam paradoxically spread this upper-class seclusion, and "the Qur'anic injunctions to propriety were stretched, by way of hadith, to cover the fashionable latter-day seclusion."[23]

The infusion of the misogynistic attitudes of the Middle East into Islam also influenced the way the Qur'an was interpreted. For example, the Qur'an presents a version of the story of Adam and Eve and their fall from grace for tasting the forbidden fruit, but, unlike the Old Testament, it doesn't portray Eve as the deceiver—Adam receives the divine reproach.[24] But in the Qur'anic commentaries written after the third century of Islam, Eve started to receive the blame. This occurred at the same time that dozens of new Hadiths appeared, defining women as cunning, insidious, and immoral creatures. No wonder that Islamic feminists of our times often uphold the Qur'an in order to challenge misogynistic Hadiths, which they see as products of the "male-domination ideology."[25]

The traditional Islamic ban on painting and sculpture also was a Hadith-induced late invention. Although the depiction of living forms was not explicitly forbidden by the Qur'an, "most jurists, basing themselves on Hadith, held that this was an infringement of the sole power of God to create life."[26] On the big debate between free will and predestination, most Hadiths supported the latter view, reflecting "ancient Arab beliefs."[27] The Qur'anic ban on usury was similarly extended by way of Hadiths, leading to the traditional position that all forms of interest are prohibited.[28] With the stagnation of the Shariah through such moves, the economic dynamism of the early centuries of Islam would also slowly fade away.[29]

The tendency toward "strictness and rigorism" showed itself vis-à-vis not only Muslim society, but non-Muslims as well. The rules regulating the affairs of the *dhimmis*—the protected Jews, Christians, and others—became less tolerant as time went by and Muslims adopted, often via the Hadiths, the attitudes of the Byzantine and Sassanid Empires.[30]

The doctrine of *jihad*, too, was emboldened by the Hadiths and their proponents. The earlier scholars tended to put greater emphasis on religious practices such as prayer and mosque attendance, and they did not see *jihad* as a religious obligation.[31] "The Arab conquests, however, gave a psychological twist to Islamic thought," notes Western historian Ann K. S. Lambton, "as a result of which the duty of jihad was exalted in the Traditions [i.e., Hadiths]."[32]

The great champion of the Hadiths, al-Shafi, was particularly influential here. He developed the theory that the more peaceful verses of the Qur'an were abrogated by "the sword verses," while it was also possible to see them referring to different contexts— war against belligerents, peace with others.[33] He also divided the world into the Abode of Islam and the Abode of War and envisioned constant warfare between them. Political theorists after al-Shafi would enshrine this concept in their writings by averring that one of the duties of the caliph was to "launch jihad at least once a year."[34] Most Hanafis would disagree, though, and argue "that non-believers could be fought only if they resorted to armed conflict."[35]

The People of Reason, unsurprisingly, sounded more reasonable.

HADITHS REVISITED

Here I should provide a brief comment in order to avoid painting merely a black-and-white picture of the Hadiths. Not all of them were forgeries, and not all of them had distasteful content. There are, in fact, many inspiring Hadiths with good moral teachings on charity, compassion, and honesty. Moreover, the idea of an Islam totally devoid of the Hadiths—as the Sola Scriptura–type radical reformists of our era suggest—is not plausible. At the very least, without the rich historical infor-mation that the Hadiths provide us, it would be impossible to understand the context of the Qur'an—which is often impera-tive to understanding its meaning.

The problem, then, is not the existence of the Hadith litera-ture, but rather the way it is handled. The People of Tradition turned these narratives into a sanctified source that must only be obeyed and not questioned. Quite intentionally, they put the Hadiths above human reason. That's why the main criterion they considered when accepting a Hadith was its chain of transmitters—and not its content.

But the People of Reason, as might be expected, used reason for judging the Hadiths. The Mutazilites, in particular, "held the rational sense of the content of these reports about the Prophet to be a more important test of their validity, along with analysis of the chain of transmitters."[36] In the course of this book, we will see that some contemporary Muslim reformers advocate such a rational reevaluation of the Hadith literature.

THE HOUSE OF WISDOM—AND INQUISITION

Having been introduced to the People of Tradition and their ideas, let's return to the story that opened this chapter: that of the "radical cleric" Imam Ahmad ibn Hanbal and his campaign against the People of Reason.

These two opposing camps of Islamdom (from here on, the Traditionists and the Rationalists) engaged in their war of ideas for at least five centuries—from the eighth to the thirteenth. Throughout this period, the Traditionists very often secured the backing of political authorities. Only during a brief period in the early ninth century did the Rationalists win the favor and even the active support of the political authority—a support that turned out to be more curse than gift.

Let's examine how this political factor played out. We have seen how the Umayyad caliphs supported the predestinarians against the defenders of free will in order to justify their corrupt rule. But, despite all such efforts, the Umayyads were overthrown by the rival Abbasid dynasty in 749. The latter brought important changes to Islamdom, ending the Arab supremacist attitude of their predecessors and allowing non-Arab Muslims, such as Persians and Turks, to hold prominent positions.

The Abbasids also moved the capital of Islamdom from Damascus, the Umayyad base, to Iraq—first to Kufa and then to the new city they built: Baghdad. With beautiful parks, gardens, villas, canals, and promenades, this new capital soon earned fame as the most beautiful city in the world. It also would be the stage for the Golden Age of the early medieval Islamic civilization, which peaked during the thirty-three-year reign of Harun al-Rashid (786–809), whose magnificent court inspired *One Thousand and One Nights*.

In 813, Harun's son, al-Ma'mun, a Rationalist by conviction, sat on the Abbasid throne. Word has it that the young caliph once had a dream in which he saw Aristotle, who told him that "reason and revelation" were not just compatible but also mutually supportive, and that a good Muslim ruler should encourage both.[37] Hence, al-Ma'mun founded an academy called the House of Wisdom, where philosophical and scientific works of ancient Greece, including all the major works of Aristotle, were translated into Arabic. Great minds such as al-Kindi, "philosopher of the Arabs," and mathematician al-Khwarizmi, from whose name the word *algorithm* comes, were also employed in this academy, along with numerous Christians.

As a Rationalist, al-Ma'mun was interested in theological debates, including interfaith ones. He invited Abu Qurra, a Greek Orthodox bishop from Syria, to his court, and the latter defended Christian theology while the caliph tried to refute his arguments —all in a civilized manner. Al-Ma'mun and his successors would continue to welcome discourse with Christians, Jews, Zoroastrians, Buddhists, and many others—helping Islamdom flourish intellectually.[38]

So far, so good. But in the ninth year of his rule, al-Ma'mun made a disastrous decision that would stain all his good works. His distaste for the Traditionists—whom he found not only "vulgar" but also politically suspicious—led him to launch the *mihna*, a sort of inquisition, in order to impose the "created Qur'an" doctrine on all scholars.[39] Prominent figures of the Traditionist camp, including Ahmad Hanbal, were arrested, questioned, and, in some cases, even flogged for their insistence on calling the Qur'an "uncreated." This tyrannical policy would last for sixteen years under al-Ma'mun and two of his successors, and, naturally, it would create havoc not just in Baghdad but throughout the empire.

The exact motivation and the culprits behind this bizarre inquisition have long been a matter of controversy. The "created Qur'an" was certainly a doctrine championed by the Mutazilites, and, although they "were not directly responsible" for the *mihna*, their doctrinal link puts them under suspicion.[40] One pertinent explanation, which also makes sense in light of our previous acquaintance with Ahmad Hanbal and his campaign against the Rationalists, comes from Nimrod Hurvitz, an expert on the formation of the Hanbali school. He suggests that the *mihna* might have been supported by the Rationalist theologians as "an act of self-defence" rather than an attack. Frustrated with the "scare tactics" of the Traditionists, who constantly declared the Rationalists heretics, the latter seem to have found the *mihna* a lifesaver, as it silenced those who harassed them and allowed them to "raise their heads, speak their minds and establish themselves in their proper role in society."[41]

Yet still, this whoever-suppresses-my-suppresser-is-right approach was certainly wrong. It should be acknowledged as a historic mistake of the Mutazilites and others who seem to have allied themselves with the *mihna*. And perhaps some reform-minded Muslims of our day who tend to support authoritarian measures against contemporary Traditionists should derive a lesson from this.

A further lesson can come from the fact that the *mihna* ended in utter failure. Not only did the Traditionists remain steadfast in their doctrines, but the inquisition helped them gain further popularity by turning them into folk heroes. And soon, they had their own chance for dominance.

THE DESTRUCTION OF REASON

In 847, the Abbasid caliphate passed to a new member of the dynasty named al-Mutawakkil. He was a nephew of al-Ma'mun but also his exact opposite. He not only ended the *mihna* but also reversed the official policy and gave full support to Traditionists such as Ahmad Hanbal, adopting their doctrines as the official view.

Now the Mutazilites were the outcasts. "Every discussion about a thing that the Prophet did not discuss," al-Mutawakkil declared, "is an error."[42] He ordered the Traditionists to preach against the Mutazilites, who were soon fired from all official posts.[43] The House of Wisdom lost caliphal favor and declined. One of its eminent scholars, al-Kindi, who had produced more than 250 treatises on philosophy, physics, chemistry, medicine, psychology, and even music theory, was beaten, and his library was confiscated. Traditionism was back with a vengeance.

Al-Mutawakkil also suppressed non-Muslims. Under his rule, Christians and Jews were stripped of much of their social status and were forced to wear distinctive clothing. Some churches and synagogues in Baghdad were demolished, and every tenth Christian or Jewish house was confiscated to make room for future mosques. Al-Mutawakkil even "ordered that wooden images of devils be nailed to the doors of their [the non-Muslims'] homes to distinguish them from those of Muslims.[44]

Even worse, al-Mutawakkil's policies were there to stay. The Traditionists continued to enjoy official support and became "the most ardent supporters of the institution of the caliphate."[45] The most radical among them, the Hanbalis, grew more and more assertive under the patronage of the throne. In 935, Muslim author Ibn al-Athir wrote:

> In that year the Hanbali affair became more distressing as their fury intensified. They began to raid the houses of the commanders and of the common people, and if they found wine they poured it away, and if they found a singing girl they beat her and broke her instruments. They hindered buying and selling and delayed men who were walking along with women and youths, to question them about their companions. If the answers failed to satisfy them they beat the men and dragged them to the chief of police and testified about their immoral acts. The Hanbalis wrought discord upon Baghdad.[46]

At the beginning of the eleventh century, al-Mutawakkil's policy was revived by one of his descendants, Abbasid caliph al-Qadir, who called on all "innovators," and especially the Rationalist Mutazilite and Hanafi scholars, to "repent" from their misguided ways. Those who refused were forbidden to do any theological or juridical work. A heavy-handed minion of the caliph, Mahmud of Ghazni, ruler of a vast area covering today's Iran, Afghanistan, and Pakistan, carried the policy to extremes.

He launched a brutal campaign to kill all the Mutazilites and other "heretics" by "crucifying them, imprisoning them, [or] exiling them." He also "ordered the cursing of them from the pulpits of the Muslims. And he threatened every group from the *ahl al-bida* (innovators) and drove them away from their homes."[47]

Back in Baghdad, the caliph soon coped with the tone. He declared that anyone who called the Qur'an created—a cornerstone of Mutazilite theology—would be deemed an infidel and his blood would be shed.[48]

Besides all this internal bigotry, the most destructive blow to Islamic reason, and actually to Islamdom itself, would be an external threat: the "Mongol catastrophe" of the mid-thirteenth century. The armies of Genghis Khan and his successors stormed the Middle East, conquering everything between Syria and India. All invaders are brutal, but the Mongols' terror was "unprecedented," for they "loved destruction for its own sake."[49] As they marched through Islamdom,

> Again and again, almost the entire populace of a city was massacred without regard to sex or age, only skilled artisans being saved and transported away; even peasants were involved, being used as a living mass of rubble forced ahead of the army to absorb arrows and fill moats.[50]

In 1258, the Mongols sacked Baghdad—then the most vibrant and polished city of Islamdom, if not the world. They massacred almost the whole Muslim population, including the caliph, and destroyed the House of Wisdom, with its magnificent collection of the works of the Mutazilites and other intellectuals of Islam. It was said that so many manuscripts were thrown into the

Tigris that the river turned black from the ink for days on end.[51] The Mongols even shattered the irrigation systems of the Middle East, reducing agricultural production to one-tenth of what it had been before.[52] This was colossal destruction that Europe was lucky to have never faced.[53]

A similar tragedy would hit Spain, the western edge of Islamdom, three centuries later. The Muslim kingdom there, called al-Andalus, had preserved the intellectual sophistication of the Rationalist school, along with magnificent works of art and architecture and a spirit of *convivencia*—cultural and civic collaboration among Muslims, Jews, and Christians.[54] As in Baghdad, though, this medieval enlightenment was afflicted first by internal bigotry and then by external invasion. The rich libraries of Muslim Spain were attacked first by the Kharijite-like militant Muslims from North Africa and then by the Spanish *Reconquista*, which expelled all Muslims and Jews from the Iberian Peninsula.[55] When Inquisitor Ximenez de Cisneros ordered the burning of some eighty thousand Muslim books in Granada in 1499, "to sweep away all the traces of the teachings of Islam," what he was really sweeping away was the best of Islam.[56]

The Not-So-United Colors of Sunni Islam

The war of ideas between the Traditionists and the Rationalists of Islam was a long and complex one, and we have covered only the headlines of this curious story. The result, in a nutshell, was that the Traditionists won and the Rationalists lost. This was the outcome of a trend that started in the third century of Islam and crystallized in the fifth.

The Traditionist victory had permanent consequences for Muslim thinking. "In the very early period the Muslims interpreted the Qur'an pretty freely," notes the late Fazlur Rahman, the prominent Muslim modernist theologian. "But after the 2nd century . . . the lawyers neatly tied themselves and the Community down . . . and theology became buried under the weight of literalism."[57] The Traditionists also swept aside the individualist spirit of the Qur'an, for they "cared little for the individual and his personal experience." Instead, they emphasized "almost exclusively the social content of Islam . . . [and] refused to allow the individual the right of creative thinking."[58]

As early as the third century of Islam (tenth century), Traditionists were already arguing that all problems that Muslims could ever face were solved, and there was no need for further inquiry. The gates of *ijtihad* (independent reasoning), they famously claimed, were closed.

The rise of Sufism, the mystical tradition in Islam, as a popular trend in the ninth century and onward was in some ways an effort to find a breath of fresh air outside this narrow and hard legalism and to create room for the individual.[59] It might be worthwhile to note that, despite views to the contrary, Sufism had its origin in the Qur'an,[60] and it had some common roots with the Mutazilites.[61]

The Traditionists were, however, far from a uniform group; the legacy of the Rationalist school did not disappear entirely and found its way into some Traditionist schools. What emerged at the end of the long controversy between reason and dogma was more of a spectrum of thought rather than a black-and-white division.

The most definitive name in the Traditionist camp, as we have seen, was al-Shafi, whose followers created the Shafi school. Their method became so dominant that soon even the less Hadith-oriented Malikis (followers of Malik) and the formerly

Rationalist Hanafis were forced to move closer to the Shafi view. Nonetheless, the Hanafi school, which would later be adopted by the Ottoman and Mughal Empires, remained relatively rational, flexible, and lenient.

In theology, the counterpart of the Shafi attitude was Asharism, created by the tenth-century scholar al-Ashari, a former Mutazilite who "repented" after seeing the Prophet in a dream. In his polemics he used the rational method, but he employed it for opposing Rationalist views and defending Traditionist ones, such as predestination, voluntarism, and occasionalism (i.e., the rejection of natural laws). He insisted that human reason could not find what is right and what is wrong—a view that justified the Traditionist jurists' efforts to find all answers in the Sunna.

The more rational Hanafi school found its theological complement in the Maturidi school, created by al-Maturidi in the early tenth century. His views show some Mutazilite influence because of the greater credit he gave to human reason and free will. In disagreement with al-Ashari, for example, al-Maturidi argued that human reason, unaided by revelation, could distinguish between right and wrong.[62]

Meanwhile, the most radical line in the Traditionist camp, the one led by Imam Hanbal, soon turned into Hanbalism, the most rigid of the four major Sunni schools. Its followers opposed all forms of "innovation" and any form of rational discussion. Theirs was such an impractical doctrine that it remained marginal among Muslims, only to be revitalized during times of crisis, such as the catastrophic Mongol invasion in the thirteenth century.

The eighteenth century would see a surprising revival of the Hanbali school in the Arabian Desert under the leadership of another radical cleric named Muhammad ibn Abd-al-Wahhab. His followers, who became known as Wahhabis, started a militant campaign against the Ottoman Empire, which they condemned for Sufism and other "innovations." The empire kept in check these latter-day Hanbalis—who also had a "Kharijite zeal"—until World War I, when the British Empire decided to destroy Ottoman power and establish Arabia as an independent state.[63]

Soon Arabia would become Saudi Arabia, and Wahhabism would be its official doctrine. It would also turn out that the country was sitting on top of the world's greatest oil reserves—a source that the Saudis could use to evangelize their rigid doctrine in the four corners of the Muslim world. This was a success that Imam Hanbal, who spearheaded "strictness and rigorism," could never have even imagined.

The Desert Beneath the Iceberg

> The dwellers of the desert are very
> hard in unbelief and hypocrisy, amd
> more disposed not to know the limits
> of what God has revealed to his
> Messenger.
>
> —*Qur'an 9:97,* Shakir translation

THE DECLINE OF THE Rationalist school in Islam, and the triumph of the Traditionist one, is a famous story—and there are various explanations for it. Some critics have argued that the Rationalist school was just an alien import from ancient Greece that would inevitably prove "incompatible with a Qur'anic worldview."[2] Yet, as we have seen, it was not the Qur'anic worldview but the post-Qur'anic tradition that overshadowed Islamic reason. Why was this so?

Some have found an answer by blaming specific individuals, such as the influential Imam al-Ghazali in the twelfth century. His magnum opus, *Incoherence of the Philosophers*, was indeed a severe blow to "philosophy," a term that then referred to all sources of secular knowledge. Al-Ghazali is also criticized for promoting a religious awareness based on unquestioning obedience rather than critical thinking.[3] But should we see al-Ghazali's impact as a cause or a result of the stagnation in Islamdom?[4] After all, other thinkers, such as the great Ibn Rushd (Averroes), who refuted al-Ghazali and defended "philosophy" in *The Incoherence of the Incoherence*, could have spearheaded a Rationalist victory. Was there a determining factor, then, that favored one of these strains in Islamic thought over the other?

We have seen that the political authority, the Umayyad and Abbasid caliphates, had played an important role in this story by frequently offering their support for the Traditionists. Yet even this might be a superficial explanation, for it leaves us wondering why the political authority acted this way and why its decisions were so definitive.

To put things in perspective, it is worth remembering that the controversy that haunted Islamdom—reason versus dogmatism—also occurred in Christendom. Early Christian theologian Tertullian, who coined the term *Trinity*, was a strong opponent of reason, which he saw as a deviant influence from pagan Greeks. "To us there is no need of curious questioning now that we have Jesus Christ," he wrote, "nor of enquiry now that we have the Gospel."[5] His insistence on "fideism"—faith devoid of reason—survived as a trend among Catholics even into the nineteenth century.

But at some point in the history of Christianity, the rationalist view became more dominant, whereas the opposite occurred in Islam. The torch, it could even be said, passed from one to the other. While Ibn Rushd's defense of rational faith had little impact in Islamdom, it greatly influenced St. Thomas Aquinas, whose synthesis of philosophy, science, and faith opened the way to modernity in the West. And al-Farabi's tenth-century antici-

pation of a democratic government to secure the rights and freedoms of the individual certainly found its destiny in the West
before anywhere else.

So, why did reason and freedom flourish in Christendom
while it declined in the lands of Islam?

Could the answer be related to the fact that Islam unfolded
into the Orient, whereas Christianity flourished in the Occident?

The Context of the Text

The doctrines of a religion do not derive just from its sacred
texts. Those texts, especially in the "Abrahamic" religions, are
of course important. Yet they come into life in the minds, and at
the hands, of people. That's why the same religion takes on different forms in different societies. All Christians read the same
New Testament, but those in New York are in many ways different from their coreligionists in, say, the Philippines, where
some flagellate and torture themselves during Holy Week to
atone for their sins. And all contemporary Christians are dis-
similar from their medieval coreligionists, some of whom burnt
"witches" at the stake or tortured "heretics" during the Inquisition. Throughout history, all such diverse followers of Christ
have given quite different meanings to his gospel, because they
understood it within quite different mindsets.

The same is true for Islam. Muslims have understood their
faith in all sorts of ways, because they had all sorts of mindsets
that were shaped by the age and the milieu in which they were
living. Their contexts, in other words, have strongly influenced
how they understood their sacred text.

No wonder when we look at the background of the "medieval
war of ideas" explored in the previous chapters we can clearly

see the influence of context in the formation of different trends and schools that contrasted and sometimes conflicted with each other. When we look at their contexts, in fact, a whole new picture emerges to explain why the Mutazilites were rationalist, the Hanbalis antirationalist, and others whatever they were. This even explains why, in the long run, the winners won and the losers lost.

The Tribes Strike Back

Let's begin with the Kharijites, the Dissenters, who, after the war between Ali and Muawiyah, blamed both parties for apostasy and thus withdrew from and fought against both. This first "terrorist" movement in Islamic history—and not the last one, as current events show—was the most fanatic of all early Islamic sects. They denounced as "infidels" every Muslim who disagreed with their doctrine and then set about killing them. They were so inclined to violence that they put it at the top of their agenda, making *jihad* the sixth pillar of Islam, in addition to the five peaceful ones that almost all Muslims accept.[6] Their most extreme wing, like today's al-Qaeda and other Islamist terrorist groups, even disregarded the distinction between combatants and noncombatants, killing not only men but also their wives and children.[7]

Now, as many historians have noted, all this fanaticism and militancy was directly linked with the Kharijites' preexisting social structure. Most of them were Bedouin, the nomadic Arabs of the desert, whose culture, in the words of a contemporary Arab scholar, was shaped by a "prolonged historical process of adaptation to the harsh conditions of the desert environment." The result was the glorification of "courage, gallantry, power, fierce vitality, confrontation, attachment to and mastery of arms, manhood, pride, rivalry, defiance, heroism, and austerity."[8] The Bedouin way of life, in other words, was "nothing but raids and wars."[9]

One of the telltale episodes about this culture comes from the life of the Prophet Muhammad. On one occasion, it was reported, he kissed his grandson in front of a Bedouin. The latter was surprised and said, "I have ten children, and I have never kissed any of them." The Prophet answered: "He who does not spread mercy will not find mercy."[10]

In other words, mercy and affection was Islam's message, but that Bedouin was not particularly inclined to internalize it. That's why the Qur'an warned the Prophet: "The desert Arabs are more obdurate in disbelief and hypocrisy, and more likely not to know the limits which God has sent down to His Messenger."[11] This did not mean that "the desert Arabs" did not become Muslims. They did. But they also brought their harshness into the religion, which was manifested in the Kharijite militancy.

If militancy was one the main characteristics of most Kharijites—albeit not all of them, to be fair—a strong sense of communalism was another. This, too, was an extension of one of their pre-Islamic traits—tribalism. They formed small groups quite similar to sub-tribes or clans, "as if they were trying to restore the former groups in which they had lived, but on an Islamic basis."[12] They also spoke of their own group as "the people of paradise" and all others as "the people of hell"—reflecting the pre-Islamic Bedouin belief that the individual's life gained significance only by membership in a closed community.[13]

This tribalism was a feature of the desert Arabs, but it also appealed to some urban dwellers who were in search of such a tightly knit group. Thus, in the cities, the Kharijites "became a focus for discontented elements" and attracted "the young, the obscure and many ex-slaves and converts."[14] The similarity of this Kharijite base to that of contemporary militant Islamism—the tribal, Taliban-like groups in the rural areas, the disenchanted youth in the big cities—is most remarkable.

THE COSMOPOLITAN VERSUS THE PAROCHIAL

Despite their appeal to the discontented, the Kharijites were a marginal force in the formative centuries of Islam. The real and definitive power struggle was between the Rationalists and the Traditionists, as explained in the previous chapter. And both schools had their own distinctive backgrounds.

The Rationalists were the complete opposite of the desert-based, tribal Kharijites. It surely was no accident that the Rationalists thrived in the big cities of first Syria and then Iraq, dynamic centers of trade and culture. The Qadarite movement, for example—the earliest defenders of the free-will idea—had emerged from the "urban culture of the new classes of merchants and educated people."[15] Their heirs, the Mutazilites, were similar: well-educated, cosmopolitan intellectuals exposed to various peoples, traditions, and philosophies. That is why they were driven to create a coherent and rational Islamic theology that would appeal to the intellects of the Christians, Jews, Zoroastrians, and Manichaeans and also cope with the works of Greek philosophers.

As a case in point, consider Abu Hanifa, the leading figure of the Rationalist school of jurisprudence. His thinking closely paralleled that of the Rationalist Mutazilites and the pluralist Postponers. Hence, his critics accused him "of neglecting the Sunnah in favor of analogical reasoning and of making immoderate use of his own opinion."[16] He was also a proponent of human freedom. "Neither the community nor the government is entitled to interfere with the liberty of the individual," Abu Hanifa held, as long as the individual has not violated the law.[17]

And these views were connected to Abu Hanifa's context. He was based in Kufa, Iraq, the Abbasid capital before the creation of Baghdad. Kufa was a center for not only intellectuals, but also tradesmen. And Abu Hanifa was both. He was a lifelong merchant, and a pretty worldly one:

> He even went to Basrah to debate the opinions of the advocates of various sects, and even of the Dahrites, who were atheist materialists. . . . In his city, Abu Hanifa rubbed shoulders with Greeks, Indians, Persians, and Arabs, and their sundry cultures came in addition to the many different trends of thought. . . . Those features were to exert obvious influence on his thought, as, indeed, was his constant involvement in trade. His legal thought was directly confronted with the reality of customs, trading, and financial practices and the difficulty, if not the impossibility, of failing to take into account the interests of the people. His reading of the [religious] texts is therefore naturally impregnated with the requirements of reality and of people's daily life.[18]

Now, compare that description, written by Tariq Ramadan, a prominent Muslim reformist of our times, to the life of Ahmad Hanbal, the radical cleric in Baghdad who denounced all "innovators." Hanbal, "a petty landlord," was not only aloof from the market but also strongly opposed to it.[19] His followers were known for two things: "a profound knowledge of hadith as well as an aversion to the outside world."²⁰ He told his followers that anyone outside their Traditionist community was corrupt. Thus, anything those outsiders built, inhabited, produced, sold, or gave away constituted contamination. Hanbal even enjoined his followers not to drink water from wells built on roadsides or buy merchandise from street vendors. The goal—and the effect—was to "isolate the community from the economic mainstream."²¹

No wonder Hanbal's message found a following not among the merchants and intellectuals of Baghdad but among the less-educated classes. Their opponents called the movement *hashwiyyah*, meaning "vulgar populace."²² Their religious vision "stressed loyalty to the past" and was "communal" in nature, which was also reflective of their class.²³ This probably also explains why the Hanbalis were "people with a taste for the concrete and specific, and a dislike for the theoretical and abstract."²⁴

Even the extreme piety of Imam Hanbal and his followers can be traced to the "antiluxurious" tendencies of the masses. For example, the most luxurious form of art, sculpture, which required "the greatest aristocratic or priestly taste and resources," was entirely banned by the Hanbalis; the art that "every class could indulge in," poetry, was almost never condemned.²⁵

In short, the war of ideas between Rationalism and Traditionism in the formative centuries of Islam had much to do with the backgrounds and contexts of the followers of these two camps. The former represented the Islam of the urban cosmopolites, who engaged with different ideas thanks to the dynamism created by commerce. The latter represented the Islam of those who were more parochial. Both camps consisted of devout believers, but they were looking at the world, and their religion, from quite different perspectives.

In fact, a similar dichotomy could also be observed in Christendom—albeit not until the seventeenth century. One of the religious controversies in Europe at that time was the issue of toleration, and some of the most tolerant views came from merchants "whose vocations exposed them to the benefits of pluralism." It was the time when "the economic dynamism of the Dutch Republic" helped create a new narrative in which "prosperity and toleration were seen as twins."[26] This economic dynamism kept on pushing for "innovations" in the West, leading to changes in religious ideas, along with developments in the arts, sciences, and philosophy; the emergence of democracy; and the advance of freedom.

Perhaps, then, the question should be: Why did the same economic dynamism fail to prevail in Islamdom?

It's the Economy, Essentialist

Mahmood Ibrahim, professor of Islamic history at California State Polytechnic University, has a compelling theory that offers a possible answer. He starts by showing what we have observed so far: The Rationalists, particularly the Mutazilites, constituted an economic class. Most were merchants, others were "artisans or were associated with artisans."[27] Their opponents, the Traditionists, were led by the opposite class: the landlords.[28] So the war of ideas between these camps was "not merely a theological or doctrinal dispute, but a social conflict fought on an ideological plane."[29]

Politically speaking, the turning point of this dispute, as noted in the previous chapter, was the arrival of al-Mutawakkil, the Abbasid caliph who ended the brief pro-Mutazilite policy of his direct predecessors and supported the Traditionists. But there was also an economic side to this change. Quite tellingly, al-Mutawakkil established a new economic system that elevated the role, and the revenues, of the landlords. This system, called *iqta*, was a form of land grant. The caliph would temporarily grant a piece of land to a landlord who could then tax the peasants who lived on the land. The landlord, to make sure that the peasants continued to produce crops for him, would recruit many soldiers.

The resulting system increased the power of landowners and the soldiers they employed—at the expense of the merchants. The caliphs after al-Mutawakkil would continue to prefer this system, for they could tax land, as visible wealth, more easily than they could tax merchants' profits.[30] The role of the soldiers would be further consolidated in the face of the threat posed and the destruction caused by the Crusaders and the Mongols in the twelfth and thirteenth centuries.

According to Dr. Ibrahim, this transition in Islamdom from "a commercially based capitalistic period" to "an agrarian based semi-feudal one beginning with the Caliphate of al-Mutawakkil" was quite fateful.[31] It was the very infrastructure of the transition from Rationalism to Traditionism.

A study on labor in medieval Middle East also reveals this structural shift. Between the eighth and eleventh centuries, the formative period of Islamic law, the Arab-Islamic lands stretching from Iraq to Spain harbored 233 distinct commercial occupations. Later, between the twelfth and fifteenth centuries, there was a slight decline in this number, whereas the occupations in the bureaucracy and the military tripled. There was, clearly, a rise in military and state power, but "inertia in regard to commercial organization."[32]

This periodization in the history of Islamdom suggests that

the obstacle to economic progress in this part of the world was not Islam itself, as some essentialists believe. "It was not the attitudes and ideologies inherent in Islam which inhibited the development of a capitalist economy," notes Sami Zubaida, emeritus professor of sociology at the University of London, "but the political position of the merchant classes vis à vis the dominant military-bureaucratic classes in Islamic societies."[33]

In the later centuries (from the twelfth onward), stagnation would deepen as Islamdom became more and more isolated and as trade, the main engine of dynamism in the Orient, gradually shifted elsewhere. First came "the loss of the Mediterranean," due to the Crusaders' occupation of the whole eastern and northeastern coastline of this commercially vital sea. This, argues the great French historian Fernand Braudel, is probably the best explanation for "Islam's abrupt reverse in the 12th century."[34] In the thirteenth century, the Mongol catastrophe would impose a much more abrupt, and tragic, reversal.

The final blow would come in the fifteenth century with the Age of Discovery, during which Western Europeans found direct ocean routes to India, China, and elsewhere. Consequently, world trade routes would rapidly shift to the oceans, enriching Western Europe. Not only did this further impoverish the Middle East, it even made the Mediterranean a backwater. This whole northwestern movement of "world capital" between the twelfth and the eighteenth centuries explains, in the apt title of one of Braudel's essays, "the greatness and decline of Islam."[35]

As trade declined so gradually, and dramatically, there remained only one major factor as a context to shape the Muslims' understanding of the Qur'anic text: the land of the Middle East—the *arid* Middle East.

DEEP DOWN, IT'S EVEN THE ENVIRONMENT

Throughout this book, I have used the term *Islamdom*. To visualize which part of the world this term describes, search for "Islamic world map" on the Internet. Then please do a second search, for "world aridity map." You will see an amazing correlation between "Islamic" and "aridity."

This is a curious phenomenon that led some observers to think that Islam as a religion was particularly suitable to a certain kind of environment—deserts and dry steppes.[36] This is wrong, for Islam has flourished in rainy and fertile lands as well—such as the Far East, the Balkans, and certain parts of Turkey and Iran. But the regions where formative developments in Islam occurred were indeed almost all arid. So, could there be a link between this type of environment and those formative developments?

The late Joseph Schacht, a leading Western scholar on Islamic law, believed so. To explain the Traditionists' passionate adherence to the idea of the *Sunna* of the Prophet, which we have seen, he referred to their mindset, which was shaped by their physical environment:

> The Arabs were, and are, bound by tradition and precedent. Whatever was customary was right and proper; whatever the forefathers had done deserved to be imitated. This was the golden rule of the Arabs whose existence on a narrow margin in an unpropitious environment did not leave them much room for experiments and innovations which might upset the precarious balance of their lives. In this idea of precedent or *sunna* the whole conservatism of the Arabs found expression. . . .

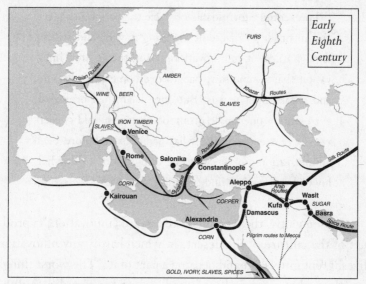

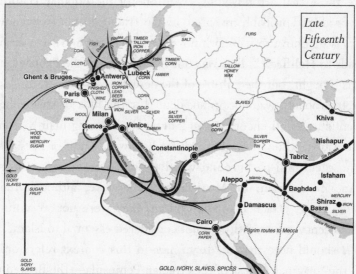

These two maps show how world trade, and the urban cosmopolitanism it fostered, shifted its weight from the Islamic Middle East to Europe between the eighth and fifteenth centuries. (Source: Colin McEvedy, *The Penguin Atlas of Medieval History* [Harmondsworth, UK, and New York: Penguin Books, 1961], pp. 43 and 89)

> [It] presented a formidable obstacle to every innovation, and in order to discredit anything it was, and still is, enough to call it an innovation. Islam, the greatest innovation that Arabia saw, had to overcome this obstacle, and a hard fight it was. But once Islam had prevailed, even among one single group of Arabs, the old conservatism reasserted itself; what had shortly before been an innovation now became the thing to do, a thing hallowed by precedent and tradition, a *sunna*.[37]

Consequently, the Arab distaste toward "innovation," a product of the culture of the desert, in which hardly any innovation lives, crept into Islam and became a part of it. "The worst things are those that are novelties," read one of the popular Hadiths favored (and probably invented) by the Traditionists. "Every novelty is an innovation, every innovation is an error, and every error leads to Hellfire."[38] This was not the wisdom of the Prophet, as was thought, but the culture of the desert.

It probably was not an accident that the idea of strict obedience to an all-encompassing Sunna was coming mainly from the Arabs, while most of the Mutazilites were Iraqis or Persians, whose cultural background was Babylonian or Persian, Christian, Zoroastrian, or Manichaean. Therefore, although they were firmly attached to the Qur'an, they were not so willing to "accept Arabian attitudes not considered essential to Islam."[39]

I should note that the term *Arab* in this context refers only to the "original Arabs" of the Arabian Peninsula—the Bedouin. The wider Arabic world of today, stretching from Morocco to the Persian Gulf, is mostly made up of "late Arabs," who, with the spread of Islam, adopted the Arabic language. I should also note that what we are speaking about here is not any inherent characteristic of any group of people, but rather certain cultural traits formed by the physical terrain where they live. Ibn Khaldun, the fourteenth-century Muslim scholar, was the first to systematically study this matter. "The Arabs, of all people, are least familiar with crafts," he wrote, for they "are more firmly rooted in desert life and more remote from sedentary civilization."[40] (Again, the term *Arab* in Ibn Khaldun's language only referred to the Bedouin.)

In the eighteenth century, Ibn Khaldun's idea was advanced, probably thanks to some direct connection, by the French liberal Montesquieu.[41] His theory of climate held that the physical environment has great influence on the shaping of cultures. British liberal Adam Smith, too, made similar suggestions.[42] The theory, known as "environmental determinism"—or, in a more modest and accurate version, "environmental possibilism"—became more popular in the late nineteenth and early twentieth centuries, influencing some Western interpretations of Islam as well. "The Koran is not in itself the conservative force in Islam," wrote an American scholar in 1924:

> Rather is that force the attitude of the Moslem toward his sacred book—and to things in general. Or shall we not say that the ultimate cause is "something more reliable and dependable than the human mind"—the eternal desert, which preserves, as in a museum of antiquities, races, customs, and religions, unchanged as the centuries come and go.[43]

The late Sabri Ülgener, the towering figure of economic history and sociology in modern Turkey, also made similar observations on the origin of some cultural attitudes in Middle Eastern societies. "Fatalism," for example, he noted, "was not the creation of religion and Islam in particular. It was the expression of the weakness of the man of the desert and the steppe in the face of the staggering odds of nature. It merged into Islam, however, and survived under the name and the mask of submission [to God]."[44]

Gérard Destanne de Bernis, a French economist who extensively studied rural life in Tunisia, agreed. If "the peasants of the Muslim countries are indeed fatalistic," he argued, this was not an irrational attitude on their part, but a just estimation of the precarious factors that determine the outcome of their efforts: "Anyone so placed would be fatalistic."[45]

The desert not only produced fatalism and an extreme conservatism distasteful of every "innovation" but also a very literalist conception of language, which had left not much room for a mind open to nuance and allegory,[46] and even a "lack of a sense of aesthetics."[47]

Later in the twentieth century, though, such environmental explanations for culture and development lost their popularity in academia, for they faced accusations—wrongly, in my view—of justifying racism or imperialism. But the idea was "not disproved, only disapproved."[48] No wonder it is having a comeback in scholarship and in popular literature, with significant books such as David Landes's *The Wealth and Poverty of Nations* and the Pulitzer-winning *Guns, Germs, and Steel*.[49] "Environment," notes the latter's author, Jared Diamond, "molds history."[50]

ORIENTAL PATRIMONY

The environment molded the history of the Middle East as well—by shaping not just the mindsets of individuals and the cultures of societies but also the political structures of states. One definitive outcome of the aridity of Middle Eastern land was infertility, and hence "the lack of surplus."[51] This made it impossible for local (i.e., feudal) rulers to gain power. Instead, power was concentrated in central governments that could organize forced labor to build irrigation systems.[52] In addition, much of the Middle East has a "flat" topography on which "armies could march unhindered"—as the Mongol armies tragically did.[53] As a result, even before Islam, this part of the world was ruled for millennia by powerful centralized states.

Now, compare this geopolitical structure with that of Europe, which, unlike the Middle East, was a rainy and fertile continent with plenty of regions that are "hard to conquer, easy to cultivate, and their rivers and seas provide ready trade routes." This topography, explains Fareed Zakaria,

> made possible the rise of communities of varying sizes— city-states, duchies, republics, nations, and empires. In 1500 Europe had within it more than 500 states, many no larger than a city. This variety had two wondrous effects. First, it allowed for diversity. People, ideas, art, and even technologies that were unwelcome or unnoticed in one area would often thrive in another. Second, diversity fueled constant competition between states, producing innovation and efficiency in political organization, military technology, and economic policy.[54]

That's how feudalism ultimately worked in favor of freedom in Europe. The fertile land produced enough revenue to allow the rise of powerful lords, who would compete with kings for power and force them to sign liberal texts such as the Magna

Carta. And when Martin Luther was excommunicated by the pope, he found support from the powerful princes of Germany who could afford to disobey Rome.

But the arid and flat Middle East only produced the "semifeudalism" of the *iqta* system. Here the land continued to belong to the central power and was granted only temporarily to the landlord, leading the latter to "mere pillage rather than to private development of the lands granted."[55] The ultimate result was the hindrance of an "independent, responsible, and non-alienated feudal class"—and the hindrance of political pluralism.[56]

In short, while the fortunate environment of Europe helped the advance of liberty, the unfortunate environment of the Middle East established what Karl Marx called "oriental despotism" and Max Weber redefined as "patrimonialism"—a system of governance in which all power flows directly from the leader.

There was nothing inherently Islamic about this authoritarian system—no wonder it also has dominated non-Islamic countries of the East, such as Russia and China. But, alas, the connection between Oriental patrimony and Islam worked in the former's favor as it left its mark on the latter.[57] According to Bryan S. Turner, a leading scholar on the sociology of Islam, here was the main reason why the religion took a less rationalist and creative form after its initial centuries:

> It was under the patrimonial dynasties of mediaeval Islam, starting with the Abbasids, that a different culture with its attendant view of appropriate motivation which stressed discipline, obedience and imitation came to dominate Islam. With the formation of an alliance of necessity between the military and the ulama [scholars], the *shari'a* as a formalized and unchanging code of life

came to embody the only legitimate language of conduct. . . . It was under these conditions that Islam was to
be characterized as a slavish, fatalistic religion, a religion
of accommodation to patrimonial rule.[58]

The problem was not, Turner adds, that Islam lacked something similar to the "Protestant ethic" that fostered capitalism
in Europe. The urban merchants of medieval Islam, after all,
"adhered to a distinctively Muslim form of rationality."[59] The
Mutazilites (or the Murjiites), as we have seen, even extracted
liberal principles from that rationalism. They just could not
overcome the constraints of the Middle East.

Islam, one could say, had produced the seeds of freedom;
regrettably, they just were not rooted in fertile soil.

GIVEN THIS BACKGROUND, one hopeful question arises: If the
fall of economic dynamism led to the decline of Islamic rationality and liberty a millennium ago, can the rebirth of economic
dynamism revive them? To put it another way, can socioeconomic progress in Muslim societies also lead to progress in religious attitudes, ideas, and even doctrines?

We will explore the answer by looking at modern-day Turkey
as a case study. But first, there are a few more stones to turn
over.

PART II

The Modern Era

When there is a general change of circumstances,
it is as if the whole creation had changed,
and all the world had been transformed.

—IBN KHALDUN, medieval Muslim scholar

CHAPTER SIX

The Ottoman Revival

We always explained that the constitutional
regime was legitimate and suitable for
the sharia. It was not banned by it, on the
contrary, our sharia ordered a constitutional
regime. . . . We tried to explain what
freedom, brotherhood meant; what the
meaning of equality was.

—ŞEYH-ÜL İSLAM MUSA KAZIM EFENDI,
top cleric in the late Ottoman Empire[1]

ONCE THE MEDIEVAL WAR of ideas between the Rationalists
and the Traditionists of Islam ended with the latter's dominance,
Islamdom entered into an intellectually stagnant age that would
last for several centuries. There were occasional bright spots, but
the overriding attitude in the Muslim world, especially among
the Sunnis, was defined by a strict obedience to custom and a
strong distaste for innovation.[2]

This equilibrium would be punctured only by the intrusion of
an outside power: the modern West, which, from the eighteenth
century on, was a colossal force of innovation, one that Muslims
could not afford to ignore. Some Muslims faced this reality and

decided to reform their ways. Others decided to resist change, and even fight back. The result would be a new war of ideas—this time, a modern one.

A telling moment in this new saga was the 1856 revolt against the Ottoman Empire in the Hejaz, the western coast of the Arabian Peninsula and the home of Islam's holiest sites. At this time, the Ottomans controlled the whole Arab world, often ruling indirectly through local chieftains. But one chieftain, Grand Sharif Abdulmuttalib of Mecca, had been stirring up opposition to the Ottoman authorities by denouncing their "irreligious" ways—such as Sultan Abdülmecid's ban on the slave trade. According to Ahmet Cevdet Paşa, the official Ottoman chronicler of the time, Abdulmuttalib even believed that "the Turks have become apostates," by simply "allowing women to uncover their bodies, to stay separate from their fathers or husbands, and to have the right to divorce."[3]

The grand sharif was also enraged by the friendly relations the Ottoman Turks established with "the infidels," and the consulates that the British and the French opened in the nearby town of Jidda.[4] One British diplomat would later describe Abdulmuttalib as "a fanatical Wahhabee" who believed that all Christians were "dogs that ought to be swept from the face of the earth."[5]

In his chronicles, Cevdet Paşa, also a scholar of Islamic law, tried to explain that the grand sharif was wrong on all these matters. Banning slavery was not against the Shariah, the Ottoman sultan was indeed the sacred law's best protector, and the maintenance of friendly relations with the infidels was not necessarily forbidden by Islam.[6] But Abdulmuttalib remained unconvinced by such arguments, and soon he launched his rebellion, declaring,

> O the people of Mecca, wage *jihad* on the Turks for that
> they have become Christians and Francs! Those who
> will be killed from you will enter heaven; those who
> will be killed from them will enter hell.[7]

His men began to attack Ottoman officials, killing them
as well as some pilgrims at the Ka'ba—only to be quickly
defeated and captured by Ottoman forces.[8] Yet this was neither the first nor the last uprising the Ottomans faced in Arabia.
Since the middle of the eighteenth century, the Wahhabis had
denounced them for "innovations" such as Sufism, the mystical
tradition that they saw as a deviation from the Shariah. In the
nineteenth century, Ottomans introduced even more disturbing "innovations"—more rights for women, more contacts with
non-Muslims, and less tolerance for slavery. For the Wahhabis,
all such reforms were heresies that needed to be fought against.

For our story, though, these reforms are inspiring—for they
constitute the most extensive, and coherent, Islamic effort to
embrace liberal democracy yet.

HERE IN THE LAND OF THE TURKS . . .

The Ottoman story goes back to the beginning of the fourteenth century, when a group of Muslim Turks led by a leader
named Osman established themselves as a tiny principality in
northwestern Anatolia. (The term *Ottoman* comes from the
Turkish word *Osmanlı*, or "the sons of Osman.") It was the time
when the Abbasid caliphate in Baghdad was destroyed, and the
Arab Middle East was devastated, by the brutal Mongol invaders. The decline of the Arabs made way in Islamdom for other
peoples, especially the Turks.

The Turks, like the desert Arabs, were nomads from an arid region—this time, the steppe. Hence they lacked a sophisticated culture to bring into their new religion. But, unlike the desert Arabs, who carried their pre-Islamic conservatism and fatalism into Islam, the nomadic Turks experienced a radical rebirth. They completely "surrendered themselves to their new religion" and "sank their national identity in Islam as the Arabs and the Persians had never done"—to a degree that even the name *Turk* came to be almost synonymous with Muslim. The result was a passionate devotion to the faith. "In the earnestness and seriousness of their loyalty to Islam," observes Bernard Lewis, "the Turks are equaled by no other people."[9]

The Turks had not only the passion but also the military skills to serve Islam by expanding the borders of Islamdom toward the West—first under the Seljuk dynasty, which ruled parts of Central Asia and the Middle East from the eleventh to the fourteenth centuries, and later the Ottomans. The latter gradually pushed back the borders of the Byzantine Empire, bringing it to an end in 1453 by conquering its capital, Constantinople (which would later be known as Istanbul). The Ottoman state grew rapidly, and, in the early sixteenth century, became an empire that extended from Budapest to Yemen, Algiers to Basra. It became, one could say, the world's superpower.

In line with Islam's acceptance of the People of the Book, the Ottoman Empire was a pluralist state that allowed non-Muslim communities to preserve their identities and religious practices. Thus, Serbs, Greeks, Armenians, or Bulgarians remained Christian. In the early sixteenth century, Selim I "the Stern," a particularly heavy-handed sultan/caliph, had considered converting all his Christian subjects to Islam forcibly, simply for the sake of homogeneity. Yet he was convinced by his Şeyh-ül İslam, the superior authority on the issues of religion, that this would have been unlawful.[10]

Thanks to their belief in the supremacy of law, along with their pragmatism, Ottomans continued to recognize the rights of their Christian subjects and even Protestants fleeing Europe—generating admiration from Martin Luther, the Christian reformist, and Jean Bodin, the French philosopher.[11] The highest praise came in the seventeenth century from the Greek patriarch in Jerusalem, who praised God for putting "into the heart of the sultan of these Ottomans an inclination to keep free the religious beliefs of our Orthodox faith."[12] (Yet such positive images of the Ottomans would be replaced by much more negative ones in the nineteenth and twentieth centuries, when more than two dozen post-Ottoman nation-states needed to glorify their genesis by depicting a "dark age" in the past.)[13]

The Ottoman Empire was even more comforting to Jews, at a time when they were routinely persecuted in Christian Europe. From the late fourteenth century onward, Jews expelled from Hungary, France, and Sicily found refuge in Ottoman lands. In the early fifteenth century, Rabbi Yitzhak Sarfati, who had emigrated from Germany to Edirne, in what is now western Turkey, felt secure enough to write to Jewish communities in Europe entreating them to leave behind the torment they were enduring under Christianity and find a safe haven in the Ottoman Empire. "Here in the land of the Turks we have nothing of which to complain," the rabbi said. "Every one of us lives in peace and freedom."[14]

In 1492, a large portion of the Sephardic Jews expelled by Spain heeded this advice and set sail for Turkey, where they were warmly welcomed by Sultan Beyazid II, one of the most pious of all Ottoman rulers. The Ottoman hospitality to Jews would con-

tinue well into modern times; prayers were said in Istanbul synagogues in the late nineteenth century for the victory of Ottoman
armies against the onslaught of Russia and its Balkan allies.[15]

The Hanafi Way

The form of Islam subscribed to by the Ottoman Empire fostered an important advantage. It had adopted the Hanafi school
in jurisprudence and the Maturidi school in theology—which
were both, as described in the previous chapters, on the Rationalist side of the Sunni spectrum. This gave the Ottomans more
freedom in interpreting the Shariah. Ottoman scholars often
employed the Hanafi principle of *istihsan* (juristic preference),
which allowed alterations in the Shariah for the public good, to
cope with new issues and problems.[16]

In the sixteenth century, for example, Şeyh-ül İslam Ebusuud
Efendi legitimized reasonable interest-charging by pious foundations because they served the welfare of society.[17] He also found
singing, dancing, whirling, and shaking hands—all banned by
various Hadiths—permissible.[18] On the other hand, another
scholar of the time, Mehmet Birgivi, who subscribed to the strict
Hanbali school, denounced these "innovations" and condemned
Ebusuud Efendi's Hanafi-based flexibility.[19]

The Ottoman system was also innovative in the sense that
it gave the state the right to enact secular laws, called *kanun*,
along with the Shariah.[20] Doing so meant that the Shariah did
not cover all aspects of public life, and the state thus had the
religiously legitimate authority to introduce new rules and regulations.[21] Thanks to this tradition, the empire would be able to
enact many modernizing laws in the nineteenth century.

Even the Shariah itself was regulated by the Ottoman kanun.

Under Sultan Mehmed II, the conqueror of Constantinople, some harsh corporal punishments (such as amputations of hands) were deemed obsolete and were replaced by beating or monetary fines assessed according to the economic status of the culprit.[22] Stoning also became difficult to implement, and it is known to have occurred only twice during the six centuries of Ottoman rule.[23]

The Ottoman flexibility also had something to do with its geography, which, as we have seen, was influential in shaping perceptions of Islam: "unlike previous Islamic states, the Ottoman Empire rose in Anatolia and the Balkans, areas of solid and steady peasantries, rather than on the edge of nomad-inhabited deserts."[24] This allowed the rise of autonomous guilds and provincial notables, saving the empire from a total surrender to patrimonialism—i.e., absolute domination by the central power—the hallmark of that arid Middle Eastern geography.[25]

On the Western Edge of Islamdom

The fact that the Ottomans were rooted in Anatolia and the Balkans also gave them a unique geostrategic position on the western edge of Islamdom, bordering with Christendom. This proximity to the West allowed them to recognize the great transformation in Europe—the rise of modernity—much earlier than did other Muslim or Eastern peoples.

For a long time, in fact, the Ottomans, overconfident in their superiority, were not particularly curious about the ways of the People of the Cross. Yet once they started to lose battles with Christian powers, being forced to retreat from lands they had conquered, the Ottoman elite began to realize that they were lacking something. Especially after their disastrous defeat at the Second Siege of Vienna in 1683, which clearly marked the revived supremacy of European powers, Ottoman statesmen started to think about reform. Initially they focused on internal corruption and disorder, hoping that the restoration of their effective former system would be enough. Yet soon it dawned on them that their decline was due not only to problems on their side but also to the innovations on the European one.

Hence, starting in the early eighteenth century, the Ottoman government sent a large number of civil servants to various European capitals to observe "Western ways." Yirmisekiz Mehmet Çelebi, a special envoy sent to the court of Louis XIV in 1720, was specifically instructed to "visit the fortresses, factories, and the works of French civilization generally and report on the modern French institutions, which might be applicable in Turkey."[26] (The French—and, fatefully, not the Anglo-Saxons—would continue to be the prime model of modernity to which most Ottomans and other Muslims were exposed.) Another Ottoman bureaucrat who spent time in Europe, Ahmed Resmi Efendi, would write in the 1770s that "the age of *jihad*" was over and that the Ottomans needed to pursue a peaceful path of diplomacy and reform.[27]

The expeditions to Europe soon led to the creation of new schools with modern curricula and the translation of some European scientific works into Turkish. Then came the *Nizam-ı Cedid* (New Order) of Sultan Selim III in the late eighteenth century, which produced important military and administrative reforms. The next sultan, Mahmud II, initiated an even more extensive new order—first by getting rid of the military establishment that resisted reforms and then by introducing European-style clothing, architecture, legislation, institutional organizations, and land reform. He also established the Grand Council of State, a precursor of the parliament that would come four decades later.

Mahmud II also introduced the concept of equal citizenship for all regardless of religious belief. This was directly linked to the Ottoman state's goal of winning the hearts and minds of non-Muslim peoples, because the latter, and especially those in the Balkans, were increasingly influenced by the ideas of modern nationalism. In order to keep the Serbs, Bulgarians, Armenians, and other Christians loyal to the empire, the sultan and his bureaucrats started to promote the spirit of Ottomanism as a common and equal identity among all citizens.

The fez, the red flat-topped cap that Mahmud II adopted as the new national headgear, became the symbol of this new ecumenism. Unlike the different types of turbans and caps that formerly differentiated religious preferences, now all Ottomans would be one nation under the fez. "Henceforth," the sultan famously announced in 1830, "I distinguish among my subjects, Muslims in the mosque, Christians in the church, and Jews in the synagogue, but there is no difference among them in any other way."[28]

ARE ALL OTTOMANS CREATED EQUAL?

These gradual reform efforts took a giant leap forward on November 3, 1839, when Sultan Mahmud's newly crowned son, Abdülmecid, announced the edict of *Tanzimat* (Reorganization), a document that has been compared to the Magna Carta in terms of its content and significance.[29] The symbolism of the edict reflected the empire's goal of reforming its ways while remaining loyal to its religion. After a public proclamation before an impressive assembly of diplomats and Ottoman notables, the young sultan and his high officials gathered in the chamber that preserved the mantle of the Prophet Muhammad and swore to uphold the Tanzimat. The text began by criticizing the nonobservance of "the precepts of the glorious Qur'an," as the cause of the empire's decline. It then proclaimed the security of life, honor, and private ownership; regular and orderly conscription into the armed forces; and fair and public trials. The sultan, who took an oath to respect these individual rights, was clearly limiting his power by law. "These imperial concessions," he also affirmed, "are extended to all our subjects, of whatever religion or sect they may be."

These liberal precepts were clearly inspired by Europe, but, in the eyes of the Ottoman elite, they also were a reaffirmation of the primal values of Islam.[30] The abolition of the sultan's right to confiscate property at will, for example, was not just a modern liberal reform but also the reestablishment of the Shariah's original guarantees on private property—which had been partly eroded by the patrimonial power structures of medieval Islamic empires, inherited, to some extent, by the Ottomans.[31]

One of the architects of the Tanzimat was Sadık Rıfat Paşa, author of *A Booklet on Conditions of Europe*, which analyzed the reasons for Europe's success and concluded that the key was a liberal state that secured the rights and freedoms of its citizens. "Government is for the public," he wrote, "but the public is not for the government." He also praised the concept of freedom of the press and the notion of natural, inalienable rights of men.[32] Most notably, he articulated these ideas in not a secular but a religious framework.[33]

In 1856, the Ottoman government proclaimed another edict, entitled *Islahat* (Reform), which removed all the remaining distinctions between Muslims and other citizens and effectively asserted non-Muslim's rights. Non-Muslims were exempted from the poll tax, gained the right to work in the government and the military, and earned the right to testify against Muslims in a court. Meanwhile, the sultan's edict forbade "every distinction or designation tending to make any class whatever of the subjects of my Empire inferior to another class, on account of their religion, language, or race." The echo of this on the Muslim street would be a common joke: "Infidels won't be called infidels anymore."

Implementations soon followed. Some Christians were appointed, and elected, to local advisory councils established in each province and also to the Grand Council of State. Christians and Muslims were accepted together as students in the newly established imperial high school of Galatasaray in 1867. Two years later, the Ottoman Nationality Law was issued, which further consolidated the principle of equal citizenship.[34]

During this period, the Ottoman bureaucracy started to employ large numbers of non-Muslims. Toward the end of the nineteenth century, at least three thousand Armenian civil servants worked in important ministries and legal institutions of Istanbul. Another six thousand were working as state officials in the countryside.[35] Many other non-Muslims were appointed to such influential positions as bureau chief, ambassador, and even minister. "Egalitarianism," a Western historian observes, "really had begun to take root in Ottoman minds."[36]

These reforms for the equality of all citizens amounted to the abandonment of the classic Islamic political system—dominant Muslims and "protected" yet second-class non-Muslims—by the prevailing power in the Muslim world. Today, critics of this clas-

sic system—*dhimmitude*—often overlook both the significance
of Ottoman reforms of the mid-nineteenth century and the fact
that equal citizenship was not established in Europe until the
same era.

Here is an irony to add: Since the non-Muslims in the Ottoman Empire weren't doing too badly under their "protected"
status, some of them resisted the equality introduced by the
Tanzimat and Islahat edicts. Equality ended the extra tax that the
non-Muslims had to pay, but it also made them eligible to serve
in the armed forces. It soon became obvious that most Christians
preferred to pay the extra tax rather than be drafted. Besides,
the leaders of the non-Muslim communities also did not want
to lose control over their people. When the Tanzimat edict was
read publicly in 1839 and then returned to its red satin pouch,
the Greek Orthodox patriarch did not look happy. "God grant,"
he reportedly said, "that it not be taken out of this bag again!"[37]

Balkan Christians, too, were uninspired by the reforms,
because they sought independence, not equal citizenship. That's
why, despite legal guarantees, equality for the empire's Christians and Muslims would not be fully realized—"not because of
bad faith on the part of leading Ottoman statesmen but because
many of the Christians wanted it [equality] to fail."[38]

Moreover, while one obstacle to the consolidation of equality
"was the innate attitude of superiority which the Muslim Turk
possessed,"[39] the other one was, ironically, the constant interference of European states, and Russia, to "protect" the rights
of the Christians of the empire. To the Ottomans, such interference implied that even if they regarded all citizens as equal,
foreign powers did not. The Muslim population became fed up
with "the support given by Christian diplomats and consuls to
thousands of protégés . . . who were shielded against the taxes

and courts of their own state and were often granted foreign passports."[40] This was a mistake Western powers made then, and one that they continue to make today: their calls for greater religious freedom in Muslim lands focused only on the rights of Christians, not on those of Muslims.

"The Musselman Is Now . . . Free . . . to Become a Christian"

One of the blessings of the Tanzimat reforms was broader religious freedom. Until then, non-Muslims had been allowed to keep and practice their religion, but conversion from Islam to Christianity was, as the Shariah decreed, punishable by death.

One of the rare implementations of this harsh penalty took place in October 1843 in Istanbul, but the reactions were mixed. "The old Mussulman party had triumphed in the most disgraceful manner," noted Cyrus Hamlin, an American missionary. "The young Turkish party," on the other hand, had cursed it "as a needless insult to Europe and a supreme folly of old fools."[41]

The latter view was more in line with the Tanzimat. Hence, although the Shariah laws on apostasy were not officially abandoned, the personal abandonment of Islam became practically free after 1844.[42] That year, after an incident in Acre, a court decreed, "No subject of the Sublime [Ottoman] State shall be forced by anyone to convert to Islam against their wishes."[43] A stronger guarantee would come with the Islahat edict of 1856, in which the sultan declared: "As all forms of religion are and shall be freely professed in my dominions, no subject of my empire shall be hindered in the exercise of the religion that he professes, nor shall he be in any way annoyed on this account. No one shall be compelled to change their religion."[44]

The next year, a government commission investigating a case of conversion from Islam to Christianity found it licit. "The Musselman is now as free to become a Christian as the Christian is free to become a Musselman," the decision read. "The government will know no difference in the two cases."[45] Consequently, during the anti-Christian riots in 1860 in Damascus, the Ottoman authorities supported the Christians who had been forced to embrace Islam be obliged to return to their original faith.[46] "The orders from the center [were] always in the same vein," concludes a Turkish historian who studied the apostasy cases of the era. "No force or compulsion is admissible in matters of conversion."[47]

But here again, the perception of Western intrusion into the empire, and the reaction to it, hindered the evolution to a truly liberal attitude. "On the one hand, the state sincerely sought to prevent the killing of apostates, yet on the other, it was desperate to safeguard its flock against foreign (missionary/diplomatic) incursions."[48] Thus, "the convert or apostate became the bone of contention in an international prestige war, in which the Great Powers sought to impose their will on the last remaining non-Christian Great Power."[49] The issue was not just religion but also sovereignty.

This political meaning attached to religious affiliation has lingered well into the contemporary era. That's why, in present-day Turkey, those who are most reactionary about missionary activity are those most obsessed with sovereignty: the nationalists, some of whom are, surprisingly, quite secular.[50] Perhaps this apparent paradox also sheds some light on the political, and not religious, origins of the ban on apostasy in medieval Islam—a point to which we will return in the upcoming chapters.

ISLAMIC LIBERALISM AND ITS CHAMPIONS

Although the Tanzimat reforms were driven mainly by state bureaucrats, they also were consolidated by two other important elements: the new middle class and the newly emerging liberal intelligentsia.

Until the nineteenth century, the Ottomans relied on a land-tenure system adapted from the *iqta* system (discussed earlier). Accordingly, the state owned all lands and any grant of land would be only temporarily and conditionally distributed to landlords and peasants. In other words, there was no private ownership of land.

But the Tanzimat reforms abolished the *iqta* system. The Tanzimat edict denounced, "[this] land tenure procedure which is one of the most destructive tools in this matter and any useful fruit of which is never seen." Soon other laws not only allowed but also promoted private ownership. The whole reform was based on "the absorption of economic liberalism," and its aim was to "create individuals who would participate in economic life as entrepreneurs."[51] It worked—at least to a degree. In the words of Kemal Karpat, professor of Ottoman history:

> As a result [of privatization], the old notables lost their preeminence and were incorporated into the new middle class led mainly by the new propertied and commercial groups that arose throughout Anatolia and Rumili (the Balkans), Iraq, Syria, and Palestine.
>
> The new individualistic and reform-minded middle class simultaneously defended change and demanded respect for tradition and culture, believing modernity

and Islam perfectly reconcilable. . . . [It] moved into the modernist age by preserving its Islamic faith and looking for ways to acquire and legitimize political power by converting the absolutist monarchy into a constitutional system based on some sort of participation. The beginnings of democracy were sown in the second half of the nineteenth century.[52]

The other agent of reform was an intellectual group of the late Tanzimat era known as the Young Ottomans—not to be confused with the higher-profile Young Turks, who came decades later and were more secularist, nationalist, and revolutionary. The Young Ottomans were Islamic rather than secular, "Ottomanist" rather than nationalist, and progressive rather than revolutionary. They supported the reforms, criticizing the government only for not being steadfast or principled enough in implementing them. When Sultan Abdülaziz gave a speech in 1868 and spoke of the newly established legal rights as if they were a part of his generosity to his people, the most prominent Young Ottoman, Namık Kemal, wrote the following:

> If the purpose is to imply that up to this day the people
> in the Ottoman Empire were the slaves of the sultan,
> who, out of the goodness of his heart, confirmed their
> liberty, this is something to which we can never agree,
> because, according to our beliefs, the rights of the people, just like divine justice, are immutable.[53]

Namık Kemal also found the basis for representative government in the Qur'anic principle of *shura*, which requires that matters concerning the community should be decided by mutual consultation. To date, this argument has been one of the basic tools for defending democracy in an Islamic frame of reference. According to Kemal, the Tanzimat edict of 1839 was good but not good enough. The empire needed "a charter for the Islamic Caliphate," which would fully establish "freedom of thought, sovereignty of the people, and the system of government by consultation."[54]

In 1868, the Young Ottomans started to publish a newspaper called *Hürriyet* (Liberty). In it, they articulated "an unmistakable liberal critique of government action, and a programme of constitutional reform."[55] Notably, they made such proposals not for a secular but for an Islamic agenda. The earliest decades of Islam, the Young Ottomans argued, had seen a protodemocracy and a protoliberalism. Europe's success came from developing these ideas while the Muslim world mistakenly neglected them. And now was the time, they said, to move forward with imports from modern Europe and inspiration from the early Islamic past.

The Young Ottomans became the first movement in the Muslim world to devise a modern ideology inspired by Islam. And, lo and behold, their ideology was a liberal one.

Bumps in the Road

The dreams of the liberals came true in November 1876, when the newly crowned Sultan Abdülhamid II accepted a "Fundamental Law," or constitution. It stated that "the religion of the state is Islam," but it also accepted the modern secular definition of citizenship. "All subjects of the empire are called Ottomans," one article read, and the next one declared: "Every Ottoman enjoys personal liberty on condition of not interfering with the liberty of others." Another article guaranteed that "all Ottomans are equal before law; they have the same rights . . . without prejudice to religion."

The sultan still had strong authority, but the new constitution also established a parliament with some legislative powers. In 1877, a general election was held—the first in Ottoman and indeed in Islamic history. The first Ottoman parliament met on March 19, 1877, with more than one-third of its seats filled by non-Muslims—Armenians, Greeks, Jews, and Bulgarians. The first Islamic liberal democracy was born.

But it soon encountered trouble.

Russia—which had long had designs on Ottoman territories—provoked the empire's Eastern Orthodox peoples, whom it considered natural allies. In 1876, the year the Ottomans unveiled their constitution, an uprising began in Bulgaria; it was quickly joined by Serbs and Montenegrins. Russia soon entered the picture, and the Ottomans suddenly found themselves at war with Russians, Serbians, Montenegrins, Romanians, and Bulgarians. Major battles occurred in the Balkans and the Caucasus, and the Ottoman military and the Muslim populations suffered huge losses. In Bulgaria alone, a quarter of a million Muslims, mostly Turks, were either slaughtered or died as a result of the war; half a million others, including thousands of Bulgarian Jews, had to flee to Turkey to survive. In January 1878, Russian troops reached the outskirts of Istanbul, creating the deadliest threat the empire had ever seen.

Then European powers intervened and a diplomatic process started. It ended with the signing of a treaty at the Congress of Berlin (July 1878). Montenegro, Serbia, and Romania became independent states and Bulgaria an autonomous one. In Anatolia's east, four cities, including Kars, were given to Russia. In the end, the Ottomans lost two-fifths of their territory, were subjected to an enormous war indemnity payment to Russia, and became responsible for more than a million destitute refugees from the Balkans and the Caucasus. It was the most disastrous moment for the Ottomans in the entire nineteenth century.

The internal impact of this external threat was reminiscent of what James Madison had warned against when he defined war as "the most dreaded enemy of liberty" and the extender of "the discretionary power of the executive."[56] When he saw Russian troops just a few miles outside of his capital, Sultan Abdülhamid II, who had never been a genuine believer in democracy, decided that the empire needed order and discipline more than anything else. So, assuming "war powers," he suspended the constitution and dismissed the parliament. The First Constitutional Period of the Ottoman Empire, as it later would be called by historians, had lasted just over a year.

This was only one of many examples of a burden that the Ottomans (and, later, other Muslims) would continually face while working toward reform: they were trying to liberalize while under foreign threat. The West, on the other hand, from the sixteenth century onward, moved toward political and economic liberalization without the pressure of a rival civilization or the insecurity of its borders. Even within the West, most liberal ideas flourished in those countries that were geographically more isolated and thus more secure than others—Great Britain and the United States.

Muslims, on the other hand, would be plagued constantly by fears for their survival (as in the Ottoman era) or by a lack of independence (as in the post-Ottoman colonial era). An additional burden would be the psychological resistance to adopting the ways of the West while the West seemed threatening or intimidating. Little wonder, then, that liberal ideas would be more popular within Muslim societies at times when they felt secure and respected, and less so when they felt insecure or humiliated.[57]

WHAT WOULD THE CALIPH DO?

Sultan Abdülhamid's thirty-year absolutist rule, which lasted until the Second Constitutional Period in 1908, ushered in a new phase of Ottoman history. The liberal democratic spirit that originated with the Tanzimat in 1839, and that peaked with the Islamo-liberal ideological synthesis of the Young Ottomans, certainly faced a setback. But the sultan was far from being a narrow-minded reactionary. He continued modernization, making positive advances in education, legal reforms, and economic development, including the construction of railways and telegraph lines. In 1895, Descartes's *Discourse on Method* was translated into Turkish under his auspices. In the same era, Western classics, as well as European political topics of the day, became part of Ottoman intellectual life. A pious Muslim, Abdülhamid nonetheless admired Western civilization and explicitly advised his fellow Muslims to learn from the Christians' successful efforts to rid their faith of dogmatism and obscurantism.[58]

A significant change under his rule was the subtle shift away from the policy of Ottomanism to what was later dubbed Islamism.[59] The latter, however, must not be confused with the totalitarian ideology of the twentieth century with the same name. Abdülhamid's Islamism was a practical policy necessitated by the new political reality faced by the empire. The revolts in the Balkans, which led to the creation of four new states at the Congress of Berlin, had disillusioned the Ottoman elite, who had hoped that liberal reforms would create national unity among all citizens, regardless of their creed. Christian peoples, one by one, were shattering that vision.

Therefore, after the Congress of Berlin, keeping the Muslims loyal to the empire emerged as the second line of Ottoman defense against the threat of collapse. Abdülhamid emphasized the Islamic character of the empire and his religious prominence as the caliph of all Muslims—appealing to, and dealing with the problems of, Muslims around the world. He transformed the ancient image of the corrupt caliph—a legacy of the Umayyads and some Abbasid rulers—and gave the institution a new respectability and authority. European statesmen raised eyebrows over his "pan-Islamic" message, but the sultan had no desire to create any new tension between Muslims and the Western powers. In fact, he would actually help establish peace between the two— even in as distant a locale as Southeastern Asia.

This took place when the Americans occupied the Philippines in 1898 and faced a troublesome insurgency in Sulu, the southern Muslim sultanate. A year later, the American ambassador to Turkey, Oscar S. Straus, received a letter from Secretary of State John Hay wondering whether "the [Ottoman] Sultan under the circumstances might be prevailed upon to instruct the Mohammedans of the Philippines, who had always resisted Spain, to come willingly under our control." Straus then paid a visit to Sultan Abdülhamid and showed him Article 11 of an eighteenth-century treaty between Tripoli and the United States, which read that the latter "has in itself no character of enmity against the laws, religion, or tranquility of Musselmen."

"Pleased with the article," Abdülhamid asserted that the "Mohammedans in question recognized him as khalif [caliph] of the Moslems and he felt sure they would follow his advice." Two Sulu chiefs, in Mecca at the time, soon received a letter from Istanbul, "forbidding them to enter into any hostilities against the Americans, inasmuch as no interference with their religion would be allowed under American rule." This message proved to be effective, and Sulu Muslims refused to join the insurrection. Soon President William McKinley thanked his ambassador for his "excellent work" and credited him with having saved "the United States at least twenty thousand troops in the field."[60]

This was only one example of Abdülhamid's peacemaking. He also "did his best to contain the popular Islamic fundamentalist movements."[61] In fact, by the end of the nineteenth century, some European statesmen regarded him as an ally who calmed anti-European feelings among Muslim masses. (His father, Abdülmecid, also had helped the British by quieting the Muslims of India during the Sepoy Mutiny of 1857.)[62]

"Changing Times Legitimize the Change of Law"

Sultan Abdülhamid, a peacemaker and a reformer, also introduced "innovations" to the Islamic tradition. The biggest task of reform under his rule was undertaken by one of his ministers, Ahmet Cevdet Paşa. This erudite scholar, whose chronicles on the Wahhabi revolt were cited at the beginning of this chapter, was one of the Ottoman Empire's most remarkable statesmen. Confidently ambitious, he reformed the Shariah by writing a modern-style legal code called Mecelle, which many Muslim nations in the Middle East applied well into the mid-twentieth century and Israel used until the 1980s.[63]

Before the Mecelle, the Shariah had been uncodified—there was no single source of Islamic law to which one could refer just by opening a book. There were, instead, countless numbers of varied legal opinions. A typical Islamic judge (a *kadı*) would use his expertise to find the right legal opinion for the specific case brought before him. This ad hoc tradition was pluralist and, in some sense, democratic, but it was becoming inefficient in the context of the modernizing Ottoman society, in which legal transactions were becoming much more complex. So, a single civil code usable throughout the whole empire was essential.

Faced with this need, some Ottoman statesmen, such as Âli Paşa, proposed to incorporate the European legal system en bloc, and they even opted for a complete translation of the French Civil Code—an idea that would be applied later by the secularists of the twentieth century. Others, including Cevdet Paşa, favored not an abandonment of the whole tradition but rather a reform of its structure and content. The latter idea prevailed, and Cevdet Paşa was appointed in 1868 as the head of a commission for codifying and modernizing the Shariah.

After ten years of meticulous work, the commission came up with a sixteen-volume magnum opus, which was based mainly on the Hanafi school of jurisprudence, but it had modernized some of its aspects and used the tools of the Rationalist school of jurisprudence to select the most convenient alternatives. In his introduction, Cevdet Paşa referred to a Rationalist maxim: "Changing times legitimize the change of law."

To convince more conservative scholars of the legitimacy of his reform, Cevdet Paşa referred to the works of Jalal al-Din al-Dawani, a fifteenth-century Hanafi scholar, who argued that the political authority had a legitimate right to introduce new legal rulings that did not exist in the Shariah but that were beneficial to the community. Al-Dawani even justified the formation of non-Shariah courts, which would help Cevdet Paşa and other

Ottoman reformists design the secular courts that the empire opened in the Tanzimat era to decide cases under new criminal and commercial legal codes.[64]

Together, these changes amounted to a reform *within* the Islamic tradition, not against it. What Cevdet Paşa did was "explain and validate the new individualistic concepts of reform and change in Islamic terms."[65] This was indeed the spirit of the whole Ottoman modernization. For this reason, with the exception of some fringe reactionaries such as the Wahhabis in Arabia, and a few isolated incidents in Istanbul, the Ottoman reforms did not face an Islamic backlash.[66]

Secularist Turks today often believe that religious authorities resisted the whole modernization effort, but this is a myth created in the Republican era in order to discredit the ancien régime. Historical research proves that the religious class collaborated on the modernization program. In fact, some religious scholars were themselves reformers, while "the protest against secularizing reforms was mainly expressed by the lower echelons of the religious class."[67] Besides, most resistance to modernization arose from mundane self-interest. The reason for the long-delayed import of printing presses, for example, was not religious bigotry, as has been claimed, but the opposition of the scribes, then a powerful class, who feared losing their jobs.[68]

NEW IDEAS, NEW THEOLOGIES

Ottoman modernization entered into a new era in 1908, when the Young Turks, an opposition movement to Abdülhamid established by officers and intellectuals, forced the sultan to restore the constitution and reconvene the parliament. The Young Turks consisted of a coalition with a range of political tendencies: although some aspired to authoritarian rule, others were genuine liberals. No wonder that the Second Constitutional Period, which they initiated, was celebrated throughout the empire as the advent of Hürriyet (Liberty).

The following decade would indeed be the most liberal one Turkey has seen to date in terms of freedom of thought. Among the numerous intellectual societies that formed in Istanbul were two feminist clubs. One of their articulate spokeswomen, Fatma Nesibe, quoted John Stuart Mill in her public lectures. Another prominent feminist, Fatma Aliye, the daughter of Ahmet Cevdet Paşa, opposed polygamy and engaged in a lively polemic with a conservative writer, Mahmut Esat Efendi. Yet none of these Ottoman feminists were far from the Muslim faith. Rather, they supported the feminist agenda by pointing to examples from the Qur'an and the days of "undistorted Islam"—the age before misogyny was introduced into religious texts by some medieval scholars.[69]

In fact, progress had already been made on women's rights since the Tanzimat edict. Modern schools for women had been established in the mid-nineteenth century, and a more modern female lifestyle had developed, leading an Egyptian feminist of the early twentieth century to call for "adopting the veil and outdoor dress of the Turkish women of Istanbul."[70] The Ottoman family law of 1917 would take women's liberty a step further, with the introduction of women's right to divorce and the effective abolition of polygamy.[71]

Another remarkable phenomenon of the final decade of the Ottoman Empire was the influx of secular European thought, including atheist and antireligious philosophies, into Ottoman society. Popular books by Ernst Haeckel, an advocate of Social Darwinism, and Ludwig Büchner, a proponent of scientific materialism, were translated into Turkish by the more secular Young Turks, who had begun to see religion as an "obstacle to progress" that needs to be replaced by science.

The response of the more religious intellectuals was not to silence these ideas by force but to refute them by reason—just as the Mutazilites had done a millennium earlier in the face of the challenge from Greek philosophy. Şehbenderzade Ahmet Hilmi wrote a book titled *Is It Possible to Deny God?*, and Ismail Fenni Ertuğrul penned *The Refutation of the Materialist School.* Another name among these Islamic modernists, İsmail Hakkı İzmirli, who studied in both classical and modern schools of the empire, promoted a "new theology" that would incorporate new philosophies.[72] "The ancient books of [Islamic] theology often mentioned Thales, Socrates, Plato, Aristotle or Xenon," he noted, and argued:

> Similarly, today ideas of thinkers such as Bacon, Descartes, Spinoza, Leibniz, Locke, Malebranche, Hume, Kant, Hegel, Auguste Comte, Hamilton, Stuart Mill, Spencer and Bergson need to be considered. . . . The Greek philosophers were easily accepted in the ancient theology books; today they should be replaced by French, British or German ones.[73]

İzmirli emphasized the value of freedom in Islam, even defining the latter as a "religion of equality and liberty."[74] This attitude was common among the Islamic modernists of the late Ottoman period. Recognizing the value of freedom thanks to their exposure to Western liberalism, they then reread the scripture from this new perspective. So, the Qur'anic verse, "Everyone acts according to his own disposition," was now interpreted as a justification for individual liberty.[75] The verse, "That man can have nothing but what he strives for," was seen as encouragement for private enterprise and the market economy.[76] The Qur'anic advice for "consultation" was taken as a basis for parliamentary democracy, and the commandment to "forbid the wrong" was reinterpreted as a limit on the powers of the sultan.[77]

One Muslim thinker who supported these interpretations, Doktor Hazık, was quite thrilled by the liberalism he discovered in Islam. "When you look at our religion with the eyes of wisdom, you will see how wide its fields of liberty are," he wrote in his 1916 book, *Din ve Hürriyet* (*Religion and Liberty*). "In the face of all this," he added, "one loses his mind with excitement!"[78] Ahmed Naim Bey, another modernist Islamist, was critical of the French Revolution, but he was also convinced that the principles it praised—Liberty, Equality, and Fraternity—were "already self-evidently true for people raised with Islamic ideas."[79]

These Muslim liberals were sometimes reading into the scripture what they wanted to hear. But medieval Muslims, too, had read into the scripture the norms of their own time and milieu. This shift in religious perceptions spurred by social change was noticed by the Ottoman intelligentsia as well. One of them, Ziya Gökalp, seeking to combine Western sociology with Islamic jurisprudence, developed a discipline that he called "the science of the social roots of law" (*içtimai usul-ü fıkıh*). The Shariah, according to Gökalp, required extensive modernization for which sociologists and Islamic scholars needed to work together.

Another prominent Ottoman, Sabahattin Bey, founder of the Party of Liberals (Ahrar), had his "aha" moment at the turn of the twentieth century while reading French writer Edmond Demolins's *À quoi tient la Supériorité des Anglo-Saxons*, or *The*

Anglo-Saxon Superiority: To What It Is Due. He pinned down the secret of progress as "individual entrepreneurship and decentralization" and promoted these ideas among the Ottoman elite. "[The] obstacle for our progress is not religion," he once said, in response to the then-nascent ultra-secularist movement that blamed religion. "The obstacle is the structure of our society."[80]

Meanwhile, prominent poet Mehmet Akif Ersoy, author of the Turkish national anthem, was writing influential poems calling on Muslims to abandon blind obedience to tradition and use their reason to understand the scripture. "We should take the inspiration directly from the Qur'an," he said in a famous line, "and make Islam speak to the mind of the [modern] age."[81]

A Tragic End—and the End of All Peace

Despite the new ideas, laws, and institutions that the Ottomans adopted in their final century, the empire failed to catch up with the industrialized nations of Europe and felt trapped when Britain and France, its former friends, allied themselves in 1907 with Russia, its perpetual enemy, in the face of rising German power. For the Ottoman elite, the only option was to ally themselves with Berlin—a fateful decision that would place them on the losing side in World War I.

The most lethal nail in the empire's coffin, though, was what ultimately tore apart its pluralist system: nationalism. One by one, the Christian peoples of the Balkans launched rebellions to achieve independence. Each was a joyful moment of national liberation for the new nation, but for those in the minority, it was a nightmare. "Serbia for the Serbs, Bulgaria for the Bulgarians, Greece for the Greeks," went a popular slogan of the early nineteenth century, along with a crucial caveat: "Turks and Jews out!"[82]

The fate of Turks and Jews converged—as the latter, who had no territorial claims, remained loyal to the empire until its end. As late as the Balkan Wars of 1912–13, the Turco-Jewish axis was operative. "In Fear of Greeks, Jews Plead for Aid," read a 1913 *New York Times* headline. The Greek nationalists, the story reported, were "punishing [the Jews] for being friendly with the Turks."[83]

During such nationalist campaigns against the empire, both the Ottoman Jews and the much more numerous Turks—a term that then referred to almost all Ottoman Muslims—faced several tides of ethnic cleansing in the Balkans, the Caucasus, and the Crimea. According to some estimates, more than five million Ottoman Muslims perished in these regions between 1821 and 1922.[84] Some of them were killed in battle, others died from starvation and disease. Those who could make it to Turkey itself (including my own great-grandfather from the northern Caucasus) brought with them many stories about the cruelty of the Russians and their allies.

Nationalism slowly crept into the minds of the Muslim peoples of the empire as well. In fact, Ottoman administration was not considered alien rule in any Muslim province of the empire until the beginning of the twentieth century. But in less than two decades, the desire for independence affected first the Albanians and then some (not many) Arabs. Hence, on the eve of World War I, Ottoman armies found themselves engaged in hopeless wars throughout a vast territory stretching from Macedonia to Yemen.

The century-long shrinking of the empire, and the enormous suffering it caused Turks, created a deep fear among the Ottoman elite and propelled them to develop their own nationalism. That's why the Young Turk party that encapsulated this trend, the Committee of Union and Progress (CUP), which took over the Ottoman state with a military coup in 1913, was ready to save the remaining part of the country—Asia Minor—by any means possible. When they entered the Great War in October 1914, the Turks, once again, faced the Russian onslaught from the east, and they found that Armenian nationalists had established paramilitary units to support the enemy. This discovery formed the basis for the catastrophic decision made by the CUP government in April 1915, when it chose to expel all Armenians in Eastern Turkey to Syria. Hundreds of thousands perished en route, due to massacres, other atrocities, famine, and disease. This awful ethnic cleansing is certainly the biggest stain on Ottoman history, and is inexcusable, but it did not happen because of the Ottoman system. Rather, it occurred because of *the fall* of the Ottoman system.

The collapse of the empire would have other tragic consequences that only time would reveal. Yet Archibald Wavell, a British officer, had the foresight to see them as early as 1918. Watching the victorious European powers happily carving up the Ottoman Empire in Paris after "the war to end war," he dismissed the optimism. What the Europeans achieved instead, he said, was "a peace to end peace."[85]

Beyond the Ottomans

Ottoman modernization was the most important Muslim step forward in the nineteenth and early twentieth centuries, but it was not the only one. "Within all the Ottoman-related areas there was a general pattern that was repeated with local variations," which was essentially "an attempt to integrate Islamic ideas and Western techniques."[86] Egypt, officially an Ottoman territory but a self-governing state since the beginning of the nineteenth century, had in place an extensive modernization program under Muhammad Ali Paşa (1805–49). Prominent Egyptian religious scholars such as al-Attar and al-Tahtawi championed the revival of Islam's early rationalism and liberation from the constraints of outdated traditions.

In Tunis, which was part of the Ottoman Empire but very much a self-governing entity, a reform program modeled on the Tanzimat was put in practice, accompanied by important reforms such as the abolition of slavery in 1846. Soon Tunisians felt themselves so advanced that on October 31, 1863, Husayn Paşa, the mayor of Tunis, wrote a letter to Amos Perry, the American consul general, urging the Americans to reconsider their attitude toward slavery in the name of "human mercy and compassion."[87] This was fifteen months before the Thirteenth Amendment, which abolished slavery, was passed by the U.S. Congress.

A decade later, another Tunisian statesman named Hayreddin Paşa published a book titled *The Surest Path to Knowledge Concerning the Condition of Countries*. "With God's help, I have collected all possible information about European inventions related to economic and administrative policies," he wrote.[88] Then, with quotations from the Qur'an, the Hadiths, and classical Muslim thinkers, as well as from Montesquieu and John Stuart Mill, he argued for the acquisition of "political institutions based on justice and liberty." He concluded:

> Freedom of person, of the press, of participation in government; without this, material prosperity is not pos-

sible. Freedom inspires men to work by giving them the assurance that they will receive the reward of their work; economic prosperity is not possible without the free movement of goods and people, and also that free economic association to which modern Europe owes its material achievements. . . . Without freedom too there can be no diffusion of knowledge.[89]

In the foreword, Hayreddin Paşa also warned "those who are heedless among the generality of Muslims against their persistence in closing their eyes to what is praiseworthy . . . simply because they have the idea engraved on their minds that all the acts and institutions of those who are not Muslims should be avoided."[90] (This criticism is still quite relevant today.) According to Hayreddin Paşa, the modern West's principles of freedom already existed during the golden age of Islam, but that era was followed by a decline, and now it was time for a revival.

In 1873, Hayreddin became the prime minister of Tunis. Four years later, Sultan Abdülhamid II, who had read and apparently admired his book, invited him to Istanbul and appointed him the grand vizier. Unfortunately, the Tunisian bureaucrat did not assimilate well into Istanbul's complicated politics, so his career there was short lived, but his ideas survived, especially in his homeland, where books such as *The Liberal Spirit of the Qur'an* were published in the early twentieth century.[91]

In the same era, Jamal al-Din Afghani (1838–97), a scholar and activist from Iran, embarked on an ambitious mission to "awake" Muslims from obscurantism and encourage them to embrace Western science and rationalism, which he considered already inherent in the Qur'an. Egyptian scholar Muhammed Abduh, a professor at the prestigious Al-Azhar University in Cairo, embraced al-Afghani's views and developed a reformist Islamic view that clearly was inspired by the Mutazilites of the earliest centuries of Islam. Abduh criticized some of the established Hadiths, including the ones that promote misogyny, and argued for the emancipation of Muslim women.[92]

The neo-Mutazilite trend grew among Arab intellectuals in the early twentieth century, leading the important Egyptian writer and intellectual Ahmad Amin to remark in 1936 that "the demise of Mu'tazilism was the greatest misfortune to have afflicted Muslims; they have committed a crime against themselves."[93]

These reformist Muslims were opposed to Europe's colonialist ambitions for Islamdom, but they were far from anti-Western. Abduh, who traveled in Europe, famously said that in Paris he saw "Islam without Muslims," and on his return to Egypt he saw "Muslims without Islam." He felt that all the good things Muslim societies should have were in the West but not in Islamdom. He and his followers were only proud that Islam did not share Europe's virulent anti-Semitism. During the infamous Dreyfus affair in France, some of the Muslim press, both in Turkish and in Arabic, sympathized with the falsely blamed Jewish captain, and one of Abduh's followers, Rashid Rida, criticized the persecution of Jews in France.[94]

Albert Hourani, probably the most prominent scholar of Arab history, defines this reformist trend as "the liberal age" in Arabic thought, which dominated the nineteenth and early twentieth centuries.[95] And not just in the Arab world. The interaction with modernity also led Muslim intellectuals from non-Arab lands to conclude that there was a problem in the tradition and that reform was necessary. Not too surprisingly, these intellectuals looked back to the earliest centuries of Islam and noticed that the Mutazilite Rationalists had been overshadowed by the Traditionists. So, criticism of the Traditionist school and the Hadith literature (and occasionally Sufism for its "laziness") became a hallmark of the reformers.

In India, Syed Ahmed Khan—whose overly pro-British stance cost him some legitimacy—argued that most Hadith sources comprised "the garbled words of previous centuries." Hoping to have a "Muslim Cambridge" in India, he opened a modern university and launched publications that inspired millions. The modernist tradition in the subcontinent would later be continued, and much refined, by Muhammad Iqbal, the wise philosopher-poet of the early twentieth century who articulated an Islamic form of individualism and empiricism.

Among the Turkic Muslims of the Russian Empire, too, an intellectual movement called Jadidism grew in the late nineteenth century. The term came from the Arabic word *jadid*, meaning "new." A prominent scholar among the Jadidists, Musa Jarullah Bigiev, a Kazan Turk who translated the Qur'an into the Tatar language, promoted gender equality and argued that God's compassion in the afterlife would extend beyond Muslims to encompass all people from all faiths—an idea that the more exclusivist Traditionists found scandalous.[96]

All these reformist Muslim thinkers are commonly referred to as "Islamic modernists." They had their differences, but their common idea was that the values of Western liberalism were compatible with, and even inherent in, the original message of Islam. Muslim societies, they believed, needed to reopen the gates of *ijtihad* (independent reasoning) and reform their Traditionist ways, in order to achieve freedom, justice, and prosperity.

Quite notably, this was the dominant intellectual trend in the Muslim world in the early twentieth century. "Nearly every leading intellectual in the Islamic world," notes historian Karen Armstrong, "was a liberal."[97] And there were few notable Islamic fundamentalists.

What happened, then, to that liberal trend? And what gave us all the militancy and authoritarianism that exists right now in many corners of the Muslim world?

One answer to this important question is that Islamic modernism was an idea whose time had not yet come. Its proponents were a small cadre of elites, and most of the societies to which they appealed were still premodern. The middle class, among whom liberal ideas tend to flourish, was still quite weak—and in some places even nonexistent.

But this is not a full explanation. The modernist elite could have continued to push for reform, and Muslim societies could have shifted gradually toward liberalization. What happened instead was that the modernist elite slowly disappeared— replaced by a more reactionary, anti-Western, and illiberal one. Even a few modernists, such as the pro-Dreyfus Rashid Rida, slowly shifted to the more strident camp.

From *Ijtihad* to *Jihad*

The reason for this marked change of spirit becomes quite clear when we look at the history of the late nineteenth and early twentieth centuries. In just a few decades, nearly the whole Muslim world was attacked, invaded, and occupied by non-Muslim nations. The Ottoman Empire, the last big Muslim power, was destroyed in World War I, and almost all the Muslim states that arose from its ashes were colonized by Britain, France, or Italy. These European countries, whose liberal values had impressed and inspired Islamic modernists, were now seen as trampling on the honor of Muslim nations, whose very borders were created arbitrarily by the new masters.

Russia and the subsequent Soviet Union also played a role by crushing the whole Islamic presence, including the Jadidist movement, in Central Asia, after brutally suppressing the Basmachi Revolt (1916–23), a Turco-Islamic uprising against Russian and then Communist rule.

The foreign invasions changed the entire intellectual landscape of Islamdom. The West was no longer a model to emulate but rather an intruder to eradicate. The question, "How can we be like the West?" would soon be replaced by "How can we resist the West?" And the push for *ijtihad* would be overshadowed by the drive for *jihad*.

In her comprehensive article on "The Revolt of Islam," Nikki R. Keddie, an American professor of Middle Eastern history, clearly sketches out the causes of the rise of this militancy. She notes that, with the curious exception of Wahhabism, militant *jihad* movements in the modern era began and grew mostly as a response to Western colonialism. The earliest ones, in the eighteenth century in Sumatra and West Africa, emerged in the face of "disruptive economic change influenced by the West." In the nineteenth century, a broader wave of *jihad* movements cropped up in Algeria, Sudan, the Caucasus, and Libya as "a direct response to French, British, Russian and Italian colonial conquest." [98]

Even the very centers of Islamic modernism were negatively influenced by Western threats. "Periodic backlashes against westernized modernism tended to come in response to Western aggressiveness, as in the dismemberment . . . of the Ottoman Empire and the occupation of Egypt and Tunisia by Britain and France." [99]

In *The New World of Islam*, written in 1922, American political scientist Lothrop Stoddard was feeling the whirlwind. "The entire world of Islam is today in profound ferment," he wrote, with "discontent at Western rule and desire for independence." "What the precise outcome of all this will be," he added, "no one can confidently predict."[100]

The outcome, as we can observe today, was deep-seated distrust and even enmity against the West, and against Western ideas such as liberalism. The latter was further eclipsed by the rise of the communitarian spirit instead of the individualistic one, as Pakistani scholar Nasim A. Jawed explains:

> After a brief period of popularity of liberal democratic values among the modern educated Muslim intelligentsia in the late nineteenth and early twentieth centuries, liberalism began to wane everywhere in the Muslim world as the focus shifted from the freedom of the individual to the freedom of the community, the achievement of which required solidarity.[101]

This would push nearly the entire Arab world into a synthesis of nationalism and socialism—which were, interestingly, also Western ideas, yet ones perceived as providing ways to resist the West. After World War II, the anti-Western tendency would be further strengthened by the Arab reaction to the establishment of the state of Israel and, more important, to its subsequent expansion and occupation of Arab territory. This reaction would also foster a fierce wave of anti-Semitism, "with an import of anti-Semitic ideas from Europe, but not with Islam as a religion."[102] The ideology that appeared last in the Middle East, Islamism, would be based on the cumulative legacies of all these missteps.[103]

Notably, only three former Ottoman states escaped colonialism in the post-Ottoman era. The first was the poor and politically irrelevant North Yemen, which no one bothered to colonize. The second was Saudi Arabia, homeland of Wahhabism, the most rigid interpretation of Islam.

The third was Turkey, the very heart of the former Ottoman Empire. Yet it would soon turn out to be a very different Turkey from what it used to be.

CHAPTER SEVEN

Romans, Herodians, and Zealots

Fundamentalism is religion under siege.
—BENJAMIN R. BARBER,
American political theorist[1]

ON DECEMBER 7, 1925, a cold winter day, a group of policemen knocked on the door of a modest house in Fatih, one of Istanbul's oldest districts. An old woman opened the door, surprised to see men in uniform. "We are looking for Atıf Hodja," one of them said. "He just needs to come with us to headquarters."

Atıf Hodja, a fifty-year-old Islamic scholar with a white beard and white turban, led a very pious life. He was originally from İskilip, a small town in central Anatolia. His sermons and books had made him a leader among the pious, and he was a teacher of Islamic sciences at the *madrasa* (classical Islamic school) in Fatih.

Atıf Hodja and his family thought that the police must have come for a simple matter. They were wrong. The teacher would be kept in police custody for weeks, banned from seeing his family. His wife and daughter were traumatized, unsure of what would happen or what to do. Then Atıf Hodja was taken to court, where he and his family discovered that his "crime" was publishing a booklet two years earlier—a booklet with the peculiar title *The Brimmed Hat and the Imitation of Francs*.

"Francs" was the name Muslims had commonly used to refer to Europeans since the time of the Crusades; to Atıf Hodja, the brimmed hat was a symbol of the Frankish—thus non-Islamic—way of life. Conservative Muslims like him were not happy to see some of their countrymen embrace that lifestyle and wear alien headgear instead of the traditional fez or turban. Moreover, the brim kept a man from putting his forehead on the floor, as the Muslims do in prayer, so it seemed to give the message: "I don't bow down to God." In his booklet, Atıf Hodja expressed all such criticisms and called on fellow Muslims to stop "imitating" the Europeans. Muslims had to acquire Western science and technology, he argued, but also to preserve their identity.

Yet, what Atıf Hodja opposed in his booklet suddenly became part of the compulsory dress code in November 1925, when Mustafa Kemal, Turkey's new ruler, introduced the brimmed hat as the new national headgear and banned all traditional Islamic ones. Atıf Hodja's booklet was clearly at odds with this cultural revolution. His "crime," in other words, was an ideological one.

However, there's a crucial detail: Atıf Hodja had written the booklet a year and a half *before* the Hat Reform. Its first edition had already sold out and there was no plan for a reprint. So, while trying him for his views was unfair, trying him for views he expressed before the revolution was absurd. That's why the first court found him innocent and granted his release.

But the new regime, eager to crush all opponents of the brimmed hat, needed a scapegoat for teaching a lesson to all dissidents. So an order came from Ankara, the new capital, for Atıf

Hodja's rearrest and retrial in the Independence Tribunal—an arbitrary court that the new regime, following the example of the French Revolution's Tribunal Révolutionnaire, had established for eliminating political opponents. After a brief trial, the Independence Tribunal announced its verdict, which came as a shock to almost everyone. Both Atıf Hodja and a cleric named Ali Rıza, his "collaborator," were sentenced to death; both were hung on the gallows on February 4, 1926. Other so-called collaborators were sentenced to prison terms.

Nor were these men the only victims of the Hat Reform. Right after Mustafa Kemal's August 1925 declaration that all Turks must wear brimmed hats, dissatisfaction grew in many parts of Anatolia. Protests in late 1925 and early 1926 were brutally suppressed. In Maraş, people marched in the streets, shouting, "We don't want hats," and twenty "reactionaries" were executed while others were sentenced to prison terms of three to ten years.[2]

In the city of Erzurum, a local sheikh and his supporters petitioned the governor for permission to continue to wear traditional headgear—which was not only culturally preferred but also better suited to the cold winters of Eastern Anatolia. After the governor's dismissal of the request and his order that the spokesmen be arrested, protests grew and gendarmes opened fire on the crowd, killing as many as twenty-three people.[3]

In Rize, a town on the Black Sea coast, a similar protest erupted, soon becoming a full-blown uprising. In response, the government sent a warship to bombard the rebellious villages. A British consular document reports that government troops suffered a hundred or so casualties while suppressing the insurgency.[4] The number of civilian casualties, which probably was much higher, is unknown.

A Tale of Two Modernizations

The Hat Reform was only one of the many components of the Kemalist Revolution, which is named after Mustafa Kemal, the war hero who saved Turkey from foreign invasion after the fall of the Ottoman Empire in World War I. When he announced the Republic of Turkey in 1923, Kemal's goal was to completely rid it of its Ottoman past and form a whole new nation that would replicate the "advanced" nations in Europe. He took the first bold step by abolishing the caliphate, which symbolized the unity of all Ottoman Muslims, if not others, in March 1924. In the next few years, he outlawed all Islamic schools, banned all Sufi orders, and closed down any society that had any Islamic identity. To mark the cultural shift, he replaced the Islamic calendar with the Gregorian one and the Arabic alphabet with the Latin one. The teaching of Arabic was banned, as was, for a while in the 1930s, the performance of Turkish music. The goal was to make everyone enjoy "modern" (i.e., Western) tunes. According to a Turkish historian at Harvard University, this was a cultural revolution whose extent and zeal paralleled that of Mao Zedong in Communist China.[5]

Alas, this is not the kind of modernization that we saw in the Ottoman Empire. How did things change so dramatically?

The story goes back to the nineteenth century. At the time, political ideas in Europe were quite diverse, and a strong illiberal trend existed alongside the liberal one, and both influenced those Muslims who looked to the West for new ideas. In the words of historian Bernard Lewis:

> In the reform movements and activities of the nineteenth
> century [in the Muslim world], two distinct trends

can be discerned, between which there was continu-
ous struggle. One derived from the Central European
enlightenment, and brought ideas which were welcome
and familiar to authoritarian reformers. They too, like
their Central European models, knew what was best for
the people and did not wish to be distracted by so-called
popular government from the business of applying it. . . .

The other view drew its inspiration from Western
rather than Central Europe, and was inspired by doctrines of political and, to a lesser extent, economic liberalism. For the disciples of this trend, first in Turkey
and then in other countries, the people had rights which
were to be secured, along with the general advancement
of the country, by means of representative and constitutional government. Freedom was seen as the true basis
of Western power, wealth and greatness.[6]

In the Ottoman Empire, the Young Ottomans were the best
example of the liberal tradition. They devised, as we saw in the
previous chapter, an ideology that was both liberal and Islamic.
But among the Young Turks, who emerged some three decades
after the Young Ottomans, the other tendency to which Lewis
refers started to emerge. It was both illiberal and anti-Islamic.

This was particularly evident in one strain of the Young Turk
movement called Garpçılar (i.e., Westernists). Almost all late-
Ottoman intellectuals were influenced by the West in one way
or another, but the Garpçılar were distinct in that their sources
of inspiration were the materialist and antireligious thinkers of
France and Germany—such as Baron d'Holbach, the passionate
eighteenth-century proponent of atheism, and Ludwig Büchner,
the exponent of "scientific materialism." These European secu-

larists attacked Christianity, while their Young Turk admirers would argue that both Christianity and Islam were "the same nonsense."[7] Abdullah Cevdet, the leading figure of the Garpçılar, was convinced that religion was one of the greatest obstacles to human progress, and that it had to be replaced by science.

While the Garpçılar proved to be a marginal movement during the Ottoman Empire, its members had a golden opportunity to advance their philosophy with the establishment of the Turkish Republic. Mustafa Kemal, one of their disciples, was determined to shape the new regime based on their agenda. "Doctor, until now you have written about many things," he said to Abdullah Cevdet in 1925, as the latter wrote in his memoirs. "Now we may bring them to realization."[8]

THE DICTATORSHIP OF THE SECULATARIAT

Although Mustafa Kemal was determined to achieve his secularist goals, his vision was not the only alternative for the Turkish Republic during its genesis. The preceding War of Liberation (1919–22) was led by a democratic parliament, convened in Ankara, which included deputies with diverse views and backgrounds. Right after the war, the deputies who supported the views and the persona of Mustafa Kemal—the Kemalists— founded the Republican People's Party (RPP). Other prominent names, including war heroes Kazım Karabekir and Ali Fuat Cebesoy and feminist writer Halide Edip, founded a competing party, the Progressive Republican Party (PRP).

The difference between the two parties was exactly what Bernard Lewis pointed to in the reform movements of the nineteenth century: One was liberal, the other was illiberal. The Kemalists believed in an all-encompassing and all-powerful state that knows what is best for society thanks to "science." The PRP, in contrast, believed that government should be limited and society should be free to accommodate diverse views. Erik Jan Zürcher, the Dutch historian who wrote a book about the PRP, notes that "it was a party in the Western European liberal mould" that opposed the Kemalists' "centralist and authoritarian tendencies." Its program instead advocated "decentralization, separation of powers and evolutionary rather than revolutionary change . . . [and] a more liberal economic policy."⁹

Since the PRP was liberal, it did not share the excessive secularism of the Kemalists. Hence, one of the articles in the party's charter expressed "respect for religious beliefs and ideas." Most members were also in favor of preserving the caliphate—not as a theocratic authority but as a symbol of unity—and they were hoping to achieve a liberal democracy similar to that of Great Britain.¹⁰ Had the party survived, it would have represented a modernization vision similar to that of the Ottomans.

But, alas, it lasted only six months. In June 1925, using a Kurdish rebellion in the East as a pretext, the Kemalist government closed down its liberal rival indefinitely. Its leaders were tried in the Independence Tribunal, the same arbitrary court that executed Atıf Hodja. The stated reason for closure was the PRP's "respect for religious beliefs and ideas" clause in its charter. This statement could, the Kemalists argued, "encourage religious reactionaries."

The leading figures of the PRP remained under police surveillance until the death of Mustafa Kemal in 1938. And no other party would be allowed to compete for power in Turkey until the aftermath of World War II. In official Turkish history, this era, 1925–46, is euphemistically called "the single-party period." A witty motto used by the Kemalists of the time put their philosophy in a nutshell: "A government for the people, in spite of the people."

The idea here was a bit reminiscent of Lenin's famous "dictatorship of the proletariat." The Bolshevik leader had promised both freedom and democracy as the ultimate goal of Communism, but he argued that first people had to be saved from the "false consciousness" into which they were driven by religion, tradition, and capitalism. So, to guide and educate the people until they attained the "true revolutionary class consciousness," the proletariat, embodied in the Communist Party, had to rule.

Kemalism, too, had to guide and educate the nation until it attained a true revolutionary secular consciousness. This ideal was exposed in *La Turquie Kemaliste* (Kemalist Turkey), a monthly journal published in Ankara in French for a foreign audience. Its eye-catching covers often presented drawings of muscular Turkish workers managing huge industrial complexes, closely resembling the Socialist realism of the Soviet Union. Other scenes, which showed empty squares with huge monuments dedicated to Mustafa Kemal, were reminiscent of Italy's Fascist art. Human photos in the journal, featuring scenes such as peasants happily looking at the sky, were all staged and posed. There was not a single spontaneous scene showing the real life of Turkish society and its traditional icons, such as mosques. Indeed, any reference to religion in *La Turquie Kemaliste* "was conspicuously absent."[11]

In the decades to come, Kemalism would vary according to political circumstances, but its attitude toward religion would remain, as "distrust added to disgust, in a way similar to Voltaire's hatred of the Church."[12] That's why the unique form of secularism that Turkey established—*laiklik*, adopted from the French *laïcité*—was, and still is, quite different from the separation of church and state in the United States. Whereas freedom *of* religion has been a cornerstone of the American model, the Turkish one would focus on freedom *from* religion by the state's authoritarian measures—such as closing religious institutions, banning religious symbols, and suppressing religious leaders. The official zeal against religion would soften, and would turn more manipulative than repressive, only at times when it was seen as a useful tool against other enemies of the state, such as the Marxist Left and Kurdish separatism.

A DISILLUSION WITH A VENGEANCE

To be sure, the Kemalist Revolution also brought positive reform to Turkey. Turkish women gained full equality before the law and were granted suffrage in 1935, well before many European nations had it. Education was further modernized and new schools were opened throughout the country. The arts and sciences were promoted, and Turkey welcomed (and employed) two hundred German professors, mostly Jewish, who were deemed "unfit to teach" by the Nazis in 1933. Mustafa Kemal, to his credit, also followed a wise foreign policy that secured peace and stability for Turkey in a dangerous world.

The main trouble with the Kemalist Revolution was its excessive secularism, which alienated conservative Muslims and cut short the Ottoman modernization program. Moreover, while trying to sweep away the influence of traditional religion in society, to replace it with "science and reason," the Kemalists in fact filled the void with a newly created ersatz religion: the cult of Turkishness.

The Turkish identity was at most a first-among-equals status in the multiethnic Ottoman Empire. But it became the only acceptable identity in Republican Turkey. "The Turk fills every space," Mustafa Kemal said in 1932, "his face enlightens every-where."[13] He also promoted extravagant theories about "the origins of the Turkish race" rooted in a supposed "superior Turkish civilization" in prehistoric Central Asia.[14] Meanwhile, a policy of Turkification was imposed on the non-Turkish groups, most notably the Kurds. Villagers, for example, were forced to pay a fine for each Kurdish word that they uttered."[15] Some Kurds reacted violently to these bans, and began to form a counter-nationalist movement, creating Turkey's never-ending "Kurdish problem."

The cult of Turkishness was accompanied by the cult of "the Father of the Turks," or Atatürk, the venerable surname Mustafa Kemal was given by law in 1934.[16] A prominent poet described him as "the god who landed on Samsun," referring to the city where he started the War of Liberation.[17] Another poet defined Atatürk's residence (named Çankaya) as the nation's new Ka'ba (Islam's "House of God").[18] This image of Atatürk as an omniscient demigod would continue to be kept alive through official propaganda and national education. Even today, every Turkish primary-school student starts each morning by publicly declaring loyalty to the persona of "Supreme Leader Atatürk, who has given us this day," and then takes an oath to "sacrifice my existence to the Turkish existence." (I, too, took those oaths, but quite halfheartedly, especially after seeing my father in a military prison filled with Atatürk portraits and sayings.)

But these are Turkey's own problems. What was more important for the rest of the Muslim world was the implicit message delivered by the Kemalist Revolution: Islam and modernity were incompatible, and Muslims had to choose between them. The Ottoman style of modernization—which was not only respectful to but even justified by Islam——was swept aside. "We don't take our inspirations from the heavens and the unknown," Atatürk declared publicly. For those who still believed in "the heavens and the unknown," this was blasphemy.

Hence, Kemalism came as a great shock to pious Muslims all around the world. At first, in fact, there was great admiration for Mustafa Kemal, a brave general who had defeated colonial powers and led the Turks to independence. This was true especially among the Muslims of India, who formed the Khilafat movement, which preached peaceful resistance to British rule and had supported the Ottoman caliphate since World War I. The leaders of the movement were close friends of Mahatma Gandhi, who joined some of their meetings during which the Qur'an was recited and solidarity with Turkish Muslims was proclaimed.[19] The Khilafat supporters hoped that the Ottoman caliphate would survive the occupation of Turkey by the allied powers and would continue to defend the rights, and guide the agenda, of Muslims worldwide.

The caliphate indeed survived the occupation of Turkey, which ended in 1922, only to be abolished suddenly by Mustafa Kemal two years later. The disillusioned Khilafat movement soon dissolved, giving way to more radical voices among Indian Muslims. Sayyid Abu al-A'la al-Mawdudi, one of the two main founding fathers of radical Islamism, emerged in the 1930s with a more strident tone. "The demise of the Khilafat movement," notes historian Eran Lerman, "seems to have set Mawdudi apart from the romantic and vague Islamism held by many of its leaders."[20] Denouncing "this Turkish revolt from Islam," Mawdudi proclaimed a totally opposite agenda: "The only state for Muslims . . . is the 'Islamic theocracy.' "[21] Islamic liberalism, the path between these two extremes, was blurred.

The Not-So-Terribly-Helpful "Turkish Model"

Another impact of Kemalism on the Muslim world was to inspire other authoritarian secularists. Admiration for Mustafa Kemal among the emergent modern Arab elites contributed to the rise of an illiberal notion of modernization in which the society is controlled by the state, which itself is dominated by the military.

This influence was clear in the 1933 founding declaration of the National Action League, one of the most important forerunners of the ideological Arab nationalist organizations. Strongly impacting the development of the Arab nationalist discourse in greater Syria and Iraq, the league emphasized the role of "the state as the righteous embodiment of the national will and the military as the savior of the nation."[22] The age of uniformed dictators had begun.

One of the bold proclamations of the new Zeitgeist was an article published in the official magazine of the Syrian military, *Army of the People*. It described Islam as "a mummy in the museum of history" and called for the advent of the "new socialist Arab man."[23]

The most enthusiastic admirer of Atatürk was probably Reza Shah of Iran. He came to power in 1925 via a British-supported coup against the Qajar dynasty, which had been ruling Persia for the previous 130 years. Encouraged by the Kemalist Revolution, the shah launched a modernization program like that of Atatürk, but he was even more radical in its implementation, ordering the forceful unveiling of all women. As a result, Tehran police started to assault veiled women, tearing off their clothes. Local authorities around the country were instructed to prevent veiled women from entering shops, cinemas, and public bathhouses; Iranian writer Reza Baraheni recalls how his father used to carry his mother and his wife to the public bathhouse secretly in a sack, until the day when they were caught by a policeman.[24] Veiled women were also barred from receiving diplomas, accepting government salaries, riding in horse-drawn carriages and cars, and receiving treatment in public clinics. Government employees were fired if they did not bring their unveiled wives to official ceremonies. Ironically, the ban even resulted in creating diplomatic tensions with Great Britain, which defended the right of Indian Muslim women to visit Iran in their traditional garb.[25]

What Reza Shah hoped to achieve with this ban on the veil was to Westernize the society and demolish gender barriers. But his tyrannical methods proved counterproductive. Rather than mix with men, "many observant women remained at home," further isolating themselves from society.[26] The most desperate even committed suicide.[27]

As would be expected, Iran's powerful clerics, the Shiite *ulema*, were horrified by such a frontal attack on their traditions. This sparked their protests, which led to further persecution. Public religious festivals and celebrations were banned, and the *ulema* were forbidden to preach in public. In one instance, in March 1928, Reza Shah personally drove from Tehran to Qum, the city of the ayatollahs. He entered the city's Holy Shrine wearing his boots—an insult to any Muslim sanctuary—and manhandled a number of seminarians before ordering a whipping for the cleric who had criticized him.[28] In Mashad, in July 1935, a group of angry but peaceful protesters was encircled by the military at the Gowharshad Mosque, shot and killed indiscriminately, and then buried in mass graves.[29]

GOD'S PEOPLE UNDER SIEGE—THEN AND NOW

For a conservative Muslim living in the late 1920s, the world must have looked grim. The Ottoman caliphate was destroyed and most Muslim peoples had become slaves to European or, worse, Communist rulers. The few independent nations, such as Turkey and Iran, were overtaken by authoritarian regimes that suppressed the faith of their own people. Moreover, the "infidel" culture was penetrating Muslim societies via imposition by the secularists and the seduction of materialistic Western mores.

This was probably the biggest crisis the *umma* had ever faced. Now, some Muslims thought, was the time to resist, and even fight back. Here lay the origins of twentieth-century Islamism, the reactionary ideology created in the name of Islam, and jihadism, its terrorist offshoot.

The late Turkish social psychologist Erol Güngör offered one of the best interpretations of this trauma. Inspired by British historian Arnold Toynbee, Güngör likened the crisis of Islam in the twentieth century to one that had occurred two millennia earlier: the plight of the Jews during the time of Christ.[30]

The Jews, like Muslims, believed that they were God's chosen people, and they had an inherent sense of superiority over the Gentiles. But this belief in what ought to be conflicted strongly with what is, as the Jews gradually lost their power in the Holy Land and became totally subjugated by the infidels. The Roman Empire, the superpower of the time, occupied the land of Israel in the first century BC, defiling not just the Holy of Holies in Jerusalem but also the dignity of its people. Consequently, Israel was turned into a Roman province ruled by the client kingdom of the Herodian dynasty—a secular collaborator of pagan Rome that persecuted its own people.

Every revolt the Jews launched to get rid of foreign rule was brutally crushed. Even worse, the political and military superiority of the invading infidels was accompanied by their cultural seduction. Those who were attracted to the Roman ways, known as Hellenized Jews, adopted Greco-Roman speech, manners, and habits, including "debauchery and riotous living."[31] In the eyes of the more conservative Jews, Hellenized Jews were traitors who had become "sinners," "scoffers," and "wicked and ungodly men."[32] God's people were besieged from without and within.

According to Erol Güngör, this two-millennia-old Jewish crisis is very similar to the one Muslims faced in the twentieth century. In the latter case, the new version of pagan Rome was the secular West; the new Hellenism was Westernization; and the new Herodians were the secularist dictators in Muslim countries.

The ways Muslims reacted to this crisis also mirror those of the Jews. Among the latter, four distinct camps emerged in the face of Roman power. The Sadducees decided to cooperate with Rome and adopt some of the Hellenistic attitudes—just as some Muslims today have done vis-à-vis the secular West. The Essenes preferred to renounce the world and devote themselves to a mystical life in isolation—like today's Sufi-minded Muslims. The third Jewish party, the Pharisees, refused to cooperate with Rome and engaged in passive rejectionism, which led them to a very strict observance of Jewish law. This, too, is very similar to what the more conservative Muslims decided to do in the twentieth century: cling strictly to the Shariah and reject anything new and foreign.

The fourth element among the Jews of the time of Christ was also interesting—and quite relevant. These were the Zealots, a more radical offshoot of the Pharisees, who decided to wage an armed struggle against not just the Romans but also their Jewish collaborators. According to Josephus, a Jewish historian of the time, these men were passionately insistent that "God is to be their only Ruler and Lord."[33] They, in other words, wanted to push out the infidels and their allies and establish a theocracy—just as the militant Islamists of today wish to do.

Certain members of the Zealots were called Sicarii (daggermen), because they hid small daggers under their cloaks. They would stab their victims in popular assemblies and then vanish into the crowd. Their targets were not just Roman soldiers and officials but "any person who appeared too friendly towards the Roman oppressor."[34] They even killed the Jewish high priest Jonathan, "a man whose moderate views they refused to tolerate."[35] They were, in our contemporary language, "religious extremists" and "terrorists" who "hijacked" the peaceful faith of those like Jonathan.

After the destruction of Jerusalem and the Second Temple by the Romans in 70 AD, the Zealots took refuge by capturing the Roman fortress of Masada. After three years of repeated sieges, the Roman military finally gave up trying to seize the fortress intact and burned down the walls. When the Romans stormed in, the Zealots and their families had all committed suicide, rather than surrender. If there had been bombs in that era, the Zealots probably would have used them—to kill not just themselves but also their enemies. And the Romans probably would have labeled them "suicide bombers."

WHY DO THEY HATE YOU?

The aim of the preceding tale is certainly not to justify terrorism in the name of Islam. There can never be any valid excuse for terrorism—i.e., violent attacks on civilians. Rather, I want to demonstrate that the Muslim extremists who resort to, or sympathize with, such deplorable violence did not come out of the blue. The political history of the past two centuries of Islamdom holds the key to their emergence. The question of why Islamic liberalism—which shared such promise in the late nineteenth century—succumbed to a radical wave of Islamism cannot be answered by examining the internal dynamics of Islam alone. The intrusion of Western powers, and the secular dictators they supported in the Muslim world, are also partly responsible.[36] Both the Romans and the Herodians, one can say, had a share in the creation of the Zealots.

What this also means is that Islamism, and its violent offshoot, jihadism, is more of a political phenomenon than a religious one. These movements certainly refer to the more violent and authoritarian strains and themes in the Islamic tradition, but what makes them choose those elements, and not others, is the way they experience and interpret the current state of affairs in the world. In her article, "The Revolt of Islam," Nikki R. Keddie is wise to suggest:

> We must accept the probability that many young educated Muslims do not so much reject the West because they are Muslims, but, rather, become Islamists largely because they are hostile to Western dominance. . . . We

can speak of radical anti-imperialism, including cultural
anti-imperialism, leading to Islamism as much as or
more than the other way around.[37]

That dynamic probably explains why even religiously indif-
ferent but politically irritated Muslims can sometimes sympathize with the jihadists. "Even young Arab girls in tight jeans,"
an American scholar observes, "praise bin Laden as an anti-imperialist hero."[38]

Such "anti-imperialist heroes" gather support with an
alarming message: the *umma*, the global Muslim community,
is under attack. The evidence, within their selective and biased
reading of recent and current history, is abundant. Osama bin
Laden, for example, routinely refers in his pronouncements to
locales where Muslims have been humiliated, oppressed, or
killed by non-Muslims (led, supposedly, by the United States),
such as in Palestine, Chechnya, or Kashmir.[39] Then he calls
all Muslims to join the *jihad*, which he defines as "an individual duty if the enemy destroys Muslim countries."[40] (In other
words, although there is a concept of *offensive jihad* in the tradition as well, what bin Laden and his ilk mainly refer to is
defensive jihad.)

Therefore, an effective way for Westerners to render Islamism
and jihadism ineffective would be to convince the world's Muslims that Islam as a religion is *not* under attack. An additional
reassuring message would be that Muslims are also not targets
of enmity, insult, or discrimination in the West—and that their
mosques, minarets, and veils are *not* banned.

Most Westerners may think that they already are spreading
this message of peace and respect—and some, like President
Obama in his helpful 2009 speeches in Ankara and Cairo, actu-

ally do. But the message does not get across enough, for several reasons.

First, most Muslims believe that U.S. rhetoric does not correspond to actual policies, and they point to certain aspects of American foreign policy that they perceive as harmful to Muslim nations. The four-decade-long plight of the Palestinians, which has become an iconic Muslim tragedy, is often at the top of the list, as the United States is perceived in the Muslim world as unilaterally, and unfairly, pro-Israel. Since 2000, the situation has worsened, in large part because of the civilian cost of the "War on Terror." Westerners euphemistically refer to "collateral damage," but most Muslims see this as the killing of innocents. "One man's collateral damage," after all, as one critic put it well, "is another man's son."[41]

On the other hand, in regions where U.S. foreign policy is seen as supportive of Muslims, such as in the former Yugoslavia, America is cherished. Kosovo, which is more than 90 percent Muslim, is one of the most pro-American countries in the world. In my country, Turkey, the United States was very popular in the late 1990s, when it was seen as a peacekeeper and a bulwark against Serbian aggression, but anti-Americanism skyrocketed among Turks after 2003, when the Iraq War made the United States take on the image of an aggressor. (In other words, while some fanatics in the Muslim world might be hating America for what it *is*, most Muslims really look at what America *does*.)

Second, Muslims often hear from the West only its most hostile rhetoric. When Republican Congressman Tom Tancredo suggested on Fox News in 2005 that America could "bomb Mecca" as an "ultimate response" to Islamist terrorism, most Americans probably did not even notice. But the next day, I looked at Islamic newspapers and websites in Turkey and read the headline: "America now dares to threaten Islam with the destruction of the Ka'ba!" This tendency to perceive the most radical elements in the other civilization as its mainstream, unfortunately, is widespread in both civilizations. The media, on both sides, focus on the lunatics.

Similarly, when Switzerland banned minarets in a nationwide vote in 2009, it created an iconic double standard for many Muslims. "Look at the West that you keep praising," a Turkish reader of mine wrote to me angrily; "their freedom is only for atheists and gays, not Muslims." I tried to explain that Switzerland's vote did not represent all of Europe, let alone America, but I am sure there were millions who thought as he did whom I could not reach. On the other side, there are millions of Americans who learn that Saudi Arabia allows not a single church on its territory and wrongly assume that this is what "Islam" commands. The fact that churches exist in almost every other Muslim-majority country gets little notice.

The gap between the East and the West is even wide with regard to the way we perceive time. Americans often think in terms of current events, which are constantly changing, whereas people in the Middle East think in terms of history. When U.S. troops occupied Iraq in 2003, many Americans thought that this was an unprecedented initiative, based on the vision of the neoconservatives and the military strategies of Donald Rumsfeld. For most people in the region, though, it was yet another invasion—after those of the Crusaders, the Mongols, Napoleon, and the European colonizers.

On the cultural level, there is also a huge gap between the materialistic and hedonistic pop culture of the West and that of traditional Muslims. But the West has another face that looks approachable to those same Muslims. I remember from my childhood that my pious grandparents and their like-minded neighbors loved watching *Little House on the Prairie*, which was then aired on Turkish television, dubbed in Turkish. The family values portrayed in that series, although Christian, looked admirable to the Islamic faithful. (*Sex and the City*, of course, would be scandalous.) Unless expressed as hostility to Islam, what offends conservative Muslims is really not the West's Christianness. Rather, it is the lack of it.

The "Romans" of our era would be wise to consider these points if they want to help calming down the "Zealots" on our side. But there are also things that we as the "Jews" (I mean of course, Muslims) also can do. And one of them is exactly what a wise Nazarene did two thousand years ago: show the Zealots, and their base, the Pharisees, that with their zeal for an earthly kingdom of God, they have lost the heavenly connection with Him.

INCORPORATING MARXISM-LENINISM

To explain what I mean, let me go back to 1992, my second year in college. One day, I encountered a distant friend I had known in high school. He had not been a particularly observant Muslim, and, like most youngsters of our age and milieu in Istanbul, he used to be more interested in girls and cars than in mosques and prayers. So I was somewhat surprised when I learned that he had recently started to pray five times a day. "That's really nice," I said, over coffee in the school's cafeteria. "But, if I may ask, how come?"

His answer was surprising. "On TV, I saw those American planes bombing Baghdad," he said. "I was so pissed that I wanted to do something to resist."

The war to which my friend was referring was the First Gulf War. (God knows what he did after the Iraq War, which turned out to be far more dreadful.) He also told me he had some Arab roots and a few distant relatives in Baghdad. Watching that city bombarded live on CNN had apparently triggered feelings in him that translated into a sudden burst of religiosity.

This political motive for prayer was new to me, though. Daily prayer, as I learned many summers ago from my grandparents, was done for religious reasons—to worship God, gain His blessing, and purify the soul. Not to protest events playing out on the evening news.

My friend's story, I believe, sheds light on a larger phenomenon that emerged in the Muslim world in the twentieth century. As Islamic liberalism waned, and resistance arose against the West and its influence, that very resistance started to replace genuine religiosity as the basis of Islam. The creators and the followers of this trend—Islamism—began to define Islam not as a path to God's blessings and eternal salvation, as it is defined in the Qur'an, but instead as a political ideology that will help Muslims fight the Western-dominated world system. "Islam is a revolutionary doctrine and system that overturns governments," wrote Mawdudi in 1941. "It seeks to overturn the whole universal social order . . . and establish its structure anew. . . . Islam seeks the world."[42]

This "Islam" sounded very much like Marxism-Leninism—no wonder, since Mawdudi was heavily influenced by that ideology. Although he denounced both liberalism and Marxism as products of the secular West, he had to fill his new "Islam" with some ideological content. Since liberal Europe was the real enemy, and he needed something totalitarian, he borrowed freely from Marxist terminology and practice.[43] In the 1940s, some of his admirers openly, and proudly, pictured him as the father of "a synthesis between socialism and Islam."[44] In fact, Mawdudi himself openly acknowledged that the "Islamic state" he envisioned "bears a kind of resemblance to the Fascist and Communist states," in the way it dominates the whole society.[45]

The main mission of this totalitarian state would be to impose the Shariah on Muslim society—and, in the Islamist utopia, on the whole world. But which Shariah? In the premodern period, this question was not answered by the state. As we have seen, diverse schools of the Shariah were developed by various scholars, and individuals and communities could choose among them. Non-Muslims in Islamdom, for that matter, already had laws of their own. In that premodern age, after all, law was personal, not territorial. The Ottomans changed this in the nineteenth century by adopting the modern principle that law is territorial and equally binding on all citizens—and they standardized the Shariah by codifying it via the Mecelle. But they did this by reforming the Shariah and conceding the need for further reform by accepting the legal maxim, "Changing times legitimize the amendment of the law."

The Islamist project, however, aimed at imposing "the original Shariah," the one developed according to the norms of a dozen centuries ago. Moreover, unlike the classical period, in which the Shariah was a check on the powers of the executive, it now became an instrument of the executive. This combination of the powerful tools of the modern state and premodern standards of law would create a quite brutal and repressive system. The question of whether this tyranny would make people more devout—the Qur'an's foremost concern—was not even asked. That wasn't the issue. Establishing a "perfect system" that supposedly would bring earthly victory to Muslims was the issue.

The Islamist Retreat from God

Despite all its religious brouhaha, then, Islamism was in fact a "secular" political project—as is apparent in its slogans. Egyptian activist Hasan al-Banna, who in 1928 founded the Muslim Brotherhood, which would become one of the two pillars of Islamism (along with Mawdudi's Jamaat-e-Islami), contrasted "Islam" to both socialism and capitalism and, of course, argued that it was superior to both.[46] The problem was not only the shallowness of this rhetoric—Islam does not provide a blueprint for governance—but also its relegation of Islam to a collectivist "system," devoid of personal religiosity.

Wilfred Cantwell Smith, the late professor of religion, observed this strange trade-off between God and politics in his study of the evolution of the Egyptian journal *Majallat al-Azhar* from 1930 to 1948. During that time, the journal had two editors. The first, from 1930 to 1933, was al-Khidr Husain, a traditional Muslim. He saw religion as "a transcendent idea rather than a political and historical entity," and he was confident enough to criticize Muslim behavior. The journal's articles were full of either moral instructions or theological contemplations. The sublime beauty of nature, for example, was interpreted as a sign of God's majesty. God, apart from everything else, was the object of veneration.[47]

In 1933, Farid Wajdi, an Islamist, took over the magazine, and the content became increasingly political. Wajdi's main goal was to assure his readers that Islam as a "system" was perfect, especially when compared to Western systems. "The human reality of Islam," in other words, was the new object of veneration, and "this earthly value had in some sense replaced the transcendent God." According to Smith, a "profound irreligiousness" pervaded Wajdi's journal, and God appeared remarkably seldom throughout its pages.[48]

Quite tellingly, this retreat from God did not bring any happiness on earth. In every country where they came to power— Iran, Sudan, and Afghanistan—Islamists failed to create the heaven they promised. For it was not "Islam" in power, but totalitarianism in Islamic garb, and any totalitarianism is doomed to fail.

Allowing Islamists to engage in this trial-and-error process is perhaps better than allowing them to cling to an untested utopia. In places where they were not allowed to compete politically, they grew more radical, and ultimately violent. In Egypt, the brutal suppression of the Muslim Brotherhood by the country's successive Herods—Nasser, Sadat, and Mubarak—created more radical offshoots of the organization. Sayyid Qutb, the Arab counterpart of Mawdudi, grew more and more strident as a result of the torture he suffered in Egypt's terrible prisons. His consequent call for *jihad* would inspire many radicals, including Ayman al-Zawahiri, who, after having had his own share of Egyptian torture, became the mastermind of al-Qaeda.[49]

The stories of these modern-day Zealots are now well known in the West—ever since some of them decided to attack the very heart of modern-day Rome on September 11, 2001. Since that tragic day, concerned Americans and other Westerners have focused on and discussed "the trouble with radical Islam."

An equally important discussion should be held on how the more inspiring interpretations of Islam will be able to flourish. We have seen that the secularist project is a part of the problem, and not the solution. The attempt to push religion out of Muslim minds creates, in its worst forms, authoritarian regimes. Even its mild forms are unhelpful, for they fall short of addressing the religious aspirations of Muslim societies, something that is here to stay in the foreseeable future. We, after all, live not in a secularizing world but a de-secularizing one.[50]

But we have also seen that these two extremes—secularist and Islamist authoritarianism—were not the only options facing Muslim societies a century ago: there was also an emerging Islamic modernism that synthesized liberal politics with Muslim values. Was that an oddity of a bygone age? Or is it still a promising idea?

This is a question many minds from all over the world, Muslim and non-Muslim, are pondering these days. And the most interesting answer comes, again, from good old Turkey.

CHAPTER EIGHT

The Turkish March to Islamic Liberalism

> Perhaps the reason why we have not seen
> the proposal of a liberal development
> paradigm for the Middle East is because
> we have assumed that it must counter the
> Islamic trend.
>
> —LEONARD BINDER, *Islamic Liberalism*[1]

TURKEY BEGAN 2008 in the shadow of a very heated debate. The issue was whether female university students could cover their hair with a headscarf—a practice allowed in the whole free world, except in Turkey, where it was banned by the staunchly secularist Constitutional Court in 1989. The incumbent Justice and Development Party (AKP, with its Turkish initials) was a "conservative" party led by devout Muslims. They had just won a sweeping election victory six months earlier, in July 2007, and were willing to permit the headscarf—which most of their wives and daughters wore—at least on campuses.

In February, the AKP, with the support of two other parties in the Turkish parliament, passed an amendment that inserted two clauses into the constitution. One of them stated that all citizens, regardless of their religion, race, or ethnicity, would "benefit from public services equally." The other amendment provided a guarantee: "No citizen can be barred from the right to higher education."

These clauses might sound like commonsense declarations to most people, but to the secularist establishment they constituted an unacceptable heresy that opened the doors of the universities to "backward-minded" conservative Muslims. Soon the Constitutional Court stepped in. It not only nullified the amendment but also levied a hefty fine on the AKP government for violating the country's self-styled secularism. The ruling party, in fact, barely survived being disbanded and buried in Turkey's political graveyard, where more than two dozen parties rest in peace simply for having failed to comply with some aspect of the official ideology.

In the middle of this peculiar political controversy—during which "freedom" and "secularism" had become opposing slogans—an interesting voice emerged from the headscarfed female students whose right to education was being discussed. On a website titled "We Are Not Free Yet," three hundred of them put their signatures under the following statement:

> What we have suffered since the day that the door of the university was shut in our face taught us something: Our real problem is the authoritarian mentality which assumes a right to interfere in the lives, appearances, words and thoughts of people.
>
> Thus, as women who face discrimination because we cover our heads, we hereby declare that we won't be happy simply by entering universities with our scarves—unless:

- The Kurds and other alienated groups in this country are given the legal and psychological basis to consider themselves first-class citizens.
- The foundations of the [non-Muslim] minorities that were shamelessly confiscated are given back.
- Or the "insulting Turkishness" cases [mostly brought against many liberal intellectuals] are brought to an end.[2]

The rest of the text continued to ask for "freedoms" for all suppressed groups in Turkey, including the Alevis, an unorthodox Muslim sect, and denounced "all forms of discrimination, suppression, and imposition." Finally, these "covered women" based their entire stance on a saying attributed to the Prophet Muhammad: "The Heavens and the earth stand on justice."

This genuinely liberal and Islamic message immediately became popular, making national headlines. The number of signatories quickly increased, reaching twelve hundred in just a few weeks. Soon, the three young women who started the initiative, Neslihan Akbulut, Hilal Kaplan, and Havva Yılmaz, published a book titled *We Are Not Free Yet*. In the introduction, they used the same slogan that appeared on their website: "If the matter is freedom, nothing is trivial."

This was just one example of a phenomenon that has emerged in Turkey since the early 1990s: the growing acceptance and advocacy of liberal political ideas by the country's practicing Muslims. In fact, the liberal and Islamic trends in the country have become so intertwined that they are now seen as allies by the radical secularists. Even some of the hate words used by the latter reflected this Islamo-liberal synthesis. While they insult covered women by calling them *karafatmalar* (cockroaches), the term they prefer for Islamic liberals is *takkeli liboş*, which literally means "liberal with a prayer cap."

And how all this came about is a story worth examining.

The "Center" versus the "Periphery"

In the previous chapter, we left Turkey at the Kemalist Revolution, the effort to remove Turkey from its Ottoman past and re-create it from scratch, based on ideas derived from the radical secularism of eighteenth- and nineteenth-century Europe. Islam, according to this vision, would be allowed no influence whatsoever in society. "The boundary of religious consideration in Turkey," wrote Recep Peker, the secretary general of the single-party Kemalist regime in 1936, "cannot exceed the skin of a citizen."[3] In other words, religion could exist only on the "inside" of citizens, and not in public life. There would be no religious education, no religious communities, no religious movements—and nothing like the First Amendment of the U.S. Constitution to protect such public expressions of religion from the state.

In just two decades, from 1925 to 1945, the Kemalist vision successfully dominated the "center" of Turkish society, which included the bureaucracy, the military, the judiciary, and the universities. The "purification" of the latter was realized by the 1933 "university reform," in which professors who disagreed with the Kemalist ideology—including its pseudoscientific theories about the Aryan origins of the "Turkish race"—lost their jobs. At Istanbul University, almost two-thirds of the scholars were deemed "backward-minded" and were fired.

Since the "center" of society became so dominated by the secularists, Islam would be able to survive only in its "periphery"—

the rural areas, small towns, and the lower classes.[4] As a result, the more sophisticated Islamic tradition of the Ottoman elite disappeared, while religion became part of the culture of the less-educated masses. As a result, for many decades upper-class secular Turks considered that being a practicing Muslim was synonymous with being a *köylü*—a peasant.

Yet still, some of the liberal ideas developed by the Ottoman Islamic elite found their way into Republican Turkey. And no one was more influential in building this bridge than an exceptional Kurdo-Turkish scholar named Said Nursi.

Said Nursi, "The Wonder of the Age"

Born in 1878 in a poor village in Eastern Anatolia named Nurs (whence comes his family name), the young Said was a devout and intellectually curious student. He learned the Qur'an, the Hadiths, and other Islamic sources in the *madrasas* of his region. His teachers were so impressed by his sharp memory and intellect that they called him Bediüzzaman ("the Wonder of the Age"), which soon became his nickname.

At the age of fifteen, Said was profoundly inspired by a book entitled *Rüya* (*The Dream*), an allegorical tribute to liberty written two decades earlier by Namık Kemal, the prominent Young Ottoman introduced in chapter 6. In the book, the Islamic liberal Kemal depicted freedom as a beautiful fairy coming down from the heavens, liberating all Ottoman citizens from authoritarian rule and blessing them with rights, progress, and wealth. Said was deeply impressed by this vision. "I woke up then," he would write years later, "with *The Dream* of Kemal."[5]

No wonder, then, that from his adolescent years to his death in 1960, opposition to authoritarian rule and commitment to freedom and democracy would be important themes for Said Nursi—and the millions of his followers who would emerge in Republican Turkey.

Another important concern for Nursi was modern science. *Madrasas* of his time had become extremely conservative and insular institutions: only "Islamic sciences" were taught, not modern ones such as physics, chemistry, and biology. The modern ones were taught in the French-style schools that the Ottoman Empire had opened early in the nineteenth century. Yet some graduates of these modern institutions were becoming the followers of not only science but also scientism—the idea that science is an ultimate guide to everything and an alternative to religion. In other words, while classical Islamic education was teaching faith without any science, modern schools were teaching science without (and even against) faith.

The solution, Nursi thought, was to open new *madrasas* with a modern curriculum; he even made plans for a modern Islamic university. In November 1907, he went all the way to Istanbul to personally talk to Sultan Abdülhamid II and seek his blessing. The sultan's secretaries, surprised by the confidence and ambition of this rural-born Kurd, thought that he was out of his mind to request a private audience with the great caliph.

So Nursi failed to obtain the official support he sought for his project, but the next two years that he spent in the capital of the empire contributed to his thinking and his reputation. It was during this time that the Second Constitutional Period—or Hürriyet (Liberty), as it was then called—was announced, and the Ottoman parliament reconvened after three decades of suspension. Nursi quickly became famous as an Islamic supporter of the Liberty cause. He made impressive speeches in Istanbul and sent dozens of telegrams to the Kurdish elders in the East, all defending constitutionalism, representative democracy, and freedom of thought.[6]

When the Ottoman Empire entered World War I, Nursi took up arms, along with his students, to protect the eastern border from the Russian Army—only to be captured as a prisoner of war. Soon after his release, he went back to Eastern Turkey to try to establish the modern *madrasa* about which he had been dreaming for decades. But fate had other plans for him.

In 1925, a Kurdish revolt broke out in the region, and the Kemalist government punished not just the perpetrators but also many other Kurdish notables, "relocating" them to western areas of Anatolia. Nursi, who had opposed the revolt, was exiled to a village in Isparta Province, in midwestern Turkey. Here, he would have time for some soul-searching and finally would define a new mission in life. This "new Said" would neglect all political matters and devote himself to saving the Islamic faith from the godless ideas and temptations of the age.

Soon Nursi started to write his famous "epistles," which, over the next three decades, would fill more than a dozen volumes with Islamic apologetics. His whole purpose was to "bring God back by raising Muslim consciousness"—in strong contrast to the thoroughly secular *Homo kemalicus* the regime wanted to create.[7] The more Nursi wrote, the more he attracted official wrath. As a result, he spent the whole "single-party era" (1925–50) in prison, under house arrest, or in some form of exile in remote parts of Turkey. His followers, who clandestinely hand-wrote, distributed, and copied his works, became known as "the students of Nur" (or *Nurcus*).

The Nur movement was not only absolutely nonviolent but also persistently apolitical. "Trying to serve religion via politics brings more harm than good," a Nurcu text argues, and rejects the "revolutionary Islamic approach, which wants to shape society from above and which even legitimizes violence." "The best way to serve Islam," it concludes, "is to advocate the truths of faith."[8] But even this was unacceptable for Kemalism. Hence, newspapers of the 1930s and 1940s often reported stories about "Nurcu retrogrades" caught by the police with such "illegal materials" as books, brochures, copy machines, and prayer caps.

The Nur movement was only able to take a deep breath in 1950, when the quarter-century-old Kemalist regime was overthrown in the first free and fair elections of the Republican era. The new prime minister was Adnan Menderes, whose Democrat Party (DP) had the famous motto, "Enough! It is the nation's turn to speak." The DP was an heir to some of the liberal ideas of the Progressive Republican Party (PRP), which had been closed down in 1925. It was therefore more tolerant of and respectful to religion, more lenient to the Kurds, and more favorable to free-market capitalism. Menderes, who had promised to make Turkey "a little America," soon embraced the Marshall Plan, sent Turkish troops to the Korean War, and joined NATO. He also created an economic boom that would grant him three election victories in a row—the second one with 57 percent of the votes, an unmatched record in Turkish political history.

But the Kemalist "center"—the bureaucracy, the military, the judiciary, and the universities—despised Menderes, regarding him as the leader of a counterrevolution. Among the prime minister's supposed misdeeds was his amicable attitude toward religious leaders, including Said Nursi. "What do you want from this ascetic man who devoted his whole life to faith?" he said in January 1960 to the Kemalists in parliament who were angrily questioning why Nursi was allowed to travel freely around the country.[9]

The response came four months later, on May 27, 1960, when the Turkish military staged a coup, established martial law, and imprisoned hundreds of DP members on Yassıada, an island on the outskirts of Istanbul. The junta soon set up a show trial, which sentenced Menderes and two of his ministers to execution, for subjective crimes including "empowering religious retrogrades." On September 17, 1961, Adnan Menderes, the most popular prime minister in Turkish history, was hung on the gallows— after, by some accounts, being beaten and abused by soldiers.[10] The rest of the DP politicians were given lengthy prison terms.

The ruling generals had to take care of one more task. Nursi had died two months before the coup, in the eastern city of Urfa, and he was buried there. His grave, which attracted visitors from all over the country, could prove to be a symbol of resistance to the junta and its ideals. So, on the night of June 12, 1960, a squadron entered Urfa, established a curfew, positioned tanks around the city, and headed toward Nursi's grave. The marble tomb was broken into pieces and Nursi's remains were removed, put on a military plane, and flown out, to be reburied at a secret location somewhere in Anatolia. His final resting place remains unknown.

The junta that staged the 1960 coup soon drafted a new constitution and allowed the return of multiparty politics. But it also took measures to ensure that the new state would be a quasi-democracy, not a real one; elected politicians would be kept under check, and, when deemed necessary, overthrown by the Kemalist establishment.

Thereafter, Turkish politics would be like a pendulum swinging between authoritarianism and democracy. And while the secularists would be the proud guardians of authoritarianism, the Islamic camp would increasingly aspire to democracy.

The Making of "Turkish-Islamic Exceptionalism"

The brief history of Said Nursi helps illustrate the "exceptionalism" of Turkish Islam, which, according to Turkish sociologist Şerif Mardin, is too often overlooked by contemporary Western scholars because of their "concentration on Arab or Salafi Islam."[11]

This exceptionalism has a lot to do with the uniqueness of Turkish political history, which created conditions that other Muslim nations of the modern era did not experience. First of all, unlike most other Muslim countries, Turkey was never colonized by European powers. For Turkey's Muslims, this meant that the "other" was not necessarily the West, as was the case for most Arab and Indian/Pakistani Muslims. The "other" for Turkish Islam was homegrown authoritarian secularism. In fact, the West would appear to Turkish Muslims, from the 1990s onward, as an ally, for it showed more respect to religious freedom than shown by Turkey's self-styled secularism.

Second, even though Turkey's secularists were unmistakably authoritarian, they nonetheless were more restrained and less arbitrary than others in the Muslim world, such as the two shahs of Iran and the secular dictators in the Arab world. Unlike those countries, Turkey had a tradition of constitutional and parliamentary rule that was rooted in the Ottoman reforms of the nineteenth century. As a result, the Kemalists could not forestall free elections forever and had to accept multiparty politics after each period of ideological restoration.

This meant that, for a pious Muslim in Turkey who felt oppressed by the regime, the proverbial light at the end of the tunnel was the ballot box, which repeatedly brought to power center-right political parties, such as the DP. But in Iran, where the shah's absolutism left no space for democratic politics, the only way out was revolution. In Egypt and Algeria, where democracy was neither deeply rooted nor allowed to grow, the option would be, at least for some, *jihad*.

A third factor contributing to the exceptionalism of modern Turkish Islam was its strong aversion to Communism, an antipathy unparalleled in the Arab world. This had two explanations. First, from the beginning of the Cold War, Moscow proved to have designs on Turkey. The idea of a Soviet invasion, evoking vivid memories of the Ottoman-Russian enmity, became the nightmare of most Turks, including the devoutly Islamic ones. Second, the Turkish Marxist Left, which became a formidable force from the early 1960s onward, was vehemently antireligious. Therefore, throughout the Cold War, for most Muslims in Turkey, the enemy was "godless Communism," whereas the West, especially America, looked much more acceptable. "Americans believe in God, they respect our religion," wrote a popular Islamic pundit in 1969. "They are the People of the Book; but the Reds are infidels."[12]

Said Nursi was the archetype of this stance. His epistles were full of denunciations of Communism, which he regarded as the political outcome of philosophical materialism. That's why he supported the DP government's decision to send troops to Korea in order to fight "the Reds," and he even encouraged one of his students to enlist as a volunteer. He also hoped to build a Muslim-Christian alliance against aggressive atheism. In 1950, he sent a collection of his works to Pope Pius XII and received, in February 1951, a personal letter of thanks. Two years later, Nursi visited Ecumenical Patriarch Athenagoras in Istanbul to pledge friendship among monotheistic believers and seek cooperation in facing the challenges of a secular age.

All these aspects of Nursi's thinking—support for democracy, sympathy for the free world, and interest in interfaith cooperation—would be preserved by his millions of followers, who kept the Nur movement alive after his death.[13] One of them, a charismatic preacher named Fethullah Gülen, would even extend Nursi's legacy and turn it into a global movement, with an impressive network of schools, nongovernmental organizations, and media outlets.

THE RISE OF TURKISH ISLAMISM

The movement of Nursi (and later of Gülen) became a major branch of Islam in modern-day Turkey, but it certainly was not the only one. Another branch was official Islam, organized under the government's Directorate of Religious Affairs (*Diyanet*, for short), which had been formed in 1924 by the Republican regime to replace the Ottoman institutions organized around the caliphate. This was one of the striking oddities of Turkey's secularism: it was not about the separation of religion and state but rather the domination of religion by the state. Kemalism wanted the citizens to be as secular as possible but also wished to control their beliefs.

Not too surprisingly, the officially endorsed Diyanet became a dry and tedious bureaucracy that maintained mosque services and organized rituals and festivals, but it hardly inspired anyone. This would not change until the turn of the twenty-first century, when the organization became more self-confident and visionary, thanks to new leadership and the political support it received from the pro-Islamic AKP government.

A third branch of Turkish Islam was formed by a diverse group of *tarikats*, or Sufi orders with traditional Sunni codes of belief. The largest *tarikat* was the Naqshbandis, who emphasized personal piety and communitarian morals. They shared Nursi's focus on godliness but not necessarily his modern, rational, and even liberal bent. The difference between the two branches was apparent even at first glance. The typical Nurcu would have a mustache but not a beard, wear a suit and tie, and speak about the manifestations of God in nature as supported by modern science. The *tarikat* member would grow a long beard, avoid the Western-looking tie, and quote from twelfth-century authorities such as Imam al-Ghazali or Abd al-Qadir al-Gaylani.

In the late 1960s, the differences between the Nurcus and the *tarikats* found their political counterparts. Most of Nursi's followers continued to support the center-right, now represented by the Justice Party (JP), which claimed to follow in the footsteps of the defunct Democrat Party. But the JP leader, Süleyman Demirel (who was rumored to be a Freemason), never gained the same trust that Menderes enjoyed. Hence the *tarikats* looked for another alternative, which they found in the *Milli Görüş* (National Outlook) movement led by Necmeddin Erbakan, a former engineer and a member of the Naqshbandi *tarikat*.

The "nation" to which Erbakan's movement referred was the *umma*, the global Islamic community of believers. As a community of faith, the *umma* naturally was dear to all Muslims, but Erbakan also envisioned it as a political community. So he proposed that Turkey withdraw from the whole Western alliance in order to form an "Islamic Union" and an "Islamic NATO." Defining the Common Market, the precursor of the European

Union, as a plot by "international Zionism," he promised an "economically independent" Turkey and a state-driven industrial leap forward.

All these ideas sounded more "Left" than "Right," so Erbakan's National Salvation Party (MSP) did not have much trouble forming a coalition government in 1974 with the then-Socialist Republican People's Party, led by Bülent Ecevit. The critics of this brief Islamist-Socialist partnership jokingly called it "the watermelon coalition": green on the outside, red on the inside.

Erbakan's statist, anti-Western, anti-Zionist, and even anti-Semitic rhetoric was much closer to the Islamist movements of the Middle East, such as the Muslim Brotherhood in Egypt, than to the line of Islamic liberals of the Ottoman era and the Nurcus who preserved traces of the latter's legacy. So it was no accident that, besides the ultraconservative *tarikats*, the sails of Erbakan's ship were filled by the nascent Islamist movement of the 1970s, inspired by the translated works of Islamist ideologues such as Mawdudi and Qutb. This movement dismissed Nursi's works as "the Islam of flowers and bugs," condemned the center-right for its "Americanism," and either supported Erbakan or, among the most extreme, rejected any party politics, calling democracy "a system of unbelief."

One of the young Turkish Islamists of the time, Mehmet Metiner, who years later would renounce the ideology and redefine himself as a "Muslim democrat," explains the mindset of his comrades in the 1970s:

> The generation before us believed that they had needed to side with America in the face of the communist threat. . . . But our generation was different. We saw the United States and the West as unbelievers and impe-

rialists who colonized the Islamic world via the puppet regimes they created in Muslim lands.[14]

Metiner also notes that he had become sympathetic to Socialist ideas thanks to *Islamic Socialism*, written by Mustafa Sibai, one of the theorists of the Muslim Brotherhood. He adds that he and his Islamist friends found the Ottoman legacy uninteresting and thus were never "Ottomanist."[15]

In this sense, Islamism in Turkey was at least partly an unintended consequence of Kemalism. The latter's zeal against Ottoman tradition impoverished Islamic thought, suppressed even its most moderate proponents (such as the Nur movement), and created a vacuum that a radical Islamism of a foreign origin could fill. The 1960 coup contributed to this void by destroying the Democrat Party, whose center-right umbrella had been uniting nearly the entire Islamic camp. Had Menderes survived, politically and literally, Erbakan and his Milli Görüş probably would not have found an audience. That's why Turkish historian Ahmet Yaşar Ocak, a respected expert on Turkish Islam, thinks that the country's radical Islamists can well be regarded as the "illegitimate sons" of its radical secularists. The Turkish Herodians, in other words, unintentionally helped create Turkish zealots.[16]

THE ÖZAL REVOLUTION—AND THE "THREE FREEDOMS"

On September 12, 1980, while the center-right Justice Party was in power, Turkey faced yet another military coup, the brutal one described in the Introduction to this book. When the generals scheduled national elections again in 1983, they allowed only newcomers to run for office. Turgut Özal, a former bureaucrat and economist, stood out, and his newly formed Motherland Party came to power. The next ten years would be "the Özal decade," a revolutionary age of liberalization during which the Islamo-liberal synthesis, almost forgotten after decades of forced amnesia, was reborn.

As a member of a Naqshbandi family, Özal was a devout believer in Islam. As a former employee of the World Bank and the private sector, he also was a genuine believer in free-market capitalism and, in a broader sense, the American idea of liberty. In the words of American journalist Robert Kaplan, Özal "loved to read the Qur'an and watch soap operas, to bang his head against the carpet in a Sufi mosque and go to Texas barbecues."[17] That helps explain why, as the most far-reaching Turkish leader since Atatürk, he would be able to "restore religion to Turkey's political space without threatening the country's pro-Western orientation."[18]

Özal based his policies on the notion of "the three freedoms"— of ideas, religion, and enterprise. The economy opened up, abandoning decades-old Kemalist policies of protectionism, "statism," and "a planned economy." Some of the authoritarian articles in the penal code, which banned "religious propaganda" and many other "thought crimes," were rescinded. The tyrannical prohibitions on the Kurdish language, which criminalized even Kurdish songs, were, at least partly, lifted. (Özal also proudly noted that his mother was Kurdish, thus breaking the taboo on the K-word.)

Özal also tried to restore respect for the Ottomans, who for decades had been the bête noire of the official ideology. He even found parallels between the Ottoman Empire and the United States, arguing that both granted diverse communities the freedom to exercise their religion, culture, and economic aspirations. In 1987, he submitted Turkey's application to the European Union. Two years later, he became the president, yet he continued to guide policy via a loyal prime minister. (In the Turkish system, the presidency is the highest post, but the prime minister holds more power.)

Most Kemalists, unsurprisingly, despised Özal, seeing him as a counter-revolutionary undoing all the great things Atatürk had done half a century earlier. The fact that he was both pro-Islamic and pro-American even led some of them to suspect a Western plot to overthrow the Kemalist Republic—paranoia that would reach its zenith in the 2000s, when the pro-Islamic AKP became the champion of the EU bid.

Özal also had his fans. Among them was the tiny group of liberal intellectuals—most of them secular but not secularist—who had been sidelined for decades in a political sphere dominated by the Kemalist state, the Marxist Left, and the nationalist Right. Also in favor of Özal were the country's millions of Kurds, whose identity had been systematically suppressed since the early years of the Republican era. The third and largest group of Özal supporters was the Islamic camp. To them, he was not only a savior who eased the burdens of the ultrasecularist regime but also, as the first Turkish prime minister to make a pilgrimage to Mecca, he was the man who returned religion to public respectability. The Nurcus were already on the center-right bandwagon, but most of the *tarikats* also sympathized with Özal and voted for his Motherland Party. He was able to reopen the great political umbrella that Adnan Menderes had formed in the 1950s.

With the Özal Revolution, people in the Islamic camp also started to realize that their yearning for religious freedom could be satisfied by adopting Western-style liberal democracy, rather than the Islamist utopia that Erbakan had been promising. For decades, most of them had perceived Kemalism, which claimed to Westernize Turkey, as a natural extension of the West. This started to change as these Islamic Turks learned more about the world. Some of the young headscarfed women, excluded from Turkish colleges, headed to universities in Europe and the United States, where they found freedom and respect. Their husbands also made the same discovery. One of them, a Turkish Muslim academic who moved to the United Kingdom during the Özal years, would later write:

> I arrived in England from Turkey at the beginning of the 1990s, after having lived and studied in Ankara where we were unable to find any prayer rooms. . . . In the UK [though], we were able to pray at chapels specifically allocated for Muslims at universities and, to our utmost surprise in government buildings, like the Home Office, when we were applying to renew our visas. These were eye-opening and life-changing experiences for us, and also for many other Turkish citizens.[19]

These religious Turks soon got their facts right. The liberal West, they realized, was better than the illiberal "Westernizers" at home.

THE DECLINE OF TURKISH ISLAMISM

In April 1993, when Turgut Özal suddenly died of a heart attack at the age of sixty-six, hundreds of thousands of people from all across Turkey flocked to his funeral in Istanbul. Some carried signs that read, "The Civilian President," "The Democrat

President," and "The Muslim President"—meaningful phrases in a country that used to see ex-military and thoroughly secular names as the state's leaders. Özal was buried at a site next to the Adnan Menderes Mausoleum—which he had had built in 1990 to honor his precursor, whom the military had executed three decades earlier.

The next nine years in Turkish politics, until the arrival of the AKP in November 2002, has sometimes been called "the lost decade," because it saw a series of inefficient and unsuccessful coalitions that ultimately led the country into a dreadful economic crisis in 2001. But this period also brought about some significant changes that transformed the Islamic camp.

One of the outcomes of Özal's death was the resurgence of Milli Görüş, the political Islamist movement led by Necmeddin Erbakan. Özal's Motherland Party was taken over by Mesut Yılmaz, a secular figure, who had little appeal for religious voters. Erbakan happily filled the gap, and his Welfare Party achieved a surprising victory in the general elections of December 1995, winning 21 percent of the votes, the highest total an Islamist party had ever received in Turkey.

Erbakan had to work until June 1996 to build a coalition with the center-right party led by Tansu Çiller, who had previously been Turkey's first female prime minister. This dual government lasted for a year, during which Erbakan found the chance to implement only a few of his ideas, such as building closer ties with other Muslim countries and hosting receptions for *tarikat* leaders in his official residence—all shocking to the secular establishment. But what provoked the secularists even more was his rhetoric, and that of his party members, which seemed to herald an Islamist regime.

In response to this Islamist challenge, on February 28, 1997, the military initiated a process that later would be dubbed "the postmodern coup." The generals orchestrated the whole Kemalist "center"—the bureaucracy, the judiciary, the universities, and the "mainstream" media—to force the government to resign, then to close down the Welfare Party, and finally to crack down on Islamic groups and their resources. In June 1997, the generals declared a long list of companies "backward-minded" (i.e., too religious) and promoted boycotts of their products. Some Islamic leaders were put on trial for "establishing anti-secular organizations." Some "undesirable" journalists were fired, and several were even discredited with fake documents prepared by the military.[20] Certain members of the Welfare Party, including its rising star, Recep Tayyip Erdoğan, then mayor of Istanbul, were given prison terms for "inciting hatred" against the Kemalist regime. "Erdoğan's political career is over," some newspapers wrote in September 1998. "From now on, he can't even be a local governor."[21]

The speech that earned Erdoğan a ten-month prison term was indeed harsh,[22] but it also included an interesting remark that hinted at the direction he would follow: "Western man has freedom of belief," Erdoğan said. "In Europe there is respect for worship, for the headscarf. Why not in Turkey?"[23]

The AKP's Path to Post-Islamism

In the aftermath of "the post-modern coup" of 1997, a more moderate group in the Welfare Party, fed up with Erbakan's radical and delusional rhetoric, looked for a new vision. Led by former academic Abdullah Gül, probably the most sophisticated figure in the party's ranks, this "reformist movement," spoke more favorably of Western-style democracy and began to argue that "the state should be in the service of the people, rather than a holy state that stands far above the people."[24] This movement soon broke with Milli Görüş and joined forces with Tayyip Erdoğan to found the Justice and Development Party (AKP) in August 2001.

From its first day, the AKP declared that it was not "a political party with a religious axis," and it defined its ideology as "democratic conservatism." This meant, according to Erdoğan, "a concept of modernity that does not reject tradition, a belief in universalism that accepts localism, and an understanding of rationalism that does not disregard the spiritual meaning of life."[25]

In November 2002, a little more than a year after its founding, the AKP won the general elections with 32 percent of the votes and took power. Soon, to the surprise of the whole world, this post-Islamist party turned out to be a most dedicated and successful pursuer of Turkey's bid to join the EU. With a staggering number and scope of democratic reforms, it even proved to be, in the words of *Newsweek* columnist Fareed Zakaria, "the most open, modern and liberal political movement in Turkey's history."[26]

Hence it was no surprise when the AKP won the 2007 general elections with an astounding 47 percent of the votes, getting the support of not only conservatives but also most secular liberals, Kurds, and even Armenians.[27] The Islamist Milli Görüş, now represented by the Felicity Party, which depicted the AKP as a "traitor" that had sold its soul to "Western imperialism," received only 2.5 percent.

This might well have been interpreted as a historic defeat for Turkish Islamism, but the Kemalists believed the exact opposite. They had never trusted the AKP, insisted on calling its members

"Islamists," and asserted that the party's transformation was just a trick to deceive outsiders. Some of their conspiracy theories were mind-boggling. In 2007, for example, a staunchly Kemalist author, Ergun Poyraz, produced a series of best sellers arguing that both Erdoğan and Gül were "secret Jews" collaborating with "international Zionism" in order to destroy Atatürk's republic and enslave the Turkish nation.[28]

This anti-Semitic lunacy was just one of the many signs of the amazing transformation occurring in the political landscape. The AKP's outreach to the West had turned the tables, and now the Kemalists, who were also horrified that the EU was asking for more rights for Kurds and other minorities, had started to turn anti-Western.

Yet the Kemalists were not alone in suspecting that the AKP had a "hidden agenda." Some Western observers also believed that any party made up of devout Muslims must necessarily be illiberal and undemocratic. Critics could certainly point to traces of Islamist sentiment in the AKP's ranks, along with the typical problems of Turkey's patrimonial politics, including nepotism and intolerance to criticism. Tayyip Erdoğan also showed signs of what can be called "Muslim nationalism"—or simply "Muslimism"—in the way he demonstrated an emotional affinity for Muslim actors around the world.[29] Yet still AKP's post-Islamist position was genuine, for a few good reasons.

First, the new direction that the AKP embraced, "democratic conservatism," was not unheard-of in Turkey. Quite the contrary; it had its roots, as we have seen, among the Islamic liberals of the Ottoman Empire as well as in the center-right tradition of Turkish politics represented by the Progressive Republican Party in 1924, by Adnan Menderes between 1950 and 1960, and by Turgut Özal between 1983 and 1993. All the AKP did was abandon Milli Görüş, a late invention with foreign roots, and return to a more established political tradition. It was not an accident that Parliament Speaker Bülent Arınç, the third most powerful member of the AKP after Erdoğan and Gül, expressed regret in 2007 that until the late 1990s, he and his friends had failed to understand Özal, and had given him "the most unfair criticisms." "Only when I learned more about the world," Arınç added in an emotional tone, "did I realize how right Özal was."[30]

Second, the AKP's political transformation was in line with the changing intellectual landscape in Turkey. Classical liberalism, an idea so popular in the late Ottoman Empire but denounced by the Kemalist Republic, was rediscovered in the late 1980s, thanks to the reforms of Özal and the efforts of new organizations such as the Ankara-based Association for Liberal Thinking. Books and academic works addressing liberal philosophy, extremely rare before the 1980s, became ubiquitous.[31] The nascent group of liberal intellectuals was critical of Kemalist secularism and in favor of broader religious freedom. Their growing interaction with Islamic conservatives gave the latter group new perspective and rhetoric. Hence, from the early 1990s onward, Islamic intellectuals started to question the idea of "an Islamic state" and instead spoke of "a nonideological state" or "a neutral state," defending "pluralism" as their social ideal. They had realized, after all, that "[the] Islamist regimes in Iran, Saudi Arabia and Afghanistan introduce[d] even more extreme repression than Turkey's secularists."[32]

In 1998, the influential Gülen movement organized a conference entitled "Islam and Secularism," attended by a handful of the most prominent theologians and Islamic pundits of Turkey. Following three days of discussion, they declared that Islam and the secular state were compatible, as long as the latter respected religious freedom. The modernist theologian who championed this view, Mehmet Aydın, who promotes "liberal democratic culture" for the whole Muslim world, would become the minister responsible for the Directorate of Religious Affairs (Diyanet) in the AKP's first term.[33]

The third factor that helps explain the transformation of the AKP was a gift from Özal to Turkey: free-market capitalism. And it was this factor that ultimately was so definitive and vital to the change in Turkish Islam.

The Rebirth of Islamic Capitalism

As we saw earlier in this book, Islam was born as a business-friendly religion. The subsequent rise of "Islamic capitalism" facilitated the dynamism and splendor of Islamic civilization, as we have seen, while its decline resulted in the stagnation and eventual decline of Islamdom. We have also seen that the Ottomans realized—albeit quite belatedly—the importance of private business and tried to jump-start it via some of the Tanzimat reforms.

However, even though the Ottoman efforts led to the appearance of a Muslim middle class, this development was very limited in scope. The bourgeoisie remained primarily non-Muslim until the fall of the empire. That's why the Young Turks, and later the Kemalists, sought to create a "national bourgeoisie" that had state support. They were successful to a certain degree, but thanks to unfair methods. An "opportunity space" for Turkish capitalists opened up because of the wartime expulsion of Armenians—a tragic decision that led to sporadic mass murders—and later a "population exchange" with Greece.[34] The Kemalist regime also imposed a hefty "wealth tax" on Jews, Greeks, and Armenians between 1942 and 1944, under a cabinet with Nazi sympathies.[35] Those unable to pay, in line with the dark standards of the time, were sent to a labor camp in Eastern Turkey.[36]

Both the formation and the composition of this state-made "national bourgeoisie" were unfair. Only urbanites who could wine and dine the secular politicians and bureaucrats received lucrative contracts and loans from the state. By the end of the 1940s, the Kemalist "center" had successfully created a business elite in its own likeness.

Meanwhile, religion had survived mainly among the less privileged. "The nation-state belonged more to us than to the religious poor," says Orhan Pamuk, Turkey's Nobel laureate in literature, recalling his childhood days in 1950s Istanbul. But, he adds, secular people like him were also afraid of "being outclassed by people who had no taste for secularism."[37]

Pamuk's fears would start to be realized a few decades later, during the Özal Revolution. By liberalizing the economy, diminishing the role of the state, and personally inspiring a religiously devout and economically entrepreneurial spirit, Özal created space for Islamic-minded entrepreneurs. As early as the late 1980s, economists started to talk about "Anatolian Tigers"—companies founded in the conservative cities of Anatolia that quickly utilized the groundbreaking opportunities for manufacturing and exporting in the brave new world of the free market.

In 1990, a group of these conservative businessmen created a union named MÜSİAD, a clear alternative to the well-established TÜSİAD (Turkish Industrialists' and Businessmen's Association), which represented the more secular "Istanbul bourgeoisie." The letter "M" stood for the word *Müstakil*, or "Independent," but many thought it actually meant "Muslim," as most MÜSİAD members are mosque-going conservatives whose wives and daughters wear headscarves.

In 1994, MÜSİAD published an Islamic economic manifesto in a booklet titled *Homo Islamicus*. The document encouraged hard work and free trade, referring to the life of the Prophet Muhammad as a merchant. It vigorously defended the freedom of the markets and opposed the state's intrusive role in the economy. It also added that theirs was a capitalism tamed by the compassionate and altruistic values of Islam, not a "ruthless" one.[38]

Since its founding, MÜSİAD has become increasingly influential and has consistently supported free-market reforms, whereas some members of TÜSİAD, who used to benefit from a "protected" economy, have remained less enthusiastic. This rift started in the early years of Turgut Özal, who supported "total liberation," while most members of TÜSİAD favored a "mixed economy," or a combination of capitalism and socialism.[39]

The "Calvinists" of Islam

One of the urban centers that gave rise to the Anatolian Tigers was Kayseri, a midsize city in the heartland of Turkey. Kayserians had always been famous for both business-mindedness and religiosity, but they had their great leap forward courtesy of the Özal Revolution. From the mid-1980s onward, the city experienced an industrial boom, with hundreds of new factories opened. By the mid-2000s, just one of its textile companies produced one percent of the world's denim for brands such as Levi's, Wrangler, and Diesel. Kayseri's furniture companies supplied 70 percent of the Turkish market and exported their wares to many countries in the Middle East.

In 2005, a Berlin-based think tank, the European Stability Initiative (ESI), studied Kayseri to understand the secret of its economic miracle. After several weeks conducting interviews with the city's prominent businessmen, the ESI team wrote a report that emphasized the curious role of religion in the motivation of these entrepreneurs. "Nine out of ten of one's fate depends on commerce and courage," one of the Kayseri businessmen said, quoting the Prophet Muhammad. Another businessman argued, "It is good for a religious person to work hard," and "to open a factory is a kind of prayer." The founder of a furniture company stated, "I see no black and white opposition between being modern and [being] traditional," and said that he was "open to innovation."[40]

"To understand Kayseri," the former mayor of the town, Şükrü Karatepe, told the ESI researchers, "one must read Max Weber."[41] Weber, of course, pointed to the role that the ascetic and hardworking ethic of early Protestants, particularly Calvinists, played in the rise of modern capitalism in Europe. According to Karatepe, one could observe the same work ethic in Kayseri and a few other Anatolian cities, thanks to the teachings of Islam. Fittingly, the ESI researchers titled their report *Islamic Calvinists*. Their conclusion was that Kayseri was only a single case study, and, in general, "over the past decade [1995–2005], individualistic, pro-business currents [had] become prominent within Turkish Islam."[42]

These "individualistic, pro-business currents" were certainly capitalist, but not materialist, hedonist, or selfish. Quite the contrary, they went hand in hand with a strong sense of social responsibility, as emphasized by Islam. Kayseri's Islamic entrepreneurs spent more than $300 million in five years to support clinics, schools, and various other charitable organizations. By

2005, sixteen separate soup kitchens in the city were serving almost ten thousand people daily. Kayseri's culture was a combination of "entrepreneurship, asceticism, and altruism."[43]

The AKP's political transformation was not unrelated to the interests of these Islamic Calvinists. The latter needed a Turkey that had been integrated into the global economy, had anchored its stability in the EU, and had closer ties with all the neighboring countries—the exact strategy of the AKP.[44] No wonder all of the "Islamic Calvinists" were supporters of Erdoğan and Gül, and Kayseri was in effect an AKP city, giving the party a staggering 66 percent of the votes in 2007.

The Muslim Middle Class and Its Changing Culture

In July 2009, the founder of MÜSİAD, Erol Yarar, a practicing Muslim, gave an interview to a Turkish newspaper, sparking a nationwide debate. The headline read, "We Are the Real Bourgeois Class of Turkey." Yarar argued that while some big businesses were supported by the state, "we grew with our own effort, much like the bourgeoisie in Europe."[45]

Yarar also noted something significant: On the one hand, Muslim entrepreneurs were creating a capitalism inspired by their religious values; on the other hand, their religious values were being altered by their engagement in capitalism. "When we held our first meeting in a five-star hotel," he recalled,

> some of our friends [in MÜSİAD] were asking, "What
> are we doing here?" . . . Most of them had never trav-
> eled abroad and were hostile to Europe, America, and
> Russia. . . . They wanted to leave their companies to

their sons, and did not care much about the education of their daughters. Since then, these wrong notions have changed a lot. Now they are traveling to Europe just to see it more and more. . . . Recently I entered a little mosque in a big shopping mall in Istanbul. I looked at the shoes; they were all high-quality brands! This is the revolution that is taking place in Turkey.[46]

In other words, engagement with the modern world as its *partner* ameliorated formerly negative attitudes toward it. The experiences of these Muslim businessmen are quite different from engagement with the modern world as its *victims*—as Muslims under Western occupation or a secularist dictatorship would see themselves. It is also different from being the modern world's *outsiders*, as many marginalized Muslim immigrants in European societies feel.

The Islamic Calvinists also created jobs for a new generation of Muslim professionals. Hence, in just two decades—from the mid-1980s to the mid-2000s—a "Muslim middle class" emerged, to the shock of the secularists. As its social context changed, this middle class started to change its political attitudes. One example was the decline of Islamism. A public survey conducted by a liberal Turkish think tank in 2006 (when the AKP was in power) showed that the demand for a "Shariah state" in Turkish society had fallen from 21 percent to 9 percent in just seven years. When questions were asked about some extreme measures of the Shariah, such as stoning, this support dropped to one percent.[47] This was an especially big change when compared to the heyday of the Turkish Islamists, when they had dreamed of imposing "a Taliban-like Shariah."[48]

"Ah, those idealist *mujahids* of the 70s," wrote an Islamic pundit in 2009, "now they all have become moneymaking *müteahhids* [i.e., building contractors]."[49]

In addition to its changed outlook on political life, the new Muslim middle class started to develop a whole new culture. An interesting study that demonstrates this transformation comes from a Turkish sociologist who examined the content of "Islamic novels" in Turkey. The change became clear when he contrasted two eras of novels—the first being the 1980s, the second starting from the mid-1990s. In the first era, all of the characters in these novels were clear-cut figures—immoral secularists versus exemplary Muslims. Each story had a hero who, after some soul-searching, saw the light and became a devotee of "the Islamic cause." Even his marriage was about "raising good kids for Islam," and not focused on romance and love.

In the second era, though, the characters in the "Islamic novels" became much more real and their stories more complex. Now the secular figures were not necessarily all bad, and the Islamic ones were more human—with sins, self-doubts, and love stories. Moreover, criticism was now directed not only to the outsiders but also to the Islamic camp itself. One of the female authors whose earlier novels idealized "the Islamic way of life" was now criticizing injustices within the Islamic community, such as misogynist husbands who adopt mistresses as their "second wives."[50]

In short, Islamic literature shifted from "a rhetoric of collective salvation" to "new individualistic Muslimhoods."[51] And this was directly related to the changing socioeconomic background of the writers and their readers. The Islamic novels of the 1980s "reflected the experiences of the newcomers to the big cities . . . people of the lower class." But in the late 1990s, those people were no longer newcomers; "they had found modern

jobs as engineers, mayors, businessmen and businesswomen."
No wonder that, in this era, the old "salvation novels" and other
"ideological books" did not sell well anymore. What instead had
become popular were books about personal development.[52] As
pious Muslims entered the urban middle class, in other words,
their understanding of religion became less ideological and more
individualistic.

"UPDATING OUR RELIGIOUS UNDERSTANDING"

This changing social landscape, and the acceptance it created
for new interpretations of religion soon found its echo when the
AKP, six months after it came to power in late 2002, appointed
Ali Bardakoğlu as the head of the Directorate of Religious Affairs
(Diyanet). An erudite theologian, Bardakoğlu was willing to
infuse the institution with new dynamism and a new outlook.
Symbolically, he dropped the boring black tunic his predecessors
wore and donned a white one with golden leaves, modeled after
the Ottoman royal style. In 2004, he spoke about the need for
"updating our religious understanding," according to changing
times. "Except for the basic religious sources," he said, "we must
not adopt religious interpretations from the past as a model to
be taken literally today."[53] The following year, for the first time
in Islamic history, he appointed two women as counselors for
mosques in Istanbul and Kayseri.

In 2006, Bardakoğlu made news again with another statement: "There cannot be a Hadith that says, 'The best of women
are those who are like sheep.' "[54] This was an introduction to the
"Hadith Project" the Diyanet had launched, in order to create a
new Hadith collection that would exclude some of the misogynistic statements in the classical literature, or at least to put

them into their right contexts.[55] Hadiths that banned women from traveling alone, for example, originated "because the desert in the Prophet's time was too dangerous for a lone female traveler," explained Mehmet Görmez, the then–vice president of the Diyanet, who would replace Bardakoğlu in November 2010. "Unfortunately, this temporal concern turned into an ever-valid religious rule."[56] (The Hadith Project—based at Ankara University's School of Theology—was still underway as this book went to press.)

The Turkish critique of the Hadith corpus had actually begun in the 1980s, but it initially lacked any real support. When a lone radical reformist, Edip Yüksel, challenged the Hadiths and proposed a "Qur'an only" formula, he was reviled by conservatives and even declared a heretic. But some of Yüksel's criticisms were hard to dismiss. In the 1990s, a theologian-turned-televangelist, Yaşar Nuri Öztürk, voiced similar criticisms about the Hadiths and promoted the more progressive "Islam of the Qur'an" versus the "Islam of tradition." His unscrupulous alliance with the Kemalists turned off the conservatives, but the notion that "some Hadiths are really problematic" became increasingly popular.

Criticism of the Hadiths accompanied the rise of feminist ideas in the Islamic camp—again thanks to social change. When faced with a Hadith depicting women as half-brained creatures whose only duty is to obey their husbands, a traditional Muslim housewife would have kept quiet. But now a middle-class Muslim woman who has a degree in economics and perhaps makes more money than her husband could say, "Wait a minute, this can't be true." In other words, the Diyanet's effort to create a new Hadith literature free of misogyny would probably have been a nonstarter without the new social status Turkish women achieved with new economic opportunities.

In fact, even bolder ideas for "updating our religious understanding" developed, beginning in the 1990s, as theologians at the "Ankara School" emphasized the distinctions between what is *historical* and what is *religious*. Often inspired by the works of Fazlur Rahman, the most prominent "neo-Mutazilite" of the twentieth century, these scholars not only take a critical look at the Hadiths but also make an argument for the contextuality of the Qur'an, as opposed to literalism. Their books have taken critical approaches to the Islamic tradition, offering more rational and liberal interpretations. Among their titles are: *The Mutazilite Interpretation of the Qur'an*, *The Golden Age of the Mutazilites*, *Rethinking the Sunna*, *Rethinking the Hadiths*, *The Behind the Scenes of Ideological Hadith-Making*, *The Road to Individualization*, and *The Individual and His Religion*.

A growing emphasis on individualism was also very noticeable in the monthly magazine published by the Diyanet. Some of the articles from the late 2000s include such titles as: "Raising the Self-Governing Believer of the Open Society," "The Responsibility of the Individual to Construct His Own Religiosity," and "A Liberating Religious Education." Their author, top Diyanet official Mehmet Şevki Aydın, advises parents not to "impose their religious understanding on their children" and suggests that the believer "should consult religious authorities but also use his own reasoning . . . and be the active master of his own life."[57]

Perhaps the most worthy defense of freedom by the Diyanet came from Ali Bardakoğlu in April 2007, following a tragic incident in which three Christian missionaries were brutally murdered by a group of Turkish ultranationalists in Eastern Turkey. In a press conference, he denounced the murderers and said, "It is their [the missionaries'] natural right to preach their faith. We must learn to respect even the personal choice of an atheist, let

alone other religions."[58] Three years later, Bardakoğlu also advocated the reopening of historic Christian churches in Turkey,
which had been closed down due to the secular state's nationalist
biases.[59]

For all these views, the new leadership of the Diyanet, and
especially the theologians of the Ankara School, are considered in Turkey to be on the "modernist" side of the theological
spectrum. But even some of the more conservative voices have
offered fresh perspectives. Prominent Islamic pundit Ali Bulaç,
for example, objected to the second-class *dhimmi* status that Muslim empires have offered to non-Muslims throughout Islamic
history. This status, he argued, was intended by the Qur'an only
for the non-Muslims who initiated war on Islam but was wrongly
extended to all of them. The Islamic ideal, he wrote, should be a
social contract based on equal statuses.[60]

Another conservative opinion leader, Hayrettin Karaman,
professor emeritus of Islamic law and a columnist for the pro-
Islamic daily *Yeni Şafak*, has defended the views that Christians
and Jews can be "saved" in the afterlife; that apostasy from
Islam should not be punishable; that Islam rejects "an all-
powerful state like that of the Nazis"; and that the "un-Islamic
beliefs and practices" of non-Muslims should be free even in
an Islamic state. He has also opposed the view that the pacifist
verses of the Qur'an were abrogated, and argued that the right
Islamic political vision is "not a world in which everybody is a
Muslim, but a world in which Muslims protect all peoples and
freedoms."[61]

In response to a question about the Islamic legitimacy of a
handshake between members of the opposite sex, from which
many conservative Muslims refrain, Karaman gave an answer
that indicates the changes in society:

> At the places and times in which there was no custom
> of handshaking, holding hands between young men and
> women was much more likely to have a sexual connota-
> tion. The old jurists can be right from that regard [in
> opposing this practice]. But today this custom is wide-
> spread, it has become natural, and thus its connection
> with sexual passion has been weakened. It has even
> become a necessity.[62]

The changes in society, in other words, leads to a reconsideration
of old religious interpretations.

In 2008, a striking example of this change came from Fethullah Gülen, leader of the largest Islamic community in Turkey,
the "neo-Nurcu" Gülen movement. When asked about spousal
abuse, a practice some orthodox scholars are known to justify
occasionally, Gülen gave a quite unexpected answer. "That
would be a reason for divorce," he said. "Moreover, it might be a
good idea for threatened women to learn karate or judo—so if
their husbands hit, they can hit back better."[63]

LESSONS FROM TURKEY FOR "REFORM" IN ISLAM

In all the new ideas and perspectives of Turkish Islam we see
a commonality: a more rationalist and individualistic outlook
toward religious texts. In 2004, an Islamic intellectual recognized what this means: "The Mutazilite perspective is becoming
the dominant and widespread mind among today's Muslims."[64]
Five years later, another intellectual noted that the modernizing
Muslims of Turkey now wanted to hear about "the Qur'an and
freedom" rather than "the Qur'an and obedience."[65]

It is important to note the loose, implicit, and informal nature of this "reform." The masses are not signing proclamations saying, "By God, we are now Mutazilites." Nor has a Muslim Luther nailed a revolutionary Ninety-five Theses on a mosque door. That scenario, which is more popular in the West than anywhere else, anticipates a doctrinal change before social change. But what is happening is the exact opposite.

This is an unprecedented experiment with phenomenal implications—not only for Turkey but also for the whole world of Islam. In its dynamic formative centuries, as we have seen in the earlier chapters, Islam was a religion driven by merchants and their rational, vibrant, and cosmopolitan mindset. But then the more powerful classes of the Orient—the landlords, the soldiers, and the peasants—became dominant, and a less rational and more static mindset began to shape the religion. The more trade declined, the more the Muslim mind stagnated. In the later stages, with the rise of powerful states such as the Ottoman Empire, modern-style bureaucrats entered the scene, followed in the nineteenth century by modern-style intellectuals. But even their valuable efforts to effect change continued as a top-down process in which the majority of the society remained uninvolved.

What was painfully lacking was a dynamic that would turn the society itself into an agent for change. The statist and socialist economic models toward which the Muslim world was mistakenly driven in the twentieth century—along with the political tyrannies of secularists and others—tragically blocked the way.

Only the Gulf states became wealthy thanks to oil money, but wealth wasn't synonymous with free-market capitalism. The latter requires opportunity and objective laws. It also requires entrepreneurial individuals capable of making rational decisions and a well-educated professional workforce that can transform not just the economy but also the society. These forces can create a more merit-based culture and undermine patrimonial structures, such as tribal affiliations. The dynamics of capitalism soon demands the contribution of a female workforce, too, leading to the empowerment of women.

Oil money does none of this. "The wealth of the oil-rich states does not produce positive political change," as Fareed Zakaria puts it, and their people remain "substantially as they had been before—uneducated and unskilled."[66] In other words, you can be an oil-rich sheikh in Riyadh, and drive a Rolls-Royce, yet still remain tribal in your social relations, continue to keep your wife at home, and arrange a marriage for your daughter with another sheikh. But if you are a Muslim businessman in Istanbul, constantly battling the dynamic challenges of the economy, you understand why your daughter wants to study business administration and make an effort to send her to an American university.

That's why the seekers of "reform" in Islam need to focus not on authoritarian efforts to "Westernize" Muslim societies—let alone wars and conquests to "liberate" them—but on supporting two crucial dynamics: democracy and free markets.

In his 2009 book, *Forces of Fortune*, Vali Nasr, an Iranian-born American Muslim scholar and an adviser to the Obama administration, makes a similar case by rightly emphasizing the importance of commerce in laying the groundwork for liberal democracy in the Muslim world. He cites two countries as successful examples: Turkey and Dubai.[67] Although Dubai is the more glamorous and eye-catching of the two, it is also a tiny city-state that only emerged a few decades ago. Turkey, on the other hand, has the history and current potential to become, in the words of American political analyst Graham Fuller, "a pivotal state in the Muslim world."[68]

And, well, it is already heading that way.

Turkish Model Goes Abroad

In May 2009, I flew to Kuala Lumpur, at the invitation of the Malaysia Think Tank, a liberal institution, to give a talk entitled "Islam and Religious Freedom." To an audience of Muslim Malays and others, I argued that anyone who wants to convert from Islam to another religion should be free to do so, since "compulsion in religion" is against not just the Qur'an but also common sense.

While the reaction from the audience was mostly positive, albeit mixed, the other speaker, a prominent member of the PAS, the Islamic Party of Malaysia, could agree with me only silently. "I and other reformists in our party agree with what you said," he whispered, "but the Erbakanist establishment in the party, who calls us Erdoğanists, are not that open-minded." Apparently, the philosophical rift between Erbakan and Erdoğan—two iconic names in Turkish politics—had inspired a debate in a Muslim country five thousand miles away.

This is just one of the many examples of a larger phenomenon. The post-Kemalist Turkey of the twenty-first century has become much more significant for Muslims all around the world. In fact, "many Muslims have long considered Turkey's break with its historical and cultural past to be so radical as to make its experience irrelevant to them," as Fuller notes. But, "the new face of Turkish Islam, particularly within its evolving political context, is increasingly intriguing Muslims everywhere."[69]

This new Turkey not only offers a successful synthesis of Islam and democratic capitalism. Under the visionary strategies devised by the AKP's foreign minister, Ahmet Davutoğlu, it also plays constructive roles in the affairs of the Muslims of the

Middle East and even beyond. In a few particular cases—such as Ankara's refusal to support the U.S. invasion of Iraq in 2003 and the U.S.-led UN sanctions vote on Iran in 2010—this new line of Turkish foreign policy differed from that of Washington, raising eyebrows in America and even leading to discussions about "who lost Turkey." In those cases, however, the Turkish government was only acting pragmatically and in tune with public opinion, further enhancing the country's prestige in the Middle East as a democracy.[70] ("Democratic," some might need to note, doesn't mean "Washington's yes-man.")

This new "Turkish model" was very much in the air in the "Arab spring" of early 2011, during which longtime dictators of first Tunis and then Egypt were overthrown by public protests. As this book was going to print, similar protests were shaking other Arab autocracies, such as Libya and Bahrain, and a more democratic era was apparently at dawn in the Arab world.

And the "Turkish model" is there not because anybody imposed it, but because the success of the AKP's post-Islamist liberalism inspired the more open-minded Islamic actors all across the region. In Tunisia, whose dictatorship very much resembled Kemalist Turkey, with bans on the veil and other Islamic practices, the leader of the Islamic movement, Rachid Ghannouchi, who is a liberal-minded thinker anyway, openly said his movement "admire[d] the Turkish case."[71] A few weeks later, a leader of the Muslim Brotherhood of Egypt, Ashraf Abdel Ghaffar, said that his organization considered "the AKP to be a model for Egypt after [Hosni] Mubarak."[72]

The Muslim Brotherhood, the mother ship of the Islamist ideology, had gone through some interesting changes to come to that point—changes that were largely driven by economic change. As French scholar Olivier Roy, a foremost expert on political Islam, noted, in the 1980s the Brotherhood "claimed to defend the interests of the oppressed classes and called for state ownership of the economy and redistribution of wealth." But then came an "embourgeoisement" period, which pushed the organization toward liberal economy, and, as a result, "towards reconciliation and compromise." Ultimately, Roy suggested, the organization would have to "reckon with a demand for liberty that doesn't stop with the right to elect a parliament."[73]

According to Roy, what was really rising in the Middle East was a "post-Islamist generation," which included many devout Muslims who understood the secular rules of the democratic game. Because, after many failed experiments, "the bulk of the former Islamists ha[d] come to the same conclusion of the generation that founded the Justice and Development Party in Turkey: There is no third way between democracy and dictatorship."[74]

THE ROAD AHEAD

Of course, as pivotal as it may become, Turkey cannot alone shape the future of the Muslim world. But what it can and does do is present an example of a synthesis of Islam, democracy, and capitalism.

Turkey's more conservative Muslim thinkers still express concern over the country's unfolding destiny, which they call "the Protestantization of Islam," and they foresee it eroding Islamic values. They do have a point. If Muslims can't build a new middle-class culture that articulates and revitalizes Islamic values within the modern context, they indeed can become secularized. But the solution is not clinging to the old and the static, which is doomed to disappear, but rather embracing the new and the dynamic, and doing so as Muslims.

This vision is certainly different from that of the Islamists, who pursue a totalitarian dream of an Islamic state, and even global hegemony for Islam. But it is also different from that of the secularists, in Turkey or in the West, who wish to see a thoroughly de-Islamized world—and, really, a world without religious values of any kind.

Yet it is also the vision that is right—and promising. Walter Russell Mead, "America's premier archeologist of ideas and their consequences," is correct when he states:

> In the end, when and if Islam makes its peace with the dynamic society, it will do so in the only way possible. It will not "secularize" itself into a mild form of atheism. It will not blend into a postconfessional unity religion that sees all religions as being fundamentally the same. Rather, pious Muslims of unimpeachable orthodoxy, conspicuous virtue, conservative principles, and great passion for their faith will show the world what dynamic Islam can be. Inspired by their example, vision, and teaching, Muslims all over the world will move more deeply into the world of their religion even as they find themselves increasingly at home in a dynamic, liberal, and capitalist world that is full of many faiths and many cultures.[75]

That is indeed the road ahead. If they want to help, Western powers should support economic progress and political liberalization in the Muslim world; both strengthen the social forces that push for positive change. But they should be careful to avoid political confrontations and especially military conflicts, which only strengthen the reactionary elements. The history of the past two centuries emphatically shows that while peaceful interactions between the West and Islamdom in cultural and economic arenas have helped further the cause of liberal Muslims, tensions, clashes, and invasions have always empowered radical ones.

But those liberal Muslims also have much work to do at home. The century-long dominance of the two opposing yet mutually enhancing ideologies—secularism and Islamism—has constrained the intellectual appeal of Islamic liberalism. That tradition needs to be revitalized. It needs to go beyond academic works and become popularized. Muslim societies need to hear more accessible arguments for liberty. They need—to borrow a term from Sayyid Qutb—some signposts for navigating this long and challenging road.

So, to do my humble part as an ordinary yet concerned Muslim, allow me to offer a few of these in the following chapters.

PART III

Signposts on the Liberal Road

The most important resource in Islamic thought for recognizing religious liberty lies in [its] basic doctrine: the very powerful Islamic insight into the greatness of Allah.

—MICHAEL NOVAK, conservative thinker

CHAPTER NINE

Freedom from the State

Social engineers start on the outside,
by first creating political and social
systems, and then move inside, toward the
individual. God starts on the inside, by
first changing the individual.

—VINCENT CORNELL, professor of Islamic studies[1]

AMONG THE MANY EPISODES from the life of the Prophet Muhammad, two are exceptionally curious.

The first is a short discussion between the Prophet and one of his companions right before the famous Battle of Badr, which took place in 624, between Medinan Muslims and Meccan pagans. The night before the battle, the Muslim army had to camp nearby, and the Prophet, as commander in chief, suggested one location. Yet one of his men, al-Mundhir, felt that staying on higher ground would be preferable. So he walked up to the Prophet and asked, "O Messenger of God, is your opinion based on a revelation from God, or is it war tactics?"

"No revelation," the Prophet replied. "Just war tactics."

"Then this is not the most strategic place to camp," al-Mundhir said. He gave advice that the Prophet liked and followed. It was advice, Muslim tradition holds, that helped win the battle.[2]

What is interesting about this story is that it illustrates the distinction the early Muslim community made between God's revelation and the Prophet's personal judgment. The latter, apparently, you could dispute—provided there was a good reason.

The second episode underlines the same principle. Here, reportedly, the Prophet advised his fellow Muslims about date farming, but his suggestions proved unhelpful. So he declined to offer further advice, saying, "I am only human. If I ask you to do something concerning religion, then accept it. But if I ask you to do something on the basis of my personal opinion, then, [remember], I am only human."[3]

From both of these anecdotes, which appear in harmony with the Qur'anic verses that emphasize the humanness of the Prophet, Muslims can derive two important lessons. First, only God is all-knowing and all-wise. All human beings, including the messengers of God, can err. Since they are most righteous and they receive God's revelation, the messengers still have authority over believers, which is why the Qur'an orders Muslims to "obey God and His Messenger."[4] Yet even the messenger of God can be disputed, with all due respect, when he acts based on his personal judgment and not from direct communication with God.

Second, in a world in which even the Prophet cannot be regarded as an unquestionable authority, nobody can. The Prophet's preeminence came from the revelations he received from God, but it is the Islamic consensus that his death marked the end of all revelation. In the post-Muhammad world, therefore, no one can be considered to be in direct communion with God, and thus an unquestionable authority for Muslims. In the post-Muhammad world, in other words, no one legitimately can claim to establish "rule by God," or a theocracy.

THEOCRACY? WHAT THEOCRACY?

To Sunni Muslims, the assertion that there has been no divinely guided human being since the Prophet should not be news—it is part of their consensus. The Sunni tradition holds that only the first four successors of the Prophet, the Rightly Guided Caliphs, possessed special wisdom and piety. But their age is long gone. Moreover, the fact that the Muslim community was drawn into a civil war during this exemplary period suggests that too much idealization of it is unrealistic. Later caliphs were even less reassuring. Most were corrupt and impious men whose excesses could be kept in check only by the moral authority of the Shariah. Some of them appropriated pompous titles, such as "the Shadow of God on Earth," but these were post-Qur'anic myths created for political motives.

In short, it is quite hard to create a theocracy based on the Sunni tradition. (The Sunni ideal is rather a "nomocracy"—i.e., a polity based on rule of law, the latter being the Shariah.)[5] No wonder those who aspired for theocracy in the Sunni world have found a basis for it only in another post-Qur'anic myth—that of the Mahdi, the Islamic version of the Jewish Messiah. But Mahdi movements are rare exceptions in Islamic history, certainly not the norm.[6]

On the other hand, Shiites are more prone to theocracy, for they believe in an unbroken chain of divinely guided imams and the *ayatollahs* (tokens of God) who assume authority in the former's absence. Even so, it took the doctrinal invention of Grand Ayatollah Khomeini to turn the *religious* authority of the ayatol-

lahs into *political* authority. Consequently, the Islamic Republic of Iran he founded is partly theocratic because it accepts "a
guardianship of the Islamic jurists" over elected politicians. But
other Shiite authorities, such as the revered Grand Ayatollah
Ali al-Sistani of Iraq, reject this Iranian invention, modestly
limiting their "guardianship" to religious matters.

The big question for Islamic politics, therefore, is not whether
the *umma* should accept theocratic rulers. Few Muslims believe
in the existence of such men who can speak on behalf of God.
But a larger number of Muslims do believe in something else: an
Islamic form of government. This, they believe, is a state based
on the "system" that Islam supposedly ordains, which they hope
will answer the problems plaguing Muslim societies. But is there
really such a thing?

AN ISLAMIC FORM OF GOVERNMENT?

For starters, the Qur'an clearly does not include a definition of government. It repeatedly counsels believers to obey the
Prophet, who was the head of the Muslim community, but it
does not specify what would happen once the Prophet was gone.
One verse merely says, "Obey . . . those in authority from among
you," but it doesn't specify who these people will be and how
they will come to power.[7] Another oft-mentioned Qur'anic concept is *shura*, (mutual consultation), which means that Muslims
should listen to each other's views, but it is, again, not specific.[8]

In other words, the Muslim scripture is almost silent on the
fundamental issues of politics. In the words of a Muslim scholar,
it instead gives the impression that "matters concerning political
rule and administration [are] not considered to be within the
purview of divine revelation."[9]

Moreover, as Muslim tradition holds, the Prophet also was silent about political theory. On his deathbed, he left neither a political heir nor even an institution like a church to help the community govern in his absence. His famous Farewell Sermon ends with a very modest declaration of heritage: "I leave for you the Qur'an," he simply said, "you shall uphold it." (The two other versions of this sentence add to the Qur'an either the "Tradition" or the "Family" of the Prophet—terms that respectively, and clearly, reflect the Sunni and Shiite perspectives. Yet, even in these versions, there is still no reference to any political entity that the Prophet left behind.)

So, when the Prophet died in the summer of 632, the Muslim community had no political blueprint to follow. So the elders of the community sat down and discussed what to do. They, not too surprisingly, did their reasoning within the political norms of their time and milieu. Finally, in line with the Arab custom of having tribal chieftains, they decided to elect one of their group, Abu Bakr, as the new head of the Muslim community.

Thus was born the institution known as the caliphate. It was a temporal body created by humans according to historic conditions. It was certainly based on Islamic norms—reflected in the belief that the caliph must rule with piety, justice, and righteousness. But it was also based on the circumstances of seventh-century Arabia. Had those earliest Muslims been citizens of an Athenian democracy, perhaps they would have created an assembly, not just a single leader, informed by Islamic norms.

Yet still, a few centuries after its founding, the caliphate came to be regarded by some Muslims as a requirement of Islam, rather than as a temporal institution to govern Muslims. The scholar who first made the argument for a caliphate as a necessity of religion was al-Ashari, who, as mentioned earlier, was one

of the founding fathers of the Traditionist school and a strong
critic of the Rationalist one.[10] Another Traditionist scholar, al-
Mawardi, further developed the idea and theorized an Islamic
form of government structured around the caliphate.

Meanwhile, the Rationalist school had a less statist attitude.
Some Mutazilites had argued that a government was not a religious obligation, and if every individual complied with the law,
justice and peace would prevail even without a state.[11] Others
said that a government was necessary—but out of rational con-
siderations, not religious rulings.

Yet, as we also saw in the earlier chapters, the Traditionist
side dominated mainstream Islam, along with the idea that the
caliphate is a part of the religion. As a consequence, the idea
that Islam is inseparable from the state became a commonly held
Muslim attitude.

A Global Caliphate (of Gold and Silver)

Debate on the caliphate reopened only in the twentieth century, particularly after 1924, when Turkish ruler Mustafa Kemal
Atatürk abolished the Ottoman caliphate. I criticized this decision in earlier chapters, for it led to a vacuum of authority in the
Muslim world, opening the way to various forms of Islamism.
Yet this is a political evaluation. Religiously speaking, the abolition of the caliphate was not an offense, for it was not a religiously
required institution in the first place, as argued persuasively first
by Seyyid Bey in the Turkish parliament and later by Ali Abdel
al-Razik at Al-Azhar University in Cairo.[12]

Seyyid Bey, a professor of Islamic jurisprudence, argued that
the caliphate—unlike Catholicism's papacy, which is "religious
and spiritual"—was a political institution and as such could be

replaced by a popularly elected government. (He also claimed: "Islam is a pro-liberty religion in law as in knowledge and sciences.")[13]

In his notable book *Who Needs an Islamic State?*, contemporary Muslim thinker Abdelwahab El-Affendi also criticizes the idea of a caliphate as a religiously required institution. "The Caliphate was not an end in itself," he reminds us, "but a means to an end, which is the achievement of justice and the preservation of the nation."[14] The Traditionist scholars who idealized the caliphate, El-Affendi argues, had simply confused the means with the end. Moreover, they regarded the "ad hoc decisions" made by the early caliphs "as precedents with normative significance."[15]

Contemporary Islamists not only preserve the same misconception—that Islam provides a blueprint for a state—but they also make it the very core of their political program. They see the caliphate as a religious obligation and declare its reestablishment as their main goal. As a model, they look not at the more recent Ottoman caliphate but the "original" one—created in seventh-century Arabia. The result is a radical utopia aimed at restoring the political conditions of that time and milieu.

Alas, there's even a push to bring back the social and economic conditions. One of the greatest champions of the "global caliphate" cause, the UK-based Hizb ut-Tahrir, "a political party whose ideology is Islam," proudly states the following on its website:

> It is the duty of the Khilafah State to make its currency in gold and silver, and to work on the basis of gold and silver, as it was during the time of the Messenger of Allah.[16]

With the same line of reasoning, one could argue that a caliphate state, "as it was during the time of the Messenger of Allah," should operate on the basis of horses and camels—and not cars, trains, planes, and other innovations of the "infidels." One could also argue that this state, "as it was during the time of the Messenger of Allah," should arrange its communications on the basis of personal couriers and homing pigeons—and not phones or the Internet. Never mind the fact that the Hizb ut-Tahrir folks themselves most probably use cars, trains, and planes, and, quite obviously, the Internet.

The nonsense of such reasoning is all too obvious. At its core lies the fundamental mistake of the Islamists: They don't realize that what they call "the Islamic state" was nothing but the political experience of the earlier generations of Muslims. That experience was informed by Islam, for sure, but it was also shaped by the temporal realities of the centuries in which they lived.

The right question, then, is: What should be the political experience of the Muslims of the twenty-first century?

We should not look for an imagined "Islamic state," in other words. We should instead seek, as El-Affendi puts it, "a state for Muslims."[17]

Embracing Democracy—and Even a Secular One

Once we start looking for "a state for Muslims," we will soon end up with a commonsense solution. Since no particular Muslim can claim to have theocratic authority, and since there are all sorts of Muslims with diverse views, ideas, and aspirations, the only system that will be fair to all would be one that would include all of them in the political process: a democracy, as Muslim thinker al-Farabi envisioned a millennium ago.[18]

Yet a fundamental question remains: Should the legal system of this "democratic state for Muslims" be based on the Shariah?

At first glance, this question is meaningless, for if a state is democratic, its legislators are free to adopt any legal tradition that they deem appropriate. If they want to incorporate elements of Roman law, let's say, that's fine, they can do it. If they want to legislate in line with the Shariah, again, that's fine. Its logic would not be too different from the reasoning used in some states of the United States to support capital punishment—that it is "the law of God."

However, incorporating elements of "the law of God" via a democratic process is one thing, enacting it as official doctrine is another. In the latter case, the system will cease to be democratic for two reasons. First, not everyone wishes to live under "the law of God." Even the most conservative Muslim societies include secular citizens and non-Muslims, who would prefer other laws. Second, not everyone agrees on a definition of "the law of God." The Shariah has always had many different interpretations, and the number of these interpretations has risen today with the advent of more modernist schools. So, whenever a state decides to make the Shariah its official legal code, it inevitably will opt for one of its many possible interpretations and dismiss all others. And, in that case, "the law of God" will cease to be the law of God. It will simply be the law of men—ones who are self-righteous and arrogant enough to claim to know the mind of God.

Thus, a "democracy based on the Shariah" will be neither a democracy nor based on the Shariah. It will be an authoritarian state that imposes its own version of the Shariah, which inevitably will serve its own subjective and earthly purposes. (Or it will lead to tensions and clashes among Muslims who believe in different versions of the Shariah. A case study for this was Pakistan's ill-fated attempt at "the Islamization of laws," which led to internal conflict because the various religious factions could not reach consensus on what the true Islamic law is.)[19]

Abdullahi Ahmed An-Na'im, a Sudanese-born professor of law at Emory University, has pinned down the problem well. "Enforcing a [Shariah] through coercive power of the state negates its religious nature," he notes, "because Muslims would be observing the law of the state and not freely performing their religious obligation as Muslims."[20] Hence, he argues, the best state for Muslims is a secular state that will allow people to "be a Muslim by conviction and free choice, which is the only way one can be a Muslim."[21]

At this point, perhaps we should note the big difference between a *secular* state and a *secularist* one. The former is a state that is neutral to religion and respects the right of its citizens to live by their faith. A secularist state, on the other hand, is hostile to religion and wants to curb its influence in public life, and even in the lives of individual citizens.[22] It is hard to reconcile Islam—or any other religion, for that matter—with secularist states. But why should Muslims not be content with secular ones that respect religious freedom?

SHARIAH WITHOUT ISLAMISM

The objection to the question above might come from a perceived conflict between the secular state and two important notions toward which many Muslims feel sympathetic: "political Islam" and the Shariah. Let's look at them one at a time.

In the past few decades, the term *political Islam* has become quite controversial, and even infamous, for good reason: It has been dominated by the Islamists, whose goal is the creation of a totalitarian "Islamic state." But in fact, there can well be a political Islam whose goal is just to represent and defend Islamic values within the rules of a democracy. Some core values of Islam— such as justice, rights, and family values—clearly have political implications, and Muslims are absolutely justified to advance them via political means such as parties.

Dr. An-Na'im agrees, noting that "separation of Islam and state," which is necessary, is not the same thing as "separation of Islam and politics."[23] The difference here is similar to the one between a Communist state, which takes Marxism as its official ideology, and a democratic state under which a Communist party exists as a part of the democratic game. The same game would also allow different versions of political Islam. In such a democratic system, for example, there could well be a "Liberal Islamic Party" that finds classical liberalism and its free economy more compatible with the Islamic values it aspires to uphold. Another political party could be named the "Socialist Islamic Party," which could defend a more state-governed economy. Both could claim that their programs would serve Islamic values (and society) better, and voters could then decide which one sounded more promising.

The Shariah, too, can be separated from the state and exist in the civil sphere as a guide for conservative Muslims who wish to organize their lives according to it—just as has been done by the Orthodox Jews who have long been living according to the Halakha, their religious code, in Western countries.

One good case study is the United Kingdom—which is practically, if not technically, a secular state, and also a very liberal one. In late 2008, the government officially allowed the establishment of Shariah courts to deal with matters of family law and make legally binding decisions if parties agreed. In just a year, more than eighty Shariah courts were opened throughout the country, and thousands of British Muslims, mostly immigrants, appealed to them on matters of marriage, divorce, and inheritance.

Of course, some elements of the classical Shariah, such as corporal punishments for crimes, are not applicable in this British system. So be it. Other aspects of the Shariah, such as matters relating to slavery, are also inapplicable, a reality that Muslims have almost unanimously accepted, acknowledging that times simply have changed. In fact, some of the laws were deemed inapplicable as early as the time of Caliph Umar, just several years after the Prophet's death, simply because conditions that had led to enactment of those rulings in the first place had changed.[24] It is inevitable that the modern context will enforce even greater changes in the Shariah.

The critical point here is the assurance that adhering to the Shariah is a voluntary choice. Those British Muslims who appeal to the Shariah courts are following the dictate of their conscience—not the dictates imposed by the government or "religious police." Other British Muslims who don't appeal to the same courts are also following the dictates of their conscience. If I were living in the United Kingdom, I, too, would skip the guidance of the Shariah courts, for the Traditionist schools to which they subscribe don't conform to my less literalist understanding of Islamic law.

All these different approaches are valid, because there is no one who can authoritatively invalidate them. The Murjiites (Postponers) of first-century Islam were right; we cannot know for sure whose interpretation of Islam is right or wrong, so we have to "postpone" the ultimate decision to the afterlife, to be given by God. We can only modestly follow the interpretation that we find most convincing. "You can say my school is most righteous," as Turkish Islamic thinker Said Nursi famously put it, "but you cannot say it is the only righteous one."

ENTER THE "ISLAMIZED UNITED KINGDOM"

However, contemporary Islamists want to impose their own interpretations of the Shariah on all other Muslims and, alas, even on non-Muslims. In Britain, a fringe group called "Islam for the UK" swears that it will "Islamize" the whole United Kingdom. It advocates such boldly outlandish steps as adding minarets to the Houses of Parliament. A rant on the group's website, titled "Trafalgar Square under the Shari'ah," vows to destroy all the great statues in that historic London plaza. "Under the Shari'ah," the site also explains nicely, "all harmful intoxicants will be banned unequivocally," apparently referring to alcoholic drinks and drugs.[25]

The totalitarian dream expressed here goes beyond even tradition. Most classical scholars have acknowledged that the Shariah is mainly a law for Muslims, and therefore most of its limitations do not hold for others. The eighth-century Hanafi scholar al-Shaybani, author of an authoritative work on the rights of non-Muslims under Islamic rule, insisted that non-Muslims were free to trade in wine and pork in their own towns, although these were deemed illegal for Muslims.[26] Hence, Muslim states such as the Ottoman Empire had taverns operated by non-Muslims serving alcohol exclusively (at least in theory) to non-Muslims.

The triumphalism of the radical Islamists, then, seems to be a modern invention. It also seems to stem not from a religious motive to serve but from a political motive to dominate.

"Authoritarianism," as British Muslim Ziauddin Sardar puts it, "is intrinsic in much of what masquerades as 'Islamic ideology' in contemporary times."[27] This authoritarianism is very much linked to the contempt that those on the fringes of modernity feel toward its elites. It is no accident that groups like Islam for the UK are formed by Muslim immigrants in European countries who feel alienated from and looked down upon by their host societies. These immigrants are "culturally uprooted," for they feel a part of neither the countries they came to nor the ones they came from.[28] Such "disaffected city dwellers" have always been prone to radical ideologies—often various forms of the radical Left—and have shown "hostility to the city, with its image of rootless, arrogant, greedy, decadent, frivolous cosmopolitanism."[29] The result is often a burning desire to defeat, dominate, and then radically transform the society that seems so corrupt.

In other words, although radical Islamists often claim, and probably believe, that all their triumphalism is rooted in their zeal to serve God, it might well be rooted in their sociopsychological issues—and, probably, their mere egos. For the implicit subtext of their ideology is that they are the most righteous people on earth, and thus they deserve to rule over all others. If the whole world gets "Islamized," the result will be, as one militant quite candidly put it, that "Muslims will win . . . and rule the whole world."[30]

The more Muslim thing to do, perhaps, is to be more modest, and to acknowledge the right of others to be different. The Qur'an promotes such tolerance by ordering Muslims to say to others: "Unto you your religion, and unto me my religion."[31] The best political system that will allow all this pluralism to coexist is a political system that will not be defined by any creed but will set all of them free. It is, in other words, a secular state—not too unlike the original Medina city-state that the Prophet Muhammad founded on the basis of equality with Jews.[32]

Accepting the secular state will allow Muslims not only to follow Islam in the way they genuinely believe but also to eliminate endless discussions over the ideal "Islamic state" and its systems, like the "Islamic economy"—a very recent invention.[33] For example, there remains disagreement among Muslims about whether accepting interest, a fundamental feature of modern banking, is the same thing as the usury (*riba*) that the Qur'an denounces. In a free economy, such a disagreement is fine, because those Muslims who disapprove of interest can opt for "interest-free banking," whereas others who don't see a problem with it can work with conventional banks. (This is the situation in Turkey today.) But if you try to replace a free economy with an "Islamic" one that you construct according to your own subjective interpretation, then you will first create conflict, and later, if you triumph, tyranny.

Accepting the secular state could also help Muslims focus on what is really important. Islamic movements have lost too much time, and caused too much tension, in the twentieth century with their endless quest for *systems* based on Islam. What they should have focused on instead was advancement of Islam's faith and culture—through arts and sciences, evangelism and advocacy, education, charity, and the media. All these can be carried out by individuals and communities without backup from a state. In fact, they are almost always done better *without* state involvement—as the American experience proves.

What Muslims really need from the state, in other words, is not religion but freedom of religion.

CHAPTER TEN

Freedom to Sin

But then what is virtue,
if not the free choice of what is good?
—ALEXIS DE TOCQUEVILLE[1]

IMAGINE THAT I am sitting on a bench in a quiet park, on a beautiful day, in an overwhelmingly Muslim country. Let's say there are other people around who are also relaxing in the same park. When the time comes for afternoon prayer, the nearby mosque raises the call for prayer. Everyone in the park, including me, heads to the mosque. Only one man remains sitting on his park bench.

Now, what would happen if I threw disapproving looks at that man? Or if I went even further and mumbled to other mosque-goers: "Huh, look at that impious guy, he's ignoring the call for prayer."

Chances are that the man would feel pressured to go to the mosque. Perhaps the next time the call for prayer sounded he would join everyone else in the mosque to avoid public censure.

If this hypothetical country were Saudi Arabia, the pressure this man would feel could be heavier and more direct. If members of the religious police were around, they could scold the man for skipping the prayer and push him to the mosque to catch up with the service.

In both scenarios, the man in question is forced to pray by the dictate of either the society or the government, not his own conscience. And if he succumbs to these pressures, then he will be praying out of a concern for image, rather than a sincere wish to worship God.

But is this what God really wants from Muslims? Quite simply, no. A passage in the Qur'an specifically addresses this issue. "Woe to those who do prayer," it reads, "those who show off."[2] In other words, God deplores worshipping for the sake of appearance. Worship should be solely for the sake of worship.

Coercion not only fails to lead to such sincere religiosity; it even blocks the way. If the man in our story were not coerced by anyone to go to the mosque, he would have a better chance eventually to find his own way to godliness. Perhaps he would be impressed by the piety of the people around him, and think about it. In fact, he certainly would be much more impressed if those mosque-goers smiled at him rather than giving him nasty looks. Respect is always more attractive than contempt.

This is just common sense. But it also is Qur'anic wisdom, reflected by verses such as, "There is no compulsion in religion,"[3] or this one: "If your Lord had willed, surely all those who are in the earth would have believed, all of them; will you then force men till they become believers?"[4]

Why, then, do some Muslim societies have a strong tendency toward "compulsion in religion"? Why do the Saudis employ the *Mutawwa'in* and the Iranians the *Basij*—official security forces whose job is to stroll the streets and punish any "impious" behavior they see?

Commanding Right, Forbidding Wrong

To be fair, neither the Saudi nor the Iranian religious police are entirely devoid of an Islamic justification. There is indeed a specific concept in the Qur'an to which they, and other authoritarian-minded Muslims, routinely refer: "commanding right and forbidding wrong." The Qur'an presents this as an obligation for Muslims: "From among you there should be a party who invite to good and enjoin what is right and forbid the wrong."[5] Several other verses call for the same duty. Scholars of the Shariah have expanded the idea over time and created detailed rules about how piety must be imposed on fellow Muslims who fail to be pious enough.

The world learned more about all this, with shock but not much awe, when Afghanistan fell under the rule of the Taliban, who, immediately after capturing Kabul in 1996, established a Department for the Propagation of Virtue and the Prohibition of Vice. Its militias soon started to ban and destroy everything they deemed sacrilegious—including wines and spirits, VCRs and cassette players, and even kites and chessboards. All-enveloping burqas were imposed on women, and long beards became obligatory for men.

The Taliban represent an extreme case, of course. Most things that they deem *haram* (illicit) would be just fine for many other Muslims. Even the most conservative Muslims in Turkey would find a headscarf and a long skirt sufficiently modest for females and certainly would see nothing wrong with flying kites or playing chess. The Taliban's list of bans and obligations, in other words, is just too long for most other Muslims.

But the length of the list of religious injunctions is not the only issue. Is it ever right to impose those injunctions on a fellow Muslim? If one Muslim sees another drinking wine, or skipping prayer, as the man in the park did, does he have the right to intervene? Is such behavior justified or even required under the Qur'anic obligation of "commanding right and forbidding wrong"?

Traditionally, yes, the Qur'an was interpreted in this way. But the Qur'an is far from being specific on what to command and what to forbid, and its earliest interpretations were much more modest and limited in the scope that they attributed to the obligation.[6]

For example, Abu al-Aliya, an early commentator on the Qur'an, argued that the verse that specifies "commanding right" was simply "calling people from polytheism to Islam." The parallel duty, "forbidding wrong," he believed, was all about "forbidding the worship of idols and devils."[7]

There is, of course, a huge difference between calling people to accept the basic tenets of a faith and imposing on them that faith along with all its detailed rules. And the early interpretation of the duty—which we can safely consider as the more authentic interpretation—had apparently focused on calling rather then imposing. Yet, as time went by, and as the Sunni orthodoxy crystallized, the scope of "commanding right" and "forbidding wrong" expanded more and more. Writing two centuries after Abu al-Aliya, the famous scholar Tabari argued "that 'commanding right' refers to *all* that God and His Prophet have commanded, and 'forbidding wrong' to *all* that they have forbidden."[8] Tabari had clearly realized that if the scope of the duty was "restricted to enjoining belief in God and His Prophet, then it [would have] nothing to do with reproving other Muslims for drinking, wenching and making music."[9]

It was, in other words, not the Qur'an's clear injunction but the preference of interpreters such as Tabari to reprove other Muslims for activities such as drinking, wenching, and making music. (The last one was not declared illicit in the Qur'an, by the way, but rather by the scholars who constantly expanded the list of bans.) The willingness to enact punishments for supposedly illicit behavior grew gradually, and Traditionist scholars such as the great Imam al-Ghazali listed sanctions for almost all forms of perceived sinful behavior.[10]

Virtue under Tyranny?

This inflation of sanctions was part of the general tendency toward strictness and rigorism that emerged in the third century of Islam, as we saw in chapter 4. It was also the product of an age in which the idea of individual freedom was little noticed and was overshadowed by the will to enforce the creation of a pious society.

In fact, other verses of the Qur'an could have prevented medieval scholars from expanding the verses about "commanding right" and "forbidding wrong" into a system of coercion. One such verse is the oft-quoted "There is no compulsion in religion."[11] Some scholars from the Rationalist camp *did* focus on this verse, arguing that in this world—which they defined as an Abode of Trial in which God tests men—people should be free to make their own religious choices. But this liberal attitude remained marginalized, and the "no compulsion" verse attracted little attention among classical scholars.[12]

That medieval lack of focus on liberty was unfortunate but also understandable. The idea of individual freedom was seldom emphasized in any premodern society. Hence, until fairly recently, the idea that a pious society can be created and preserved through coercion did not appear terribly wrong to most believers, including those in the West. As late as the mid-nineteenth century, popes were still condemning religious freedom as "a heresy that no Catholic can accept."[13] In 1927, the Pennsylvania Supreme Court upheld a law against professional basketball on Sunday, ruling that it was an "unholy activity that defiled the Christian Sabbath."[14] In the same era, America was trying the "Noble Experiment" (the prohibition of alcohol), which proved that imposing virtue via the state's coercive powers not only fails but also creates other problems, such as the black market and organized crime.

The Muslim world needed to come to a similar conclusion in the modern age, but the Islamist movement did the opposite— not just preserving the classical interpretation of "commanding right" and "forbidding wrong" but also pushing it to new extremes. Classical scholars had at least acknowledged the privacy of homes, a right strongly guarded in the Qur'an.[15] The Islamists, though, paid little attention to privacy and advocated a much more concerted and systematic effort to command and forbid, "something like industrial planning."[16]

Meanwhile, though, Muslim societies in the modern world have moved in the exact opposite direction. As Muslims grew more individualistic, their reaction to repression came not as acceptance but defiance. The Iranian author of a popular book advocating the duty of "commanding right and forbidding wrong" complains about this widespread resistance. The duty inevitably means interfering in other people's affairs, he says, but "people with their heads stuffed full of Western ideas don't like it."[17]

Those "Western ideas" are not exclusively Western but rather universally modern—they emerge from the strengthening sense of individualism, which is a product of wider literacy, education, technology, and exposure to other cultures. In medieval times, only a tiny group of Muslim elites, such as the Mutazilites, had the chance to find a library to study foreign philosophies. Now, almost everyone can do that—it just takes an Internet connection. The world now has many individuals who have both the mindset to think independently and the means to act accordingly.

Such individuals not only dislike coercion but respond in rebellious ways. Some upper-class Iranians and Saudis, for example, are famous for flying to European capitals to indulge in wild nightlife. When they return home, they may appear to be pious, continuing to condemn what the regime considers as sin, but all the while they may be continuing to sin in secret. Private drinking and pornography are common examples of this. Reportedly, the obsessive seclusion of women in Saudi Arabia even has led to lesbianism.[18]

What coercion produces, in other words, is not genuine piety but hypocrisy—something the Qur'an considers to be worse than disbelief. Perhaps this is not a big problem for the regimes that I mentioned, for they seem more concerned about how people *appear*. The Saudi regime especially takes great pride in, and justifies itself by, not allowing any "un-Islamic" practice on its soil. From this political perspective, a puritan demeanor might be good enough, but from a religious perspective, what should matter most is what people have in their hearts.

And that's why Muslims need to reconsider how we interpret "commanding right" and "forbidding wrong" in today's world.

Sin versus Crime

Let us go back to the story of the man in the park. Most of us would agree that he should be left alone with his choice of not praying, despite realizing that, by abstaining from daily prayer, as a Muslim he would be committing a sin. But what if we saw that he was hitting a child, or trying to start a fire in that park? We would be more than justified in trying to stop him, for he would be committing a crime.

Instinctively, then, we understand that sin and crime are two different things. The former is about the violation of the individual's responsibility to God. The latter is about the violation of his responsibility to other individuals. Most crimes, such as murder, theft, and fraud, are also sins according to most religions, including Islam, but this overlap should not blur the basic difference between the two categories.

Traditionally Islamic scholars have also made this distinction by separating "the rights of God" from "the rights of men." As a Muslim, if I do not fast during Ramadan, for example, then I am disobeying God and violating His "rights" over me. If I refuse to repay a debt to my neighbor, though, it not only is a sin but also is a violation of his property rights.

Although this distinction was made in classical Islam, the scholars of the Shariah enacted punishments for both violations, according to the duty of "commanding right" and "forbidding wrong." But what does the Qur'an, the core of Islam, say (or at least hint) about this?

The answer is quite interesting. The Qur'an bans gambling, usury, and intoxicants and forbids eating carrion, blood, pork, and animals sacrificed to idols. It also orders Muslims to perform certain duties, such as daily prayers, fasting during the month of Ramadan, a pilgrimage to Mecca once in a lifetime, and giving alms (*zakat*) to the poor.

Violating any of these bans, or failing to perform any of the duties without good reason, would be a sin—which is serious, because it may bring punishment in the world to come. But in this world, the Qur'an prescribes no punishment at all for the sins mentioned above.

It does, however, specify punishments (*hudud*) for four specific sins: theft, brigandage, calumnious accusation of adultery, and adultery.[19] The penalties are all corporal, which is quite understandable, given the milieu in which the Qur'an was revealed—a desert-based tribal society with no correctional facilities. Today, though, we can interpret these penalties less literally, as some modernist theologians are already arguing.

Yet what is crucial for us at this point is the nature not of the penalties but of the sins for which they stand. Here is the curious point: These four punishable sins are categorically different from the other ones that the Qur'an leaves unpunished. For, in these four cases, not just the rights of God but also the rights of men are violated. Someone, in other words, gets wronged.

This is quite obvious in the first three cases—theft, brigandage, and calumnious accusation of adultery, so we should take a closer look at adultery (*zina*). Traditionally, Muslim scholars tended to consider adultery as any form of sex between unmarried persons. But a rereading of the Qur'an suggests that the term might be limited to extramarital sex—which is "cheating" on a spouse, and thus hurtful to a second person.[20] There is another Qur'anic term, after all, for sexual indecency in general (*fahsha*), and although the Qur'an denounces that as sin, it does not prescribe a specific punishment for it.

If this interpretation is true—that the Qur'an penalizes extramarital sex but not the premarital kind[21]—then we can safely reach a remarkable conclusion: The Qur'an only penalizes crimes that are violations of the rights of men. The consequences of sins, which are violations of the rights of God, are left to God, to be dealt with in the afterlife.[22]

And this makes it possible to argue, with Islamic justification, for "freedom to sin."

VIRTUE UNDER FREEDOM

"Freedom to sin" might be an appalling concept for some Muslims, but it is gaining acceptance in Turkey. In 2008, Dr. Ali Bardakoğlu, the top cleric as the head of Turkey's Directorate of Religious Affairs, said on TV: "We, as the Directorate, communicate the known rules of Islam. It is free to observe or not to observe them, no one has the right to interfere."[23] Other Turkish figures, including the minister of culture, a popular theologian, and a female Muslim pundit have also publicly defended the freedom to sin.[24]

The reasoning behind their recognition of this freedom is purely theological. The Qur'an teaches that, in the afterlife, God will judge the life led by every individual in this world. It is the responsibility of the individual to obey God's commandments and refrain from actions that He prohibits. But all individuals quite often will fail this test, so the Qur'an calls on them to repent and to appeal to God's forgiveness. It also says that the test goes on for life, and no sin, no matter how deadly, cuts it short. "If God had destroyed men for their iniquity, He would not leave on the earth a single creature," says one verse. "But He respites [postpones] them till an appointed time."[25] Since this "appointed time" is assigned to each person by God, it would be wrong to interfere in any individual's life and shorten or terminate his test.

Of course, Muslims can—and, according to the Qur'an, should—preach the faith and encourage fellow Muslims to be more pious. The Qur'an indeed praises those who "believe and do good, and enjoin on each other truth, and enjoin on each other patience."[26] But enjoining the truth is one thing and imposing it is another. The latter is useless, counterproductive, and tyrannical.

Religious virtue, in other words, should be sought under the umbrella of freedom. It should not be the job of Muslims to forcefully prevent people from sin—with methods such as banning alcohol, closing down bars, or enforcing a particular dress code. Their job should be to invite people to refrain from sin and then let them make their own decisions.

One could even argue that the means to commit sin should be available, so that the world will remain an Abode of Trial, where people are tested by God. In a country where alcohol is forbidden, for example, there is no chance for Muslims to prove they are observant by freely choosing to abstain from it. A particular verse in the Qur'an may be illuminating in this regard. This verse specifies that Muslims should not hunt any animal during the time of pilgrimage. Then it says, "God will test you with game animals which come within the reach of your hands and spears, so that God will know those who fear Him in the unseen."[27] One can infer that the existence of the means to sin, "within the reach of your hands," is the very medium in which the fear of God will be tested—and proved.

Replacing the fear of God with the fear of state or community would only be an obstacle to heartfelt piety. Everyone should have freedom from both the state and the society, in other words, to have genuine religiosity.

CHAPTER ELEVEN

Freedom from Islam

> If your Lord had pleased, surely all
> those who are on the earth would have
> believed, all of them; will you then force
> men till they become believers?
>
> —Qur'an 10:99, Shakir translation

IN MARCH 2006, a modest Afghan citizen named Abdul Rahman made global headlines with an unpleasant story. The poor man was on the verge of execution for the "crime" of converting from Islam to Christianity. His prosecutors, who called him a "microbe," were pretty straightforward in their indictment: "He should be cut off and removed from the rest of Muslim society, and should be killed."[1] The court, which did not hesitate to agree, gave Abdul Rahman three days to rethink and recant. If he still insisted on apostasy, he would be sentenced to a public hanging.

Miraculously, Abdul Rahman survived. Under heavy pressure from foreign governments, the court returned his case to prosecutors, citing "investigative gaps." Meanwhile, he was released from prison and escaped to Italy, where he was granted asylum.

This infamous story, however, was just the tip of an iceberg.

As noted in a 2008 report by a Christian human-rights organization, "apostates from Islam to another religion suffer a host of
serious abuses from their families, communities and nations."[2]
These renegade Muslims may well face the death penalty in
countries such as Saudi Arabia, Iran, and Sudan, and other forms
of oppression in many other Muslim societies.[3]

The reason for this systemic violation of religious freedom
is, unfortunately, religious. Most classical schools of the Shariah
consider apostasy from Islam a crime punishable by death. A
Hadith attributed to the Prophet Muhammad is quite clear on
this: "If somebody [among Muslims] discards his religion, kill
him."[4] The implication is that Islam is a religion with free entry
but no free exit.

For this reason, some Muslim countries have had difficulty
accepting the Universal Declaration of Human Rights (UDHR),
adopted by the UN General Assembly in 1948. Among its pro-
visions is the "freedom to change [one's] religion or belief."
Spokesmen for Saudi Arabia, in particular, have consistently
opposed this clause, noting that it "might be interpreted as giving missionaries and proselytizers a free rein."[5]

As an alternative to this "free rein," the Organization of the
Islamic Conference (OIC), of which all Muslim-majority states
are members, adopted in 1990 a Universal Declaration of Human
Rights in Islam. It denounced efforts "to exploit [one's] poverty
or ignorance in order to convert him to another religion, or to
atheism." Deserting Islam was not welcome nor was calling for
its desertion.

The disparity between the UDHR and the "Islamic" version still exists, and this thorny issue of apostasy is the biggest
obstacle to resolution. It even has led some conservative Muslims to condemn the UDHR as evil. Grand Ayatollah Khamenei,

the supreme leader of the Islamic Republic of Iran, for example, denounced it as "mumbo jumbo by disciples of Satan." He explained his reasoning explicitly: "When we want to find out what is right and what is wrong, we do not go to the United Nations, we go to the Holy Qur'an."[6]

I have to admit that, as a Muslim, I can understand why the grand ayatollah put the Word of God above a declaration of men. I just don't understand why he dismissed the possibility that there might be no contradiction between the two.

REVISITING APOSTASY

Yes, there might be no contradiction between the modern idea of religious freedom and the Qur'an, for the latter includes nothing that penalizes apostasy. It threatens apostates and other unbelievers with divine punishment in the hereafter, to be sure, but it decrees no earthly retribution.

Quite the contrary, in fact. There are Qur'anic verses that seem to suggest that rejecting Islam is a matter of free choice. "The truth is from your Lord," a verse reads, "so let him who please believe, and let him who please disbelieve."[7] Another verse speaks about "those who believe then disbelieve, again believe and again disbelieve, then increase in disbelief," implying that there were people who could go back and forth between Islam and disbelief during the time of revelation.[8]

One of the interesting figures who stressed the leniency of the Qur'an on this matter was Stratford Canning, the longtime British ambassador to the Ottoman Empire in the mid-nineteenth century. While trying to persuade the Ottoman statesmen to annul the Shariah laws on apostasy, Canning referred to the Muslim scripture. "We have researched this matter," he said to Sultan Abdülmecid. "There is no clear Qur'anic basis for execution."⁹

However, as we have seen in previous chapters, the Qur'an defined only a small part of the mainstream Islamic tradition. And the earthly punishment for apostasy came as part of the post-Qur'anic literature, namely the Hadiths.¹⁰

Some scholars think that this late invention was born out of the political needs of the early Muslim community. Right after the Prophet's death, when Abu Bakr became the first caliph, the first problem he faced was the rebellion (ridda) of a few Arab tribes who had formerly sworn allegiance to Medina. In fact, the rebel tribes had not renounced their loyalty to Islam; they just declared that with the death of the Prophet, their commitment to Medina as a city had ceased. In particular, they were no longer willing to pay zakat, which they had been paying to Muhammad's envoys to finance military campaigns and to be distributed to the needy.¹¹

Different opinions surfaced in the face of this rebellion, and some, including Umar, who would soon become the second caliph, thought that the rebellion should be tolerated. Abu Bakr, however, insisted on imposing zakat on the rebellious tribes and then launched military campaigns to subdue them.¹² The later jurists who interpreted these events understood ridda not just as a political rebellion against the state but also as a rebellion against Islam as a religion. It was this interpretation that "transferred the punishment for apostasy from the hereafter to this world."¹³

The concept also proved to be politically useful, as despotic caliphs of the Umayyad and later the Abbasid dynasties could get rid of their critics simply by accusing them of apostasy. The Hadiths that order the killing of apostates were probably put into circulation at this time, more than a century after the Prophet's death. They were, in other words, "apocryphal" narratives made up later to justify what the political authority had been doing.[14]

On the other hand, there were other Hadiths suggesting that the Prophet in fact did not consider apostasy to be a crime. One of them is a narrative about a Muslim named Husayn, whose two sons were converted to Christianity by Byzantine merchants who had come to Medina to sell their goods. Following their conversion, the two sons left for Syria with the merchants. When this happened, their father asked the Prophet to pursue them and bring them back, apparently in order to make them embrace Islam again. On this occasion, the tradition holds, the famous Qur'anic verse, "There is no compulsion in religion," was revealed. Consequently, the Prophet did not send anyone to pursue the two converts.[15]

Because of these complexities in the Hadith literature, and the total lack of any Qur'anic earthly punishment for apostasy, Muslim scholars have disputed the mainstream view on this matter for centuries. In the eighth century, Ibrahim al-Nakhai, a prominent jurist, and Sufyan al-Thawri, a Hadith expert, wrote that the apostate should be reinvited into Islam but should never be condemned to death.[16] The noted Hanafi jurist Shams al-Din al-Sarakhsi also disregarded any temporal punishment for apostasy.[17] The death penalty, these scholars noted, deprives the apostate of the right to reconsider his decision, which can happen at any moment during his lifetime.[18] The Prophet, the same commentators pointed out, had never ordered anyone put to death for apostasy alone.[19]

Even Ibn Taymiyyah, the thirteenth-century scholar regarded as strict and militant on many other issues, argued that the Hadith stating, "Whoever changes his religion, kill him," was meant to address high treason against the political community—i.e., joining forces with a deadly enemy—and not apostasy as such.[20]

In the nineteenth century, as noted in previous chapters, the Ottoman Empire made it uncomplicated for its citizens to abandon Islam and accept another religion. Modernist thinkers such as Rashid Rida openly argued that the death penalty for apostasy should be abandoned.[21] Two months before his death in the Islamic Republic of Iran, Grand Ayatollah Hossein-Ali Montazeri, a liberal cleric who fell out with the regime for his defense of human rights, argued in a BBC interview that an apostasy based on conviction was different from "desertion of Islam out of malice and enmity toward the Muslim community"—and that the former deserved no punishment.[22]

The list of Muslim scholars, clerics, and thinkers who challenge the classical notion of apostasy can go on and on.[23] Yet the problem remains. Apostates from Islam, or unorthodox Muslims who apostatize from orthodox interpretations, still face the death penalty in some countries, vilification in others. Despite the Qur'anic injunction, "There is no compulsion in religion," a great deal of compulsion still occurs.

It is crucial to recognize that the earthly punishment for apostasy is not Qur'anic but post-Qur'anic. The latter reflects a historical context in which one's religious affiliation also determined his political allegiance. No wonder other civilizations of the time, such as the Sassanids and the Byzantines, also punished apostasy with death.[24] The early Muslims merely adopted the norms of their time.

Now, of course, we live in a very different world with very different norms. Religious affiliation and political allegiance are regarded as totally separate. Insisting on keeping a medieval notion of apostasy is pointless. It is also damaging, for it leads to the persecution of innocent people (such as the Afghan convert Abdul Rahman) as well as the portrayal of Islam as a tyrannical religion.

Here Muslims also need to think how they would respond if, say, Christians ordered death sentences for their apostates who chose to accept Islam. What would they think, for example, if someone like Yusuf Islam—formerly Cat Stevens, who became a Muslim in 1977—had been put on trial in a British court and given three days to recant before being executed?

Converts to Islam don't face such treatment in the Western world, because the West has embraced freedom of religion, which includes freedom from their own religion as well. Muslims need to do the same.

REVISITING BLASPHEMY

If one aspect of freedom from Islam is the right to apostatize from it, another is the right to criticize it. And this "criticism," sorry to say, can sometimes come in the form of satire, mockery, and even insult.

Insult, of course, is never acceptable. When a non-Muslim curses God, the Qur'an, the Prophet, or any other sacred value of Islam, he is, at the very least, being disrespectful. Muslims would be considered disrespectful, too, if they insulted other people's faiths. "Do not curse those they call upon besides God," the Qur'an warns them, "in case that makes them curse God in animosity, without knowledge."[25]

If we were living in an ideal world, everyone would listen to this fair advice and respect each other's religion. In real life, however, people do satirize, mock, and insult each other's religion, including ours. Moreover, what other people put forward as a fair criticism sometimes might sound offensive, simply because of the differences between perspectives and cultures. What, then, should Muslims do?

This matter has grown testy in the past few decades, as some Muslims' reactions to real or perceived insults to Islam have made global headlines. In 1989, Ayatollah Khomeini issued a death *fatwa* on author Salman Rushdie for his contentious novel, *The Satanic Verses*. In 2004, Dutch filmmaker Theo van Gogh was murdered by a militant Muslim who was offended by van Gogh's film *Submission*. A year later, *Jyllands-Posten*, a Danish newspaper, published a series of cartoons depicting the Prophet Muhammad as a terrorist, sparking attacks on Danish embassies and death threats to the newspaper and its cartoonists.

In all these cases, the Muslims who reacted with anger and violence probably were sincere in their zeal to defend their faith. Yet, alas, the practical result of their actions was to vindicate the very accusation brought against them—that Islam is an intolerant and aggressive religion. So, if they really want to change that negative perception about their religion, they must begin by changing their course of action.

But, common sense aside, one needs to accept that those Muslims who react violently against perceived offenses are not devoid of religious justification. Traditional schools of the Shariah have a concept called *kufr* (blasphemy), which is considered a crime punishable by death. It is to this concept to which angry Muslims who want to "behead those who insult Islam" refer.[26]

To put matters in perspective, one should recall that other Abrahamic traditions also used to follow the same concept. The Torah clearly states that those who speak blasphemy "shall surely be put to death."[27] St. Thomas Aquinas wrote that blasphemy, "a sin committed directly against God, is more grave than murder."[28] Yet, in modern times, both Judaism and Christianity have abandoned earthly punishment for blasphemy, whereas Islam, as with some other aspects of the Shariah that we have examined, has remained largely unchanged.

Of course, adapting to the modern world simply because it is modern would not make sense to a Muslim—or to anyone else who believes in a moral law unbound by the fluctuations of time. But the same believer does not have to insist on preserving the elements of his tradition that are historical rather than divinely mandated.

In the case of Islam, these two separate categories roughly correspond to, as we have seen, the Qur'an and the post-Qur'anic tradition. All elements of the latter are somehow "manmade." And, tellingly enough, on the issue of blasphemy, as with the matter of apostasy, the Qur'an is surprisingly lenient. Its verses threaten blasphemers with God's punishment in the hereafter but do not impose on them any earthly punishment.

As with apostasy, the punishment for blasphemy comes from certain narratives in the Hadith literature and the way they were interpreted by classical scholars. These narratives are about certain individuals, mostly satirical poets, who mocked the Prophet Muhammad during his mission and claimed that the Qur'an was a fraud. Some of them, the narratives go, were executed by the nascent Muslim community for being "enemies of God and the Prophet." But besides the fact that the very accuracy of these historical accounts can be challenged, they can also be regarded as limited by their specific context. As Muslim scholar Mohammad Kamali shows, the executions of the satirists were political, rather than religious, events. At a time when the early Muslim community was battling for survival with hostile pagans, mockery had become a part of war propaganda.[29] But "blasphemy today can in no sense threaten the existence or continuity of Islam as a great religion, a legal system and a major civilisation."[30]

JUST "DO NOT SIT WITH THEM . . ."

Beyond the Hadith literature, a response to blasphemy that is more compatible with the liberal standards of the modern world actually comes from the Qur'an. The Muslim scripture not only lacks any suggestion of earthly punishment for blasphemy, it also advises a nonviolent response: "When you hear God's revelations disbelieved in and mocked at, do not sit with them until they enter into some other discourse; surely then you would be like them."[31]

What is described here is a clearly peaceful form of disapproval: Muslims are not supposed to be part of a discourse that mocks Islam, but all they have to do is stay away from it. Even then, the withdrawal should last only until the discourse changes into something inoffensive. Once mockery ends, dialogue can restart. (We should note that this verse is from a chapter of the Qur'an that was revealed in the "Medinan" phase. In other words, it reflects a time when Muslims had political and military power. So its nonviolent character can't be explained, and explained away, as resulting from necessity.)

A few other Qur'anic verses, too, order similar acts of nonviolent disapproval in the face of blasphemous talk. "When you see those who enter into false discourses about Our communications," one of them commands the Prophet, "withdraw from them until they enter into some other discourse."[32] Another verse describes Muslims as quite nonconfrontational: "When they hear idle talk they turn aside from it and say: We shall have our deeds and you shall have your deeds; peace be on you, we do not desire the ignorant."[33]

I believe that the Muslim response to blasphemy in the modern world should be based on the spirit of these verses. For example, Muslims can boycott anti-Islamic rhetoric by refusing to join conversations, buy publications, or watch films and plays that mock the values of their faith. They can also organize peaceful protests. All of that is right, but trying to silence the anti-Islamic rhetoric with threats and attacks is not.

Meanwhile, the Muslims who are willing to resort to violence in the face of mockery should reflect on the source of their motivation: a genuinely religious commitment or a nationalistic zeal? The latter option comes to mind because of a curious pattern. In the modern era, the Muslim response to mockery has been most zealous when the subject is the Prophet Muhammad, rather than other prophets and, most strangely, God. According to the Qur'an, though, Muslims should "believe in God and His messengers, and make no distinction between any of the messengers."[34] Therefore, they should stand up for Abraham, Moses, or Jesus Christ as passionately as they do for the Prophet Muhammad. And, to be sure, they should stand up most passionately for none other than God Most High.

I suspect that the selective attention to the Prophet Muhammad comes from the fact that he is revered only by Muslims, which makes him an exclusive symbol of the Muslim community. In other words, the offense to the Prophet Muhammad comes off as an offense to the Muslims' own selves. A reaction to such a personal offense certainly is an understandable human phenomenon, but it is a secular phenomenon, not a religious one—and one that has the tendency to go to extremes, especially in the Orient. The secular Turkish Republic, for example, used to have laws banning "insulting Turkishness," and the courts prosecuted intellectuals—such as the novelist Orhan Pamuk—for offending the honor of the nation simply by making critical remarks about its history.[35] Some ultra-nationalists in Turkey have even assassinated liberal critics for the same "crime."[36] All this nationalist zeal looks quite similar to that of the Muslim militants who attack those who offend the Prophet. Their motivation, one might say, is just another form of nationalism—the nation being the *umma*.

On the other hand, more theologically minded Muslims have reacted to insults to other sacred figures as well, and they have done this peacefully. When a blasphemous picture of the Virgin Mary was painted in Adelaide, Australia, in 2007, a representative of Muslim communities voiced a protest, with restraint and civility, receiving praise in Turkey from none other than Ecumenical Patriarch Bartholomew I.[37]

Besides all that, those Muslims who are prone to react with fury to criticism or mockery should also see that this only helps portray them as immature and insecure. If all they can do in the face of an antagonistic book, film, or cartoon is to destroy it by brute force, then what they really display is a lack of self-confidence. They will serve Islam much better if their response is solemn and sensible. The power of any faith, after all, comes not from its coercion on critics and dissenters but from the moral integrity and the intellectual strength of its believers.

WILL ISLAM CONQUER THE WORLD?

Finally, we should rethink what the ultimate goal, and the destiny, of the *umma* should be on this earth.

The answer given by the Islamist movement is often a triumphalist one: Islam will simply conquer the whole world; sooner or later, the whole world will be Muslim.

Yet this ambitious rhetoric might be reflecting the ambitions of the people who happen to be Muslims, rather than the intentions of the Divine. The Qur'an, in fact, clearly states that the whole world will *not* be Muslim. "What has been sent down to you from your Lord is the Truth," a verse tells the Prophet, "but most people have no faith."[38] Another verse refers not to the lack of faith but to the variety of faiths, explaining that this diversity is exactly what God desired for mankind:

> And We have sent down the Book [the Qur'an] to you with truth, confirming and conserving the previous Books. . . . We have appointed a law and a practice for every one of you. Had God willed, He would have made you a single community, but He wanted to test you regarding what has come to you. So compete with each other in doing good. Every one of you will return to God and He will inform you regarding the things about which you differed.[39]

This striking Qu'ranic passage clearly describes a world in which Islam is one religion among others, not the only one.[40] The differences between them will be reconciled only in the afterlife. Meanwhile, people of different faiths—Muslims, Christians, Jews, and all others—are expected to "compete with each other in doing good."

To be able to realize this pluralist vision, what we would need is a world in which all faiths could freely express and advance themselves.

Granted, such a pluralist world sounds different from the

ideal of the medieval Muslim scholars—the Abode of Islam. This term, as we saw in chapter 4, referred to lands ruled by Muslims and governed according to the Shariah. Only such places then looked safe for practicing Islam. The rest of the world was either hostile (Abode of War—i.e., lands ruled by non-Muslims) or only conditionally safe (Abode of Treaty—i.e., lands ruled by non-Muslims who made treaties with a Muslim state).

Yet none of these medieval categories can explain the modern world. Today, in fact, some Muslims seem to find it easier to live by their religion in the non-Muslim countries of the West, which grant more safety and freedom than some of the Muslim-majority countries with dictatorial regimes.

So it is time to stop seeing the world as divided between an Abode of Islam versus an Abode of War. Rather, what exists now is an Abode of Freedom versus an Abode of Tyranny. The former is what Muslims should seek.

In this free world, there surely will be ideas that Muslims, including me, will not like. What we need to do is to respond to them with reason and wisdom—an effort that might help us revitalize the intellectual dynamism of our earliest generations, as in the way the Mutazilites dealt with the challenges, and the contributions, of Greek philosophy.

In this free world, there also will be people with lifestyles that we will find misguided and abhorrent. We need to try to share with those people the values that we uphold. How they will react is not our business. "If they become Muslim, they have been guided," God told the Prophet. "If they turn away, you are only responsible for transmission."[41]

And, ultimately, we need this free world for our individual selves. Each of us has a personal life to live—an amazing journey that starts with our birth and continuously unfolds while we grow up to experience a mind-boggling drama. We learn and discover, we achieve and enjoy, and we fail and suffer. For the believer, none of these ups and downs of life are devoid of meaning—all are meant to be lessons to make us more mature and wise and, we hope, more godly.

Liberty is what every individual needs to be able to live such a fulfilling life, based on his own choices and decisions, successes and failures.

Liberty is, you could also say, what everyone needs to find God.

Arab Revolutions, Democracy, and Liberalism

THIS BOOK WAS written right before the "Arab Spring"—the label given to the chain of revolutions against longtime dictators in Tunisia, Egypt, and Libya in early 2011. Yet this unpredicted epoch in the Middle East not only confirmed the book's predictions but also highlighted its main premise: that Muslim societies need a case not only for *democracy*, which has been made abundantly, but also for *liberalism*, which has rarely been addressed.

The difference between these two concepts is worth emphasizing, for it is often blurred. In popular media, liberalism (a political philosophy based on individual liberties) and democracy (a political system based on representation) often are intertwined. Some texts even use the terms interchangeably, assuming that democracy and liberalism always go hand in hand.

It is possible, however, to have a democratic political system without fully acknowledging individual liberties—such as freedom of speech, assembly, religion, or property ownership. Political thinkers who have pointed out this risky situation have even coined a term for it: *illiberal democracy*. This implies a system in which free and fair elections would be held, resulting in majority rule, but minorities and dissenting individuals could nonetheless be suppressed.

Notably, the West, including the United States, has its own history with illiberal democracy. One terrible example was Jim Crow legislation, which institutionalized racism in Southern states for almost a century. The Jim Crow laws were "democratic" only in the sense that they were supported by the majority of the local populations. But they were grossly illiberal and were abolished only by a restoration of liberalism promoted by the civil rights movement and established by the US Supreme Court.

Meanwhile, that civil rights movement had an important feature relevant to the theme of this book: Its liberalism was inspired not only from the modern secular doctrines of human rights but also from the Christian beliefs about "God's children," articulated by church leaders such as Reverend Martin Luther King Jr. It was, in other words, a religion-inspired liberalism.

I had noticed this important nuance many years ago, when I was first studying the history of liberalism in the West. Consequently, I wondered whether the same thing—a religion-inspired liberalism—would apply in Islam as well. The curiosity turned into a passion and led me to write *Islam without Extremes: A Muslim Case for Liberty*. And then the Arab Spring made that book's arguments even more relevant—and more necessary—as I will explain in this epilogue.

ISLAMISM MEETS DEMOCRACY

Let's begin with a short background of the Arab Spring. As I explained in chapter 7 of this book, the Muslim Middle East was haunted by a series of secular dictators during much of the twentieth century. Although some of these dictators were hailed in the West as "progressive," or "moderate," they proved to be a curse rather than a blessing for their societies. One of their many unintended consequences was the radicalization of their main opponents: the Islamists. Being silenced, jailed, and even tortured by secular tyrants, Islamist parties grew only more angry, reactionary, and utopian. Subsequently, some of them hoped for a violent, religion-based revolution and thus resorted to armed *jihad*.

In other words, the radicalism of the Islamists was partly a creation of their political context. Yet it was also partly a matter of doctrine, for many Islamists rejected democracy on principle. They simply saw an irreconcilable conflict between "the sovereignty of people" and "the sovereignty of God." Hence many of them condemned democracy as an "idolatrous" philosophy that considers the ideas of mortal men superior to the decrees of the Almighty Allah.

However, while this condemnation of democracy is still alive today among some hard-core Islamists, others began to warm to the idea from the late 1980s onward. First, some Islamic thinkers noted that "the sovereignty of people" and "the sovereignty of God" were not necessarily conflicting ideas—God, after all, has given men a "mandate" on Earth and ordered Muslims to "consult" with each other. Second, most Islamist parties in the Middle East realized that democracy could ultimately work for their own benefit: Their piety and their charitable works were heightening their profile and increasing their popularity in Arab societies, which would give them a big advantage in the event of free and fair elections.

That is the short story of why mainstream Islamist parties such as the Muslim Brotherhood in Egypt and Ennahda in Tunisia had already made their peace with democracy in the wake of the Arab Spring. Thus, they willingly joined the revolutionary tide when masses rallied against their dictators—Zine El Abidine Ben Ali in Tunisia and Hosni Mubarak in Egypt. When these dictators fell, the same Islamists continued to support democracy by calling for free and fair elections. Even the more dogmatic Salafis—the theological descendants of the antirational and ultraliteralist Hanbalis that I discussed in chapter 4—proved willing to participate in the democratic process.

All this indicated that the Islamist attitude toward democracy as a political system had changed dramatically from condemnation to advocacy. As a Western scholar observed in a 2011 book on the Arab Spring:

> Where once Islamist groups dreamed of revolution, quietly developed paramilitary cells, and assassinated their secular opponents, mainstream Islamist groups today, most of which are descended from Egypt's Muslim Brotherhood, see elections as a means for society to maintain its *akhlaq*, the mores that define good Muslims.[1]

However, there was a catch: The acceptance of democracy did not necessarily imply an acceptance of liberalism. Quite the contrary. The political vision of the Islamists still included various illiberal elements that were partly rooted in their interpretation of Islamic law, or *shariah*. Oft-feared examples were the imposition of piety with bans on alcohol or "immodesty," the degrading of women and non-Muslim minorities, and punishments for blasphemy and apostasy.

No wonder that, in all postrevolutionary Arab states, tension emerged quickly between the Islamists and "the liberals."[2] In Egypt, for example, the latter group insisted on establishing "supra-constitutional principles" first, before the drafting of a constitution by an elected assembly dominated by the Islamists. These principles would uphold basic freedoms, human rights, and the "civil state" (as opposed to a religious one). The Islamists, on the other hand, rejected enacting any political principle above "the will of the people," which they were happy to represent in a majoritarian sense.

This political tension in Egypt escalated with the electoral ascendancy of Islamists, including Mohamed Morsi, a former member of the Muslim Brotherhood elected as president in June 2012. In one year, however, Morsi's rule frustrated not just the remnants of the old authoritarian regime but also the liberals and even a few disenchanted supporters. Hence, in late June 2013, the latter initiated massive protests against the elected president, which paved the way for a military coup against him on the night of July 3. For Morsi's supporters, most of them members of the Muslim Brotherhood, the president was "elected," so his rule was deemed "democratic." For most liberals, simply being elected did not amount to legitimacy, because they worried, rightly or wrongly, that Morsi's rule threatened some of their liberties.

On this particular tension in Egypt, still escalating as I write these lines, with worrying acts of military violence against pro-Morsi protesters, I understood the concerns of the liberals yet I still condemned the military coup. The military's ousting of an elected leader not only disrupted Egypt's democratic evolution but also pushed the Muslim Brotherhood toward a more reactionary stance.[3] In fact, the coup made it very easy for them, and other Islamists, to conclude: "Democracy is not for us."[4]

So, I argued, President Morsi should have been allowed to govern Egypt for the four-year term to which he was elected, and his opponents then should have tackled him at the ballot box.[5]

However, the concerns of the liberals—that elected Islamists can curb liberties—were not unimportant. Therefore, they deserved a closer look.

THE RISK OF "DEMOCRATIC AUTHORITARIANISM"

The problem discussed here is in fact not unique to the Arab or Muslim world; it is a problem of most new democracies. The democratic process begins with free and fair elections, but the winners of these elections tend to use political power in authoritarian ways, such as the suppression of the opposition or the silencing of critics. Many of the post-Communist states in Eastern Europe have gone through such phases of illiberal democracy, while Russia, under the elected despotism of Vladimir Putin, exemplifies its zenith.

Some of the worries caused by the election-winning Islamists stem from such simple and typical dynamics of political power. Olivier Roy, an expert on political Islam, points out this nuance by reminding us that when President Mohamed Morsi was denounced in Tahrir Square in November 2012 for overextending his powers, he was condemned by the liberals as "the new Mubarak" and not "the new Khomeini."[6] Morsi's move, in other words, reflected not a specific Islamist ideology but Egypt's long-standing authoritarian traditions.

This is also true for Turkey, where troubles with the post-Islamist Justice and Development Party (AKP)—whose elected but growing authoritarian rule sparked massive antigovernment protests in late May and June 2013—come from adopting some of the habits of the old secular establishment—such as nepotism, confrontation, political paranoia, and hubris.[7] "Power corrupts," as Lord Acton wisely observed, and it corrupts regardless of ideology or theology.

Yet even after these universal problems are noted, Islamists still have a specific reason to raise concerns among liberals about illiberal democracy: their willingness to impose Islamic norms on society. Turkish political scientist Ihsan Dagi, a self-declared classical liberal, defines this problem as the "post-modern authoritarianism of democratic Islamists." In his words:

> It is an Islamism that is not justified by a reference to the "text" but to the "people" and its will. Such Islamism in the aftermath of the Arab Spring Middle East is "democratic and representative" in justification and process, but authoritarian in content and outcome.[8]

Dagi finds this "democratic" Islamism authoritarian because it is willing to use "the state apparatus to impose its choice of morality, lifestyle, value system" and enact "Islam's social code as the only legitimate way of life."[9]

In the face of this risk, optimistic observers have put their faith in the moderating influence of democracy, and they are mostly right to do so. The urge to win votes will inevitably make Islamist parties more responsive to the concerns of social groups that are outside of their ideological sphere. This dynamic has worked well in Turkey by pushing the Justice and Development Party toward the center right, and it can work in Egypt as well. The Muslim Brotherhood, for example, realized after coming to power that a nationwide alcohol ban would hurt the all-important tourism industry—a problem that they had never considered (or needed to consider) before they assumed power.[10]

However, pragmatism might not be enough to nurture liberalism out of an inherently illiberal worldview. This is especially true for the Muslim Middle East, in which the majority of the population is "moderate but illiberal"—they reject political violence but also are suspicious of political, social, and civil liberties.[11] Therefore, if the current trends continue, it is possible that illiberal democracy might become the norm in the Muslim Middle East. Authoritarian Islamists can "democratically" dominate, whereas the liberals, the defenders of individual liberty, can prove to be a losing minority.

Yet there might also be a fortunate breakthrough in the rise of "Islamic liberalism"—an idea that would synthesize the Islamic faith with political liberalism and thus make the latter more acceptable in Muslim societies and even among some of the Islamists.

THE CASE FOR ISLAMIC LIBERALISM

Luckily, there are already opinion leaders in the Middle East who seem prone to embracing Islamic liberalism. The most prominent among them is probably Rashid al-Ghannushi, the founder and "intellectual leader" of the Ennahda Party in Tunisia. Ghannushi is known for this emphasis on "freedom" as the basis of Islam, acknowledging that apostasy from Islam cannot be considered a crime, and that women and non-Muslims should have equal rights with Muslim men. It is notable that he was defending these views even in the late 1990s, more than a decade before the onset of the Arab Spring.[12] That is one of the reasons why Ennahda, among all the Arab Islamist parties, has proven to be the most liberal-leaning one—and Tunisia appears to be the most promising case arising out of the whole Arab Spring. (The most traumatic case, Syria, was still in the midst of a bloody civil war between the ruthless tyranny of Bashar al-Assad and his diverse opponents as I was writing these words.)

On the other hand, social change in Muslim societies is preparing the ground for liberal ideas to flourish, as I explained in chapter 8 by using Turkey as a case study. Even in Saudi Arabia, the home of the most oppressive interpretation of Islam, a liberal-leaning generation is emerging, thanks to "easy access to the Internet and exposure to other cultures during study overseas." [13] One example of this is the "Statement of Saudi Youth Regarding the Guarantee of Freedoms and Ethics of Diversity," a manifesto that was posted online in March 2012 and supported by thousands of signatories. In a bold defiance of the "religious police" in the country, the signatories declared:

> No one can claim monopoly of truth or righteousness in the name of Islamic law. . . . We reject this patriarchal guardianship which forbids us from practicing our God-given right to think and explore for ourselves, as we can listen and judge. [14]

As a Western journalist observed, these young Saudis were not secular, but they "favor[ed] a religious practice that is more voluntary, less enforced by the state, and more respectful of differences among Muslims." All in all, they had embraced "freedom and human rights" and "want[ed] to have these ideas connected to Islamic thinking." [15]

Making that connection is what *Islam without Extremes* is all about. And, to summarize in a nutshell, here are the three pillars of the Islamic liberalism that it offers:

1. *Reason.* As summarized in the early chapters, there was a great "war of ideas" in early Islam within the adherents of reason

and the advocates of blind obedience. The latter camp, best represented today by the Salafis, believes that religious texts should be obeyed literally without any question or revision. The rational camp, on the other hand, grants that the religious texts arose in a particular historical and geopolitical context and sees that the radically new context of the modern world begs for a great deal of reinterpretation.

For example, blind literalists will execute apostates from Islam, based on the hadith that says, "If somebody discards his religion, kill him." The rationalists, however, would first question the authenticity of this saying attributed to the Prophet Muhammad. Then they would also reason that this injunction was most probably related to the context of war: In the early Muslim community, "discarding one's religion" also implied changing sides in a battle by joining the enemy, an act that we call "high treason" today. In today's world, however, a change of religion is simply a matter of persuasion, and it should be respected as such.

Such reinterpretations are a must if Islamic law is to become compatible with universal notions of freedom and human rights. And the path to that reinterpretation will be opened only when reason, as a God-given faculty, is restored to its more prominent place in early Islamic jurisprudence.

2. *Pluralism.* Not all Muslims, however, will be rationalists. Nor will they agree on the diverse interpretations that reason can provide. What they really need to do, therefore, is not to force all fellow Muslims to agree on "true Islam" but rather to allow Muslims to live and let live with different versions of the faith. In other words, just like the *Murjiites* ("Postponers") of early Islam discussed in chapter 3, what Muslims need is to "postpone" ultimate judgments to the afterlife, to be resolved by God, while following in this life the interpretations of Islam that persuade them best.

In short, Muslims need more pluralism within the faith. Not only will this ease the tensions between different sects, such as Sunni versus Shiite, it also will erode the basis of religious authoritarianism. After all, if no one can claim to know indisputably what "true Islam" is, then no one can dictate it to fellow Muslims. No "religious police" can impose on me what they see as Islamic, for my view of what is Islamic can be very different.

Acknowledgment of this pluralism would also desacralize all "Islamic states," because it would show that such states only institute the version of Islam they prefer—and often to venerate themselves rather than Islam. And since no state can rightly claim to represent truth, the best political model will prove to be a secular (or "civil") state, under which different interpretations of Islam, and of other faiths, can coexist.

3. *Godliness.* This third pillar of Islamic liberalism comes from commonsense logic and a simple observation: The imposition of religion does not make people religious. Rather, it makes them hypocritical or outright antireligious. Therefore, genuine religiosity, which comes from the individual's faith in God and his willingness to worship Him, can and should be promoted only by noncoercive means, such as preaching, sharing, and showing by example. With such methods, Islam can be effectively *proposed*, but it should never be *imposed*.

The modern Islamist movement often overlooked this crucial fact, because it focused on "establishing the Islamic system"—a purely political goal—rather than on saving Muslim souls. No wonder the Islamic movements that focused on the latter—such as Sufi orders or the Said Nursi and Fethullah Gülen movements in Turkey—often distanced themselves from the Islamists. Today, the historical experience shows that the politics-focused Islamists were wrong, and the faith-focused Muslims were right. The former only created violence, tension, authoritarianism, and hatred against Islam. The latter created modern schools, charities, soup kitchens, and sympathy for Islam.

Those Muslims who insist on using authoritarian measures for preserving godliness—such as bans on alcoholic drinks or atheistic books—should also recognize that even if such measures kept Muslim societies pious for centuries, times have changed dramatically. The world is inevitably becoming more open, transparent, individualistic, and—obviously—globalized. Whatever is banned will be accessible somehow, only to become more attractive and appealing. Meanwhile, immutable dictates will only prove the dictator crude, feeble, and tyrannical, thus staining the very image of the religion supposedly being upheld.

Islamic liberalism is an idea that, based on such premises, will defend individual liberty in Muslim societies—not at the expense of Islam, as secularists in the Middle East have often done, but for the sake of Islam (as well as other persuasions). It has its roots in the Qur'an, some of the early schools of Islam, the late Ottoman Empire, nineteenth-century Arab reformists, and various liberal movements in the Islamic world of today.

For sure, it still is a novel and marginal idea. But it is promising, and much needed. Because, as Leonard Binder, one of the academics who has focused on this subject, wrote in 1988, "Without a vigorous Islamic liberalism, political liberalism will not succeed in the Middle East."[16] And without a strong current of political liberalism, mere democratization cannot help overcome the region's burning freedom deficit.

Istanbul
July 2013

Acknowledgments

There are many individuals I have to thank for making this book possible—and here are only some of them.

First, I thank Phillip E. Johnson, who, several years ago, encouraged me to write about Islam in America, despite living thousands of miles away. I also thank Jay Richards and Claire Berlinski for helping me take the first steps, and Walter Russell Mead for opening the way for more. I thank fellow writer Mark Scheel, too, whose gracious friendship not only improved my writing but also enriched my spirit.

I also thank my agent Jeff Gerecke for all his support, and Maria Guarnaschelli, along with Melanie Tortoroli and Kathy Brandes, for doing a terrific job as my editors at W. W. Norton. They not only corrected my not-so-native language but also made many suggestions and criticisms that made the book much more compelling and articulate. I thank Nuri Tınaz for his help for my research at the ISAM library in Istanbul.

I also am thankful to Bruce Chapman, İskender Öksüz, Fuat Andıç, Linda Whetstone, Morgaan Sinclair, Alper Bilgili, Ahmet Kuru, and Bilal Sambur, who took the time to read the galleys and made very helpful comments. The support of my father, Taha Akyol, who not only inspired some of the ideas in this book but also helped me articulate them, was particularly invaluable. So was the emotional support of my gracious mother, Tülin Akyol, my young brother, Ertuğrul, and, most importantly, my beloved wife Riada, the light of my life.

Finally, the highest praise should go for God the Almighty, from whom, I believe, come all our gifts. As we say in the Islamic tradition; it is us who show the effort, it is Him who grants the success.

MUSTAFA AKYOL
Istanbul, June 2013

Notes

INTRODUCTION

1. Qur'an 23:78. Mohammedali H. Shakir, *The Qur'an Translation* (Elmhurst, NY: Tahrike Tarsile Qur'an, 1983); hereafter, Shakir translation.

2. Page Rockwell, "Secret Cutting," Salon.com, October 30, 2006.

3. Warner Todd Huston, "Muslim Mutilation of Little Girl in Atlanta, Georgia," Americandaily.com, October 27, 2006.

4. Bettina Shell-Duncan and Ylva Hemlund, *Female 'Circumcision' in Africa: Culture, Controversy, and Change* (Boulder, CO: Lynne Rienner, 2000), p. 168.

5. Richard Pankhurst, "A Historical Examination of Traditional Ethiopian Medicine," *Ethiopian Medical Journal* 3 (1965): 157–72.

6. Frances A. Althaus, "Female Circumcision: Rite of Passage or Violation of Rights?," *International Family Planning Perspectives* 23, no. 3 (September 1997).

7. Soli Özel, "Geleceği Kurmak (3)," *Habertürk*, September 10, 2010.

8. By "secularism police" in Turkey, I refer to the policemen whom some Turkish universities used to post at their gates. Until 2010, when the headscarf ban virtually ended, one of their jobs was to make sure that no student with "unmodern outlook" (particularly the female students who wear headscarves) could get onto the campus.

9. In his 1905 book *The Protestant Ethic and the Spirit of Capitalism,* German sociologist Max Weber argued that Puritan ethics and ideas in Europe had positively influenced the development of modern capitalism. The term *Islamic Calvinists* comes from a report by the European Stability Initiative (*Islamic Calvinists: Change and Conservatism in Central Anatolia*, September 19, 2005, Berlin/Istanbul).

10. Dücane Cündioğlu, "Düşünürken modern, inanırken geleneksel" [Modern when Thinking, Traditional when Believing], *Yeni Şafak*, December 13, 2009. Cündioğlu, a conservative who is highly critical of Islamic capitalism, says this somewhat disapprovingly.

CHAPTER ONE: A LIGHT UNTO TRIBES

1. Robert A. Sirico, *Toward a Free and Virtuous Society* (Grand Rapids, MI: Acton Institute, 1997), p. 2.

2. Ibn-i Ishak's *Sira* [Life of the Prophet], quoted in Karen Armstrong, *Muhammad: A Biography of the Prophet* (San Francisco: HarperSanFrancisco, 1992), p. 85.

3. Western Christians sometimes regard Allah as a uniquely Islamic name for God, or even a name for a deity totally separate from the one they worship. In fact, Allah is Arabic for "the God." No wonder it is used by Arabic-speakers of all Abrahamic faiths, including Christians and Jews. Arab Christians today, having no other word for God than Allah, use terms such as Allah al-'Ab, or "God the Father."

4. For an example of this argument, see Caner Taslaman, *The Quran: Unchallengeable Miracle* (Istanbul: Çitlembik/Nettleberry Publications), 2006.

5. Hans Küng, *Islam: Past, Present and Future* (Oxford: Oneworld Publications, 2007), p. 75.

6. Albert Hourani, *A History of the Arab Peoples* (London: Faber and Faber, 2002), p. 17.

7. Qur'anic verses 17:73–75 refer to this incident.

8. W. Montgomery Watt, *Muhammad: Prophet and Statesman* (Oxford: Oxford University Press, 1964), p. 232.

9. Armstrong, *Muhammad*, p. 59.

10. See Qur'an 2:30–34. It is notable that in these verses, Adam, the first man, is elevated over the angels by the "names" taught to him by God. Some Muslim scholars have interpreted these "names" as the faculty to conceptualize things, which distinguish mankind from other creatures. "The Qur'anic view of Adam's *khilafa* [viceroyship]," further argues Muslim thinker Parvez Manzoor, "is a supremely humanistic doctrine, without the hubris and arrogance of errant humanism which according to the critics of modernity is its bane and the source of its nihilism." S. Parvez Manzoor, "Faith beyond Political Correctness: Islam's Commitment to Humanity," *IslamOnline*, August 4, 2003.

11. Qur'an 90:4–17, with Arabic words anglicized. Abdalhaqq Bewley and Aisha Bewley, *The Noble Qur'an: A New Rendering of its Meaning in English* (Norwich, UK: Bookwork, 1999); hereafter, Bewley translation.

12. Qur'an 6:164.

13. Qur'an 6:94, translation from Fazlur Rahman, "The Status of the Individual in Islam," *Islamic Studies* 5, no. 4 (1996): 321.

14. Fred M. Donner, *Muhammad and the Believers: At the Origins of Islam* (Cambridge, MA: Belknap Press of Harvard University Press, 2010), p. xii. In his book, Donner opposes some Orientalist views, such as the idea that Islam emerged as a "social, economic, or 'national'" movement rather than a religious one.

15. Küng, *Islam*, p. 153.

16. Asma Afsaruddin, *First Muslims: History and Memory* (Oxford: Oneworld Publications, 2007), p. 23.

17. As for the Islamic change in the Arabic custom of vendetta, Tor Andrae notes: "Mohammed was unable completely to abolish blood-vengeance. Apparently it was too deeply rooted in the legal conceptions of the Arabs. But he attempted to check the most striking abuse of this primitive custom by stipulating that only *one* life could be taken, the life of a free man for a free man, of a woman for a woman, of a slave for a slave. Unintentional homicide does not give one the right to blood-vengeance. The kinsmen of the victim must be satisfied with a settlement consisting of one hundred camels for a man and fifty camels for a woman." Tor Andrae, *Mohammed: The Man and His Faith*, trans. Theophil Menzel (New York: Harper Torchbooks, 1960), p. 79.

18. Marshall G. S. Hodgson, *The Venture of Islam*, vol. 1, *The Classical Age of Islam* (Chicago: University of Chicago Press, 1977), p. 181.

19. For an example of this argument, see Rodney Stark, *The Victory of Reason: How Christianity Led to Freedom, Capitalism, and Western Success* (New York: Random House, 2006), especially pp. 24–26.

20. Qur'an 5:48, Bewley translation.

21. Qur'an 2:164, Bewley translation.

22. Qur'an 59:14, Bewley translation.

23. Maxime Rodinson cites Henri Lammens's comment in his *Islam and Capitalism* (London: Saqi Books, 2007), p. 115.

24. Martin Lings, *Muhammad: His Life Based on the Earliest Sources* (Cambridge, UK: Islamic Texts Society, 1995), pp. 258–59.

25. Hodgson, *Venture of Islam*, vol. 1, p. 181.

26. Noted by Fazlur Rahman in "A Survey of Modernization of Muslim Family Law," *International Journal of Middle East Studies* 11, no. 4 (July 1980): 451. The Qur'anic verse is 30:21.

27. Armstrong, *Muhammad*, p. 191.

28. Ibid., p. 199.

29. Noah Feldman, "Does Shariah Mean the Rule of Law?," *International Herald Tribune*, March 16, 2008.

30. Bernard Lewis, *Race and Slavery in the Middle East* (New York: Oxford University Press, 1994), chapter 1, http://www.fordham.edu/halsall/med/lewis1.html.

31. Armstrong, *Muhammad*, p. 231.

32. Mohammad Hashim Kamali, *Freedom of Expression in Islam*, rev. ed. (Cambridge, UK: Islamic Texts Society, 1997), p. 21. Kamali criticizes the common Western notion that Islam is essentially a system of duties. He argues that rights are equally central to Islam, and that this has only been obscured by the medieval Muslim jurists' legalistic approach, which tended to look for and explicate duties rather than rights.

33. One example is a book by a Turkish professor of Islamic law: Hayrettin Karaman, *Mukayeseli İslam Hukuku* [Comparative Islamic Law, vol. 1] (Istanbul: Nesil Publishing, 1996), pp. 75–77.

34. Qur'an 7:188, Bewley translation.

35. Qur'an 6:107, Bewley translation.

36. Qur'an 18:29, Bewley translation, with Arabic words anglicized.

37. Afsaruddin, *The First Muslims*, p. 5.

38. F. E. Peters, *Muhammad and the Origins of Islam* (Albany, NY: State University of New York Press, 1994). p. 200.

39. Qur'an 22:39–40, Bewley translation, with Arabic words anglicized.

40. Indian Muslim scholar Barakat Ahmad argues that Muslim historians have failed to take into account the fact that the historical source of the Banu Qurazya affair, the biography of Muhammad by Ibn Ishaq, written during the Abbasid caliphate, some 120 to 130 years after the Prophet's death, was strongly influenced by the environment in which it was written. Ahmad argues: "Ibn Ishaq's view regarding Muhammad's relation with the Jews were strongly influenced by his own reaction to Jewish life under the Abbasids." Harold Kasimow, "Muhammad and the Jews: A Re-Examination," *Journal of the American Academy of Religion* 50, no. 1 (March 1982): 157.

41. Walid N. Arafat, "New Light on the Story of Banu Qurayza and the Jews of Medina," *Journal of the Royal Asiatic Society of Great Britain and Ireland*, 1976, pp. 100–107. Arafat relates the testimony of Ibn Hajar, who denounced the massacre of Banu Qurayza and other accounts as "odd tales" and quoted Malik ibn Anas, a contemporary of Ibn Ishaq, whom he rejected as a "liar" and an "impostor" for seeking out the Jewish descendants for gathering information about Muhammad's campaign against their forefathers.

42. The two passages of the Qur'an (33:26 and 8:55–58) that traditionally have been regarded as referring to the Banu Qurayza incident are quite vague. They do speak of retribution to some People of the Book, but, as Arafat notes, "there is no indication whatever of the killing of a large number."

43. Norman A. Stillman, *The Jews of Arab Lands: A History and Source Book* (Philadelphia: Jewish Publication Society of America, 1979), p. 16.

44. Ibn Qutaybah in the ninth century and al-Qarafi in the thirteenth century had distinguished between the religious and political missions of the Prophet and noted the latter's contextuality. Interview with Şaban Ali Düzgün, professor of theology at the Ankara University School of Theology, *Star* [Turkish daily], April 19, 2010.

45. There are different views on this, but traditional sources write that Aisha was six or seven years old when betrothed to Muhammad, and that she was nine or ten years old when the marriage was consummated. Yet some scholars have argued against this view. Turkish Islamic law professor Hayrettin Karaman argues that it is more reasonable to assume that Aisha was fourteen at her marriage and eighteen when it was consummated. Hayrettin Kara-

man, "Hz. Aişe kaç yaşında evlendi?" [At What Age Did Aisha Get Married?], *Yeni Şafak*, January 25, 2009. For another unorthodox assessment of this issue, see T. O. Shanavas, "Was Aisha a Six-Year-Old Bride?," in *Critical Thinkers for Islamic Reform*, ed. Edip Yuksel et al. (Brainbow Press, 2009).

46. Colin Turner, *Islam: The Basics* (Oxford: Routledge, 2005), pp. 34–35.

47. Watt, *Muhammad*, p. 233.

48. Qur'an 18:110, Bewley translation.

49. Qur'an 17:81, Bewley translation.

50. Armstrong, *Muhammad*, p. 243.

51. Qur'an 110:2, Bewley translation, with Arabic words anglicized.

52. Armstrong, *Muhammad*, p. 251.

53. Rose Wilder Lane, *Islam and the Discovery of Freedom*, introduction and commentary by Imad-ad-Dean Ahmad (Beltsville, MD: Amana Publications, 2001), p. vi–vii, 1.

54. David Forte, "Islam's Trajectory," http://www.realclearpolitics.com/articles/2006/08/islams_trajectory.html, accessed October 23, 2006.

CHAPTER TWO: THE ENLIGHTENMENT OF THE ORIENT

1. Bernard Lewis, *What Went Wrong? Western Impact and Middle Eastern Response* (New York: Oxford University Press, 2002), p. 156.

2. Afsaruddin, *First Muslims*, p. 14.

3. Qur'an 2:256, Shakir translation.

4. Bernard Lewis, *The Middle East: 2000 Years of History from the Rise of Christianity to the Present Day* (London: Weidenfeld & Nicolson, 1995), p. 234. Lewis also notes: "There are some parallels between the Muslim doctrine of *jihad* and the rabbinical Jewish doctrine of *milhemet mitsva* or *milhemet hova*, with the important difference that the Jewish notion is limited to one country whereas the Islamic *jihad* is worldwide." Bernard Lewis, *The Jews of Islam* (Princeton, NJ: Princeton University Press, 1984). p. 21.

5. Bernard Lewis, *The Middle East*, p. 234.

6. See Afsaruddin, *First Muslims*, pp. 41–44.

7. Thomas Brown, "The Transformation of the Roman Mediterranean," in *The Oxford History of Medieval Europe*, ed. George Holmes (Oxford: Oxford University Press, 1988), pp. 11, 12.

8. Andrew Wheatcroft, *Infidels: A History of the Conflict Between Christendom and Islam* (London: Penguin Books, 2004), p. 46.

9. There are medieval Christian accounts of "violent conquests" by Muslims, but Near East historian Fred Donner argues that these accounts probably only reflect the plundering by "undisciplined" tribal soldiers in Muslim armies, rather than the general tendency. He adds: "The problem is that an increasing burden of archaeological evidence has turned up little or no trace of destructions, burnings, or other violence in most localities, particularly in geographical Syria, which is the area both most fully described by the

literary sources and most thoroughly explored by archaeologists. Instead, the archaeological record suggests that the area underwent a gradual process of social and cultural transformation that did not involve a violent and sudden destruction of urban or rural life at all. In town after town, we find evidence of churches that are not destroyed—but, rather, continue in use for a century or more after the 'conquest'—or new evidence that new churches (with dated mosaic floors) were being constructed." Donner, *Muhammad and the Believers*, p. 107; also see p. 116.

10. Afsaruddin, *First Muslims*, p. 39.

11. "There is nothing in Islamic history to compare with the massacres and expulsions, the inquisitions and persecutions that Christians habitually inflicted on non-Christians and still more on each other. In the lands of Islam, persecution was the exception; in Christendom, sadly, it was often the norm." Bernard Lewis, *The Multiple Identities of the Middle East* (New York: Schocken Books, 1998), p. 129.

12. Noah Feldman, *The Fall and Rise of the Islamic State* (Princeton, NJ: Princeton University Press, 2008), p. 54.

13. Under the Shariah, "no one can claim any immunity for his or her conduct merely on account of social and official status." John L. Esposito, ed., *The Oxford History of Islam* (New York: Oxford University Press, 1999), p. 149.

14. Norman Barry, "Civil Society, Religion and Islam," in *Islam, Civil Society, and Market Economy*, ed. Atilla Yayla (Ankara: Liberte Books, 2002), p. 30.

15. Rashid Rida, a reformist Muslim of the early twentieth century, critically wrote that "the men of learning (*ulama*), who were charged with the responsibility for maintaining the [Shariah], became corrupted through compromise with temporal authority (*sulta*) and consequently often lent themselves to the support of tyrants." Dale F. Eickelman and James Piscatori, *Muslim Politics* (Princeton, NJ: Princeton University Press, 1996), p. 31.

16. Fazlur Rahman, *İslami Yenilenme, Makaleler II* [Islamic Renewal, Articles II], trans. Adil Çiftçi (Ankara: Ankara Okulu, 2000), p. 106.

17. Haim Gerber, *State, Society, and Law in Islam: Ottoman Law in Comparative Perspective* (Albany, NY: SUNY Press, 1994), p. 57.

18. Haim Gerber, *Islamic Law and Culture, 1600–1840* (Leiden: Brill, 1999). p. 65.

19. The *mufti* was Khayr al-Din al-Ramli. Gerber, *Islamic Law and Culture*, p. 65.

20. Ibid.

21. Feldman, "Does Shariah Mean the Rule of Law?"

22. Feldman, *Fall and Rise of the Islamic State*, pp. 48–49.

23. Hodgson, *Venture of Islam*, vol. 1, p. 339.

24. Franz Rosenthal, *The Muslim Concept of Freedom Prior to the Nineteenth Century* (Leiden: Brill, 1960), pp. 36–37.

25. *Imam Al-Shatibi's Theory of the Higher Objectives and Intents of Islamic Law*, trans. Ahmed al-Raysuni (Herndon, VA: International Institute of Islamic Thought, 2006).

26. See Fazlur Rahman, *Islam and Modernity: Transformation of an Intellectual Tradition* (Chicago: University of Chicago Press, 1982).

27. It is not too hard to see how stoning made its way from the Torah, via the Hadiths, to Islam. A Hadith in *Sahih Bukhari* says that in Medina (then a Muslim-Jewish city), Jews brought an adulterer and an adulteress from among them to Muhammad (then the head of state), asking for his verdict. He asked what the Jewish scripture said about adultery, and when he was told that stoning was the rule, then the Prophet of Islam reportedly ordered the execution. For the classical scholars of Islam, this incident made stoning a part of the Sunna (tradition) of the Prophet.

28. Bernard Lewis, *The Crisis of Islam: Holy War and Unholy Terror* (London: Weidenfeld & Nicolson, 2003), p. 30.

29. Ibid.

30. Qur'an 2:190.

31. This is a Hadith in Sunan Abu-Dawud, book 14, number 2608. Also quoted in Gérard Chaliand, *The Art of War in World History: From Antiquity to the Nuclear Age* (Berkeley: University of California Pres, 1994), p. 390.

32. "[R]adical [jidahist] groups are guilty of taking exceptions listed in the classical texts and making them the rule—for example, with regard to killing innocents." David Cook, *Understanding Jihad* (Berkeley: University of California Press, 2005), p. 164.

33. Karen Armstrong, *Holy War: The Crusades and Their Impact on Today's World* (New York: Anchor Books, 2001), p. 178.

34. Ibid., p. 259.

35. Feldman, *Fall and Rise of the Islamic State*, pp. 46, 47.

36. Ibid.

37. Louay M. Safi, "Overcoming the Religious-Secular Divide," in *Muslim Contributions to World Civilization*, ed. M. Basheer Ahmed et al. (Herndon, VA: International Institute of Islamic Thought, 2005), p. 21.

38. Qur'an 62:10. For more on the Qur'an, wealth, and trade, see Rodinson, *Islam and Capitalism*, pp. 41–42.

39. Fernand Braudel, *Civilization and Capitalism, 15th–18th Century*, vol. 2, *The Wheels of Commerce* (Berkeley: University of California Press, 1992), p. 558.

40. Hamid Hosseini, "Understanding the Market Mechanism before Adam Smith: Economic Thought in Medieval Islam," *History of Political Economy* 27, no. 3 (1995): 544.

41. Rodinson, *Islam and Capitalism*, p. 51.

42. Ira Lapidus, Review of *Merchant Capital and Islam* by Mahmood Ibrahim, *American Historical Review* 97, no. 1 (February 1992): 257.

43. Rodinson, *Islam and Capitalism*, p. 8. In addition, one should note that "the contrast between capitalism as a 'commercial system' and capitalism as a 'mode of production' is schematic and overstated." Jairus Banaji, "Islam, the Mediterranean and the Rise of Capitalism," *Historical Materialism* 15 (2007): 67. The same author (p. 62) explains: "Islam made a powerful contribution to the growth of capitalism in the Mediterranean, in part because it preserved and expanded the monetary economy of late antiquity and innovated business techniques that became the staple of Mediterranean commerce."

44. Abraham L. Udovitch, *Partnership and Profit in Medieval Islam* (Princeton, NJ: Princeton University Press, 1970), p. 171.

45. Joseph Schacht, *An Introduction to Islamic Law* (Oxford: Clarendon Press, 1998), p. 78.

46. Braudel, *Civilization and Capitalism,* vol. 2, *The Wheels of Commerce*, p. 559.

47. Timur Kuran, "The Islamic Commercial Crisis: Institutional Roots of Economic Underdevelopment in the Middle East," *The Journal of Economic History* 63, no. 2 (June 2003): 439. Kuran's argument is that Islamic law failed to update itself after the initial centuries and thus became a roadblock to economic progress.

48. The theory is that the British common law, which was created by King Henry II of England in the twelfth century and was notably less state-oriented than the civil law tradition in Europe, might be rooted in Islamdom, via a route from Islamic law in North Africa to the Norman law of Sicily and from there to the Norman law of England. See John A. Makdisi, "The Islamic Origins of the Common Law," *North Carolina Law Review* 77, no. 5 (June 1999): 1635–1739. For the resemblance to the common law and the Shariah, see Bryan Turner, *Max Weber: From History to Modernity* (London: Routledge, 1993), p. 49.

49. Marshall G. S. Hodgson, *Rethinking World History: Essays on Europe, Islam and World History* (Cambridge, UK: Cambridge University Press, 2002), p. 167.

50. Lewis, *Crisis of Islam*, p. 40.

51. This had something to do with the intellectual revolution that the Qur'an brought to the Orient. Before Islam, Arabs and most other peoples of the region used to perceive nature as a chaos of sacred yet fearful entities. "Snakes and other dangerous animals were worshipped to avert potential harm from them." The Qur'an reserved sacredness only to God and decreed that man, the highest of His creation, is destined to both subdue and utilize nature and also reflect upon its ways. From this came the spirit for scientific endeavor. Dilnawaz Siddiqui, "Middle Eastern Origins of Modern Sciences," in *Muslim Contributions to World Civilization*, ed. M. Basheer Ahmed et al., pp. 55–56.

52. Martin Kramer, "Islam's Sober Millennium," *Jerusalem Post*, December 31, 1999.

53. In the words of a Christian commentator, "[medieval] Muslim thinkers addressed a series of philosophical and theological topics—God and the world, creation out of nothing, the freedom of God, faith and reason—that Christian thinkers would also take up. The resulting dialogue raised the level of sophistication of Western thought and helped Christian thinkers clarify and deepen their own approach to similar issues." Robert Louis Wilken, "Christianity Face to Face with Islam," *First Things*, January 2009.

54. Maria Rosa Menocal, *The Ornament of the World: How Muslims, Jews and Christians Created a Culture of Tolerance in Medieval Spain* (New York: Back Bay Books, 2003), p. 12.

55. Hodgson, *Rethinking World History*, p. 106.

56. Jonathan Lyons, *The House of Wisdom: How the Arabs Transformed Western Civilization* (New York: Bloomsbury Press, 2010), p. 59.

57. Graham Fuller, *A World Without Islam* (New York: Little, Brown, 2010), p. 247. As Fuller notes, this imbalance in the number of cities occurred despite the fact that the populations of the Middle East and Europe in the ninth century were roughly equal—around thirty million each.

58. Zachary Karabell, *People of the Book: The Forgotten History of Islam and the West* (London: John Murray, 2007), p. 67.

59. Later the term came to imply all Christians living under Muslim rule. Menocal, *Ornament of the World*, p. 69.

60. One should even note that Charles lived four centuries after al-Hakam. Fernand Braudel, *A History of Civilizations* (New York: Penguin Books, 1993), p. 72.

61. Wheatcroft, *Infidels*, p. 47.

62. Tariq Ramadan, *Radical Reform* (New York: Oxford University Press, 2009), p. 168.

63. Daniel Pipes, *In the Path of God: Islam and Political Power* (New Brunswick, NJ: Transaction Publishers, 2002), p. 177.

CHAPTER THREE: THE MEDIEVAL WAR OF IDEAS (I)

1. Leonard Binder, *Islamic Liberalism: A Critique of Development Ideologies* (Chicago: University of Chicago Press, 1988), p. 4.

2. Taha Akyol, *Hariciler ve Hizbullah: İslam Toplumlarında Terörün Kökenleri* [Kharijites and Hezbollah: The Origins of Terror in Islamic Societies] (Istanbul: Doğan Publishing, 2000), p. 7.

3. Ismail A. B. Balogun, "Relation Between God and His Creation: Revelation and Authority," in *The Concept of Monotheism in Islam and Christianity,* ed. Hans Köchler. Papers of the International Symposium on "The Concept of Monotheism in Islam and Christianity," held in Rome, Italy (Vienna: Wilhelm Braumüller, 1982), p. 82.

4. Qur'an 5:48, Bewley translation, with Arabic words anglicized.

5. Speaking of different claims of truth by "Arminians," and Calvinists, John Locke wrote: "The controversy between these churches about the truth of their doctrines and the purity of their worship is on both sides equal; nor is there any judge, either at Constantinople or elsewhere upon earth, by whose sentence it can be determined. The decision of that question belongs only to the Supreme judge of all men, to whom also alone belongs the punishment of the erroneous. In the meanwhile, let those men consider how heinously they sin, who, adding injustice, if not to their error, yet certainly to their pride, do rashly and arrogantly take upon them to misuse the servants of another master, who are not at all accountable to them." John Locke, *A Letter Concerning Toleration* (Indianapolis: Liberal Arts Press, 1955), pp. 25–26).

6. Al-Shahrastani, *Al-Milal Wa'l-Nihal*; quoted in Majid Fakhry, ed., *A History of Islamic Philosophy*, 3rd ed. (New York: Columbia University Press, 2004), p. 40.

7. Duncan B. MacDonald, *Development of Muslim Theology, Jurisprudence and Constitutional Theory* (New York: Charles Scribner's Sons, 1903). p. 126.

8. Fakhry, *History of Islamic Philosophy*, p. 41.

9. Ibid., p. 40.

10. The Murjiites have been unjustly accused for their political leanings: "In some early sources and older orientalist studies, they have been described both as loyalist supporters of the Umayyads and as political quietists. This is clearly mistaken. Their suspension of judgment concerning Ali clashed with the official Umayyad condemnation of him, and their insistence on their right to criticise the injustice of the rulers quickly led to conflict." *The Encyclopedia of Islam*, vol. 7 (Leiden/New York: E. J. Brill, 1993), p. 606.

11. "Fatalism, the supreme negation of human free will, was the most noticeable metaphysical concept embraced by pre-Islamic Arabs." Rosenthal, *Muslim Concept of Freedom*, p. 12.

12. Küng, *Islam*, p. 222.

13. Rosenthal, *Muslim Concept of Freedom*, p. 78.

14. Esposito, ed., *Oxford History of Islam*, p. 277.

15. Küng, *Islam*, p. 225.

16. Patricia Crone and Martin Hinds, *God's Caliph: Religious Authority in the First Centuries of Islam* (Cambridge, UK: Cambridge University Press, 2003), p. 68; Afsaruddin, *First Muslims*, p. 86.

17. *Encyclopedia of Islam*, vol. 12, p. 312.

18. John L. Esposito, *Islam: The Straight Path* (New York: Oxford University Press, 1998), p. 79.

19. Eric E. F. Bishop, "Al-Shafi'i (Muhammad ibn Idris) Founder of a Law School," *The Muslim World* 19, no. 2 (April 1929): 160.

20. Richard C. Martin et al., *Defenders of Reason in Islam* (Oxford: Oneworld Publications, 1997), p. 32.

21. Majid Fakhry, *Ethical Theories in Islam* (Leiden: Brill, 1991), p. 47.

22. Ibid., p. 49.

23. "Without Islamic Aristotelianism there would certainly be no Christian Aristotelianism," and "the influence of Averroes (and also of Avicenna) on the development of Later Medieval Christian thought is therefore unequivocal. But this intellectual debt to Islam is very rarely mentioned in our times." Jones Irwin, "Averroes' Reason: A Medieval Tale of Christianity and Islam," *The Philosopher* 90, no. 2 (Autumn 2002). For the influence of Averroes and Avicenna on St. Thomas Aquinas, see also Lyons, *House of Wisdom*, pp. 190–93.

24. Martin et al., *Defenders of Reason in Islam*, p. 11.

25. Rémi Brague, *The Law of God: The Philosophical History of an Idea*, trans. Lydia G. Cochrane (Chicago: University of Chicago Press, 2007). p. 152.

26. Steven Wasserstrom, *Between Muslim and Jew: The Problem of Symbiosis under Early Islam* (Princeton, NJ: Princeton University Press, 1999), pp. 142–43.

27. "Like many of the philosophers of the Enlightenment, the Mu'tazili mutakallimun were also men of religious faith, although their faith and status as good Muslims was constantly criticized by their opponents." Martin et al., *Defenders of Reason in Islam*, p. 12.

28. Ibid., p. 29.

29. John Mikhail, "Islamic Rationalism and the Foundation of Human Rights," Georgetown University Law Center, Public Law & Legal Theory Working Paper Series, no. 777026.

30. Sunni theologian Fakhr al-Din al-Razi had identified this argument as a Mutazilite view, and prominent Qadari and Mutazilite scholars, such as Hasan al-Basri and Zamakhshari, were known to support it. Patricia Crone, *Medieval Islamic Political Thought* (Edinburgh: Edinburgh University Press, 2005), p. 381; Yohanan Friedmann, *Tolerance and Coercion in Islam: Interfaith Relations in the Muslim Tradition* (Cambridge, UK: Cambridge University Press, 2003), p. 106 (note 97).

31. Qur'an 2:256, Shakir translation. "Action of the heart" is from Friedmann, *Tolerance and Coercion in Islam*, p. 106.

32. Crone, *Medieval Islamic Political Thought,* p. 381; Friedmann, *Tolerance and Coercion in Islam*, p. 100.

33. Crone, *Medieval Islamic Political Thought*, p. 381.

34. Al-Farabi's views are summarized in Rosenthal, *Muslim Concept of Freedom*, pp. 100–101.

35. Ibid., p. 100.

36. Ibid., p. 101.

37. Arnold J. Toynbee, *A Study of History*, vol. 3, 2nd ed. (London: Oxford University Press, 1935), p. 322.

38. Ibn Khaldun notes: "Greater production and maximum efficiency can be obtained by trade and specialization through profit-seeking entrepreneurs

who bear the consequences of their actions in terms of gains and losses . . . . [And] the best State is the one that has minimal bureaucracy, minimum mercenary armies to keep law and order, and minimal taxation on its citizens to finance the activities of the State." Selim Cafer Karatas, "The Economic Theory of Ibn Khaldun and the Rise and Fall of Nations," MuslimHeritage .com, May 18, 2006.

39. Stephen Glain, "Islam in Office," *Newsweek International*, July 3, 2006.

CHAPTER FOUR: THE MEDIEVAL WAR OF IDEAS (II)

1. Christopher Melchert, "The Adversaries of Ahmad Ibn Hanbal," *Arabica*, tome 44, fasc. 2 (April 1997), pp. 234–37.

2. Ibid., p. 240.

3. Ibid., p. 236.

4. Qur'an 39:12, Bewley translation.

5. Noel James Coulson, *A History of Islamic Law* (Edinburgh: Edinburgh University Press, 1994), p. 71.

6. Michael Cooperson, *Classical Arabic Biography: The Heirs of the Prophets in the Age of Al-Mamun* (Cambridge, UK: Cambridge University Press, 2000), p. 112.

7. The Arabic principle is "al-asl fi-l-ashiya al-ibaha." Ramadan, *Radical Reform*, p. 89.

8. David de Santillana, "Law and Society," in *The Legacy of Islam*, ed. T. Arnold and A. Guillaume (London: Oxford University Press, 1931), pp. 295–99; quoted in Marshall G. S. Hodgson, *The Venture of Islam*, vol. 2, *The Expansion of Islam in the Middle Periods* (Chicago: University of Chicago Press, 1977), p. 352 (footnote).

9. An article on an Islamist website has the title: "The Messenger Muhammad . . . Is Our Example—Did He Ever Vote?" It argues: "Only actions based upon the Shar'iah are accepted by Allah . . . , and certainly the Messenger Muhammad . . . never voted for anyone in the Quraish parliament in his time." http://www.islamic-truth.co.uk/islamicstore/pdf_files/Did_ SAAW_vote.pdf.

10. Melchert, "The Adversaries of Ahmad Ibn Hanbal," pp. 248–49.

11. Küng, *Islam*, p. 273.

12. Hasan Hanefi, "Geleneksel İslam Düşüncesindeki Otoriteryenliğin Epistemolojik, Ontolojik, Ahlaki, Siyasi ve Tarihi Kökenleri Üzerine" [On the Epistemological, Ontological, Moral, Political, and Historical Sources of Authoritarianism in Traditional Islamic Thought], trans. İlhami Güler, *İslamiyat* 2, no. 22 (April–June 1999): 34.

13. Beytullah Çetiner, "Hüküm Vermede Hadisin Kullanılışı" [The Use of Hadith in Jurisprudence], *Anadolu* 4, no. 4 (Winter 1994).

14. Suleiman Ali Mourad, *Early Islam Between Myth and History: al-Hasan al-*

Basri (d. 110AH/728CE) and the Formation of His Legacy in Classical Islamic Scholarship (Leiden: Brill, 2006), p. 163.

15. Qur'an 18:110, Shakir translation.

16. Qur'an 11:31, Shakir translation.

17. Küng, *Islam*, p. 222.

18. John Kelsay, "Divine Command Ethics in Early Islam: Al-shafi'i and the Problem of Guidance," *The Journal of Religious Ethics* 22, no. 1 (Spring 1994): 110.

19. For a critique of the theory of abrogation, and the argument that no Qur'anic verse is in fact abrogated, see Abdulaziz A. Sachedina, *The Prolegomena to the Qur'an* (New York: Oxford University Press, 1998), pp. 186–248.

20. Rodinson, *Islam and Capitalism*, pp. 138, 137.

21. Schacht, *Introduction to Islamic Law*, p. 35.

22. Lewis, *The Middle East*, p. 210.

23. Hodgson, *Venture of Islam*, vol. 1, pp. 342–43.

24. Qur'an 20:115–121.

25. See Fatima Mernissi, *The Veil and the Male Elite: A Feminist Interpretation of Women's Rights in Islam* (New York: Basic Books, 1992); Hidayet Şefkatli Tuksal, *Kadın Karşıtı Söylemin İslam Geleneğindeki İzdüşümleri* [The Impact of Misogynist Rhetoric in Islamic Tradition] (Ankara: Kitâbiyat, 2001).

26. Hourani, *History of the Arab Peoples*, p. 56.

27. W. Montgomery Watt, *Freewill and Predestination in Early Islam* (London: Luzac and Co., 1948), pp. 17–30.

28. Mohammad Omar Farooq, "Riba, Interest and Six Hadiths: Do We Have a Definition or a Conundrum?," *Review of Islamic Economics* 13, no. 1 (2009): 105.

29. Timur Kuran, professor of economics and Islamic studies at Duke University, notes: "Starting around the tenth century, Islamic legal institutions, which had benefitted the Middle Eastern economy in the early centuries of Islam, began to act as a drag on development by slowing or blocking the emergence of central features of modern economic life—including private capital accumulation, corporations, large-scale production, and impersonal exchange." Timur Kuran, *The Long Divergence: How Islamic Law Held Back the Middle East* (Princeton, NJ: Princeton University Press, 2010).

30. See Friedmann, *Tolerance and Coercion in Islam*, pp. 197–98; Bat Ye'or, "Jews and Christians under Islam: Dhimmitude and Marcionism," published in French as "Juifs et chrétiens sous l'islam: Dhimmitude et marcionisme," by Bat Ye'or, *Commentaire*, no. 97 (Spring 2002). (Translation available at http://www.dhimmitude.org/archive/by_dhimmitude_marcionism_en.pdf.) Duncan B. MacDonald also notes: "The harsher views developed by western Muslims, and especially by the theologians of Spain, were due, on the other hand, to Augustinian and Roman influence." Duncan B. Mac-

Donald, *Development of Muslim Theology, Jurisprudence and Constitutional Theory* (New York: Charles Scribner's Sons, 1903), p. 132.

31. Afsaruddin, *First Muslims*, p. 116.

32. Ann K. S. Lambton, "A Nineteenth Century View of Jihād," *Studia Islamica* 32 (1970), p. 181.

33. "The conflicting Qur'anic verses cannot prove an evolution of the concept or sanction for religiously authorized warring in Islam from a nonaggressive to a militant stance. To suggest that they do is nothing more than an interpretation." Reuven Firestone, *Jihad: The Origin of Holy War in Islam* (New York: Oxford University Press, 1999), p. 64.

34. Afsaruddin, *First Muslims*, p. 118.

35. Ibid.

36. Martin et al., *Defenders of Reason in Islam*, p. 15.

37. Lyons, *House of Wisdom*, p. 77.

38. Karabell, *People of the Book*, p. 48.

39. Cooperson, *Classical Arabic Biography*, pp. 34, 39.

40. That comment is by Josef van Ess, who has been cited as "the world's most distinguished scholar of classical Islamic philosophy." See Josef van Ess, *The Flowering of Muslim Theology* (Cambridge: Harvard University Press, 2006), p. 5.

41. This interpretation is suggested by Nimrod Hurvitz in "Mihna as Self-Defense," *Studia Islamica* 92 (2001), pp. 93–111. Here, Hurvitz argues that the winners of the Mutazilite-Traditionist confrontation, i.e., the latter camp, wrote its history and showed itself as the persecuted victim, whereas a closer reading reveals that the situation was much more complex: "Despite the centrality of the Hanbali-Sunni narrative and its posthumous victory, it was not the sole historiographic trend among Muslims who wrote about the *mihna*. The *mutakallimun* [Mutazilite theologians] viewed this event differently and their writings give vent to their interpretation. Their emphasis was on the missing piece of the Hanbali-Sunni narrative: its historic background. They did not see the *mihna* as the outcome of court intrigue nor did they emphasize the initiative of any single individual. Rather, they focused on wider intellectual and political developments such as inter-factional strife among the 'ulama. They maintained that during the decades that preceded the *mihna*, the *mutakallimun* and *muhaddithun* [People of the Hadith] jockeyed for power. In the course of this struggle the *muhaddithun* succeeded in landing a sequence of hard blows on the *mutakallimun*. After al-Ma'mun came to power and extended his support to the *mutakallimun*, the pendulum of power swung in their favor and it was their chance to strike at the *muhaddithun*. Such a narrative implies that the *mutakallimun* were not the original aggressors but rather the victims of the *muhaddithun* . . . . It is the *mihna* that enabled the *mutakallimun* to raise their heads, speak their minds and establish themselves in their proper role in society. Such justice could come about only

after the *mihna* reversed the power relations between the previously perse-cuted *mutakallimun* and their oppressors, the anthropomorphists. It was only when the *muhaddithun*'s scare tactics collided with the more powerful impe-rial apparatus, that they changed their behavior and in some cases fostered a respectable debate with the *mutakallimun*." (pp. 95–96, 100)

"Therefore," concludes Hurvitz on p. 102, "the *mihna* is not so much about an article of faith such as the createdness of the Qur'an, as it is about the *mutakallimun*'s right, better yet obligation, to debate its createdness."

42. S. M. Deen, *Science Under Islam: Rise, Decline and Revival* (www.lulu.com, 2007), p. 121.

43. Christopher Melchert, "How Hanafism Came to Originate in Kufa and Traditionalism in Medina," *Islamic Law and Society* 6, no. 3 (1999): 340.

44. Al-Tabari, quoted in Norman A. Stillman, *The Jews of Arab Lands: A His-tory and Source Book* (Philadelphia: Jewish Publication Society of America, 1979), p. 168.

45. Jonathan P. Berkey, *The Formation of Islam: Religion and Society in the Near East, 600–1800* (Cambridge, UK: Cambridge University Press, 2003), p. 129.

46. Ibn al-Athir, *Al-Kamil* 8:307; quoted in Nimrod Hurvitz, "From Schol-arly Circles to Mass Movements: The Formation of Legal Communities in Islamic Societies," *American Historical Review* 108, no. 4 (October 2003): 1003–4.

47. Ibn al-Jawzi, *al-Muntazam fi ta'rikh al-muluk wa al-umam*, vol. 15 (Beirut: Dar al-kutub al-ilmiyya, 1992), pp. 125–26; quoted in Eric J. Hanne, *Putting the Caliph in His Place: Power, Authority, and the Late Abbasid Caliphate* (Madison, NJ: Fairleigh Dickinson University Press, 2007), p. 70.

48. Ibid.

49. Hodgson, *Venture of Islam*, vol. 2, p. 288.

50. Ibid.

51. R. H. Lossin, "Iraq's Ruined Library Soldiers On," *The Nation*, April 9, 2008.

52. David McDowall, *A Modern History of the Kurds* (London: I. B. Tauris, 1996), p. 24.

53. According to British historian Christopher Catherwood, "Western Europe was fortunate that the Mongols turned back before going on to seize the rest of Europe. One only has to look at the history of Russia, the part of Europe that was conquered by the Mongols, to see the devastating effects that a Mongol invasion could have. Westerners should realize that there was nothing intrinsically better about them, and that if Hulagu had not stopped, the Mongol Empire would have stretched from the Pacific to the Atlantic. We in the West are not in any way superior, simply very lucky!" Christopher Catherwood, *A Brief History of the Middle East* (New York: Carroll & Graf, 2006), p. 112.

54. David Levering Lewis, *God's Crucible: Islam and the Making of Europe, 570 to 1215* (New York: W. W. Norton, 2008), pp. 202-7.

55. The Almoravids of North Africa, who arrived in Muslim Spain to help the Muslims against their Christian enemies, soon established their own dominance and imposed their own strict version of Islam. They did not even tolerate the works of Imam al-Ghazali, a Traditionist thinker by any reckoning, and they burned his works publicly in Cordoba in 1109. Menocal, *Ornament of the World*, p. 44.

56. Estimates on the number of books burnt in Granada in 1499 vary from five thousand to a million. Haig A. Bosmajian, *Burning Books* (Jefferson, NC: McFarland & Company, 2006), p. 64. Turkish historian Hilmi Ziya Ülken also gives the number as eighty thousand. Hilmi Ziya Ülken, *İslam Felsefesi, Kaynakları ve Tesirleri* (Istanbul: İş Bankası Books, 1967), p. 317.

57. Fazlur Rahman, *Islam* (Chicago: University of Chicago Press, 1979), pp. 39–40.

58. Fazlur Rahman, "The Status of the Individual in Islam," *Islamic Studies* 5, no. 4 (1996): 319–30; in Bryan S. Turner, ed., *Islam: Critical Concepts in Sociology*, vol. 1 (Oxford: Routledge, 2003), pp. 240, 241.

59. According to Fazlur Rahman, by emphasizing the religious experience of the individual, Sufism upheld the "individualist trend" in Islam. Ibid., p. 241.

60. Karen Armstrong, *A History of God: The 4000-Year Quest of Judaism, Christianity and Islam* (New York: Ballantine Books, 1993), p. 225.

61. "Contrary to all appearances, Sufism and the Mu'tazila share common roots. Al-Hasan al-Basri (d. 110/728), considered one of the founding fathers of Sufism, is known to have been the teacher of Wasil b. Ata, who is associated with the origins of the Mu'tazila . . . . [Later on] [t]here were some Mu'tazile who wore the woolen Sufi frock and manifested ascetic traits . . . . However, as the Mu'tazila and the ahl al-sunna wa'l-jama'a developed into separate denominations, with the Sufis by and large being members of the Sunni community, their common heritage was soon lost sight of. Traces of a corps of Sufis within the Mu'tazila cease to be discernible." Florian Sobieroj, "The Mutazila and Sufism," in *Islamic Mysticism Contested: Thirteen Centuries of Controversies and Polemics*, ed. Frederick De Jong and Bernd Radtke (Leiden/Boston: Brill, 1999), pp. 68, 70. Also see Osman Aydınlı, "Ascetic and devotional elements in the Mutazilite tradition: The Sufi Mu'tazilites," *The Muslim World* 97, no. 2 (2007): 174–89.

62. "Maturidi's reasoning is nearer to that of the Mu'tazila than Ash'ari's." Joseph Schacht, "New Sources for the History of Muhammadan Theology," *Studia Islamica* 1 (1953): 35.

63. Marshall G. S. Hodgson, *The Venture of Islam*, vol. 3, *The Gunpowder Empires and Modern Times* (Chicago: University of Chicago Press, 1977), p. 181.

CHAPTER FIVE: THE DESERT BENEATH THE ICEBERG

1. X. de Planhol, *The Cambridge History of Islam*, vol. 2B (Cambridge, UK: Cambridge University Press, 1970), p. 443.

2. Francis Robinson, ed., *The Cambridge Illustrated History of the Islamic World* (Cambridge, UK: Cambridge University Press, 1996); Catherwood, *Brief History of the Middle East*, p. 92.

3. Hanefi, "Geleneksel İslam Düşüncesindeki Otoriteryenliğin Epistemolojik, Ontolojik, Ahlaki, Siyasi ve Tarihi Kökenleri Üzerine," *İslamiyat*, p. 28.

4. Fernand Braudel makes the same suggestion in *A History of Civilizations*, p. 85.

5. C. Dodgson, *Tertullian* (Oxford: John Henry Parker, 1842), p. 442; quoted in Rodinson, *Islam and Capitalism*, p. 125.

6. David Bukay, *From Muhammad to Bin Laden* (New Brunswick, NJ: Transaction Publishers, 2008), p. 186. I should note that I disagree with this author's depiction of Islam as incompatible with democracy in toto.

7. Taha Akyol, *Hariciler ve Hizbullah*, p. 17.

8. Halim Barakat, *The Arab World: Society, Culture, and State* (Berkeley: University of California Press, 1993), pp. 50, 53.

9. The quote is from Ali al-Wardi, cited in Barakat, *The Arab World*, p. 53.

10. Hadith reported by both al-Bukhari and al-Muslim, quoted in Ramadan, *Radical Reform*, p. 188.

11. Qur'an 9:97, Bewley translation, with Arabic words anglicized.

12. W. Montgomery Watt, *Islamic Political Thought: The Basic Concepts* (Edinburgh: Edinburgh University Press, 1980), p. 57.

13. Ibid.

14. Clive Foss, "Islam's First Terrorists," *History Today*, December 2007.

15. Küng, *Islam*, p. 223.

16. Ramadan, *Radical Reform*, p. 53.

17. Mohammad Hashim Kamali, "The Shari'a: Law as the Way of God," in *Voices of Islam*, ed. Vincent J. Cornell (Westport, CT: Praeger Publishers, 2007), p. 159.

18. Ramadan, *Radical Reform*, pp. 50–51.

19. Ibid., p. 192.

20. Cooperson, *Classical Arabic Biography*, p. 151.

21. Ibid., p. 113.

22. Hodgson, *Venture of Islam*, vol. 1, p. 391. Hodgson notes, with reference to another historian, that the term might also mean "redundant speech."

23. S. Sabari, *Mouvements Populaires à Baghdad a l'epoque 'Abbasside ix–xi siècle* (Paris: Adrien Maisonneuve, 1981), pp. 102–3; referred to in Nimrod Hurvitz, "Schools of Law and Historical Context: Re-Examining the Formation of the Hanbalī Madhhab," *Islamic Law and Society* 7, no. 1 (2000): 50–51.

24. Michael Cook, *Commanding Right and Forbidding Wrong in Islamic Thought* (Cambridge, UK: Cambridge University Press, 2001), p. 87.

25. Hodgson, *Venture of Islam*, vol. 1, p. 369. This is most curious, because nothing in the Qur'an bans sculpture; there is indeed a passage in which the "statues" that Prophet Suleyman (King Solomon) had built for himself are mentioned in a positive tone. Qur'an 34:13 (Bewley translation) reads: "They made for him [Suleyman] anything he wished: high arches and statues, huge dishes like cisterns, great built-in cooking vats. 'Work, family of Dawud, in thankfulness!' But very few of My servants are thankful." And if there is any form that can be disapproved through a literal reading of the Qur'an, that is poetry. "And as for poets," reads Qur'an 26:224 (Bewley translation), referring to the Arab "poets" who mocked the Qur'an, "it is the misled who follow them."

26. Joseph Loconte, "Economic Prosperity: A Step of Faith," *The American*, November 10, 2009.

27. Mahmood Ibrahim, *Merchant Capital and Islam* (Austin: University of Texas Press, 1990), pp. 192, 193.

28. Ibid., p. 192.

29. Ibid., p. 193.

30. Ibid., p. 194.

31. Mahmood Ibrahim, "Religious Inquisition as Social Policy: The Persecution of the 'Zanadiqa' in the Early Abbasid Caliphate," *Arab Studies Quarterly* 16, no. 2 (1994): 53–54.

32. Maya Shatzmiller, *Labour in the Medieval Islamic World* (Leiden: Brill, 1994), pp. 255–318; quoted in Kuran, "The Islamic Commercial Crisis," p. 425.

33. Binder, *Islamic Liberalism*, p. 222.

34. Braudel, *History of Civilizations*, p. 87.

35. Ibid., p. 69 ff. Also see Abdelwahab Meddeb, "Islam and Its Discontents: An Interview with Frank Berberich," *October* 99 (Winter 2002): 4.

36. Hourani, *History of the Arab Peoples*, p. 98.

37. Schacht, *Introduction to Islamic Law*, p. 17.

38. Muhammad Ibn al-Hajj, *Madkhal Al-shar' Al-sharif* [Introduction to the Noble Law], vol. 1 (Cairo, 1929), p. 79. Quoted in Jonathan P. Berkey, "Tradition, Innovation and the Social Construction of Knowledge in the Medieval Islamic Near East," *Past and Present* 146 (February 1995): 42.

39. George F. Hourani, "Islamic and Non-Islamic Origins of Mu'tazilite Ethical Rationalism," *International Journal of Middle East Studies* 7, no. 1 (January 1976): 87.

40. Ibn Khaldun, *The Muqaddimah: An Introduction to History*, trans. Franz Rosenthal, vol. 2 (Princeton, NJ: Princeton University Press, 1967), p. 353.

41. Jean-Baptiste Chardin, "author of one of the greatest travel books of all time," seems to be "a highly credible link between Ibn Khaldun and Montes-

quieu." Warren E. Gates, "The Spread of Ibn Khaldûn's Ideas on Climate and Culture," *Journal of the History of Ideas* 28, no. 3 (July–September 1967): 422.

42. Adam Smith "underscored the role of geography in shaping the growth of commercial arrangements in parts of ancient Greece. Not only, he claimed, did the relatively easy access to the sea allow these city-states to trade with each other, but they also enjoyed a landscape that lent itself more easily to self-defense against more bellicose, agrarian peoples." Samuel Gregg, *The Commercial Society* (Lanham, MD: Lexington Books, 2007), pp. 149–50.

43. William Harmon Norton, "The Influence of the Desert on Early Islam," *The Journal of Religion* 4, no. 4 (July 1924): 395–96. Norton's approach was quite Orientalist, in the Edward Saidian sense, and not admiring of the Qur'an either, but his distinction between the Qur'anic text and the environment-influenced mindset is notable.

44. Sabri Ülgener, *Zihniyet ve Din: İslam, Tasavvuf ve Çözülme Devri İktisat Ahlakı* [Mentality and Religion: Islam, Sufism and the Ethics of Economy in the Era of Decline] (Istanbul: Derin Publications, 2006), p. 10.

45. Rodinson, *Islam and Capitalism*, p. 153.

46. Muhammed Abid el-Cabiri, *Arap-İslam Aklının Oluşumu* [The Formation of the Arab-Islamic Mind] (Istanbul: Kitabevi Publishing, 1997).

47. Mehmet Yaşar Soyalan, "Egemen İslam Kültüründeki Estetik Yoksunluğu Üzerine" [On the Lack of Aesthetics in the Dominant Islamic Culture], *Bilge Adam*, September 2006.

48. Erhard Rostlund, "Twentieth-Century Magic," in *Readings in Cultural Geography*, ed. Philip L. Wagner and Marvin W. Mikesell (Chicago: University of Chicago Press, 1962), p. 49.

49. See Dwayne Woods, "Latitude or Rectitude: Geographical or Institutional Determinants of Development," *Third World Quarterly* 25, no. 8 (2004): 1401–14. Also see Eric Jones, *The European Miracle: Environments, Economies and Geopolitics in the History of Europe and Asia* (Cambridge, UK: Cambridge University Press, 2003).

50. Jared M. Diamond, *Guns, Germs, and Steel: The Fates of Human Societies* (New York: W. W. Norton, 1997), p. 352. The other book is David S. Landes, *The Wealth and Poverty of Nations: Why Some Are So Rich and Some So Poor* (New York: W. W. Norton, 1998).

51. J. Russell Smith, "The Desert's Edge," *Bulletin of the American Geographical Society* 47, no. 11 (1915): 831. Smith also argued that aridity was a hindrance to courtesy: "'After you, sir,' means, in the long run, that there is enough for both."

52. For a famous example of this argument, see Karl Wittfogel, *Oriental Despotism: A Comparative Study of Total Power* (orig. published 1957) (New York: Vintage Books, 1981).

53. Fareed Zakaria, *The Future of Freedom: Illiberal Democracy at Home and Abroad* (New York: W. W. Norton, 2003), p. 36.

54. Ibid.

55. *Encyclopedia of Islam*, vol. 3, p. 1088.

56. Hassan Shaygannik, "Mode of Production in Medieval Iran," *Iranian Studies* 18, no. 1 (Winter 1985): 81.

57. Ira M. Lapidus, eminent historian of Islamic history, agrees that patrimonial authoritarianism is a late development in Islam, rooted in the rise of Islamic empires. Under these empires, he explains, the classical Islamic theory of sovereignty retreated to provide a space for a theory of patrimonialism where "power is not an expression of the total society but the prerogative of certain individuals or groups." This historical legacy of authoritarianism, Lapidus argues interestingly, continued into the modern period, as, for example, "many features of the Turkish republic and the Ataturk program may be derived from the patrimonial premises of the Ottoman Empire." Ira Lapidus, "The Golden Age: The Political Concepts of Islam," *Annals of the American Academy of Political and Social Science*, November 1992, pp. 17, 23.

58. Bryan S. Turner, *Weber and Islam* (London: Routledge & Kegan Paul, 1974), pp. 142–43; cited in Binder, *Islamic Liberalism*, pp. 222–23.

59. Quotes are from Binder, *Islamic Liberalism*, p. 221.

CHAPTER SIX: THE OTTOMAN REVIVAL

1. Sadık Albayrak, *Türkiye'de Din Kavgası* [The Fight over Religion in Turkey], Istanbul, 1973, p. 100; translated and quoted in Necmettin Doğan, *The Origins of Liberalism and Islamism in the Ottoman Empire (1908–1914)*. Dissertation zur Erlangung des Doktorgrades der Philosophie am Institut für Soziologie, Fachbereich Politik- und Sozialwissenschaften der Freien Universität Berlin, December 2006, p. 121.

2. One exceptional bright spot was the seventeenth-century Mulla Sadra, a Shiite thinker from Iran who synthesized Aristotelian logic, Sufi metaphysics, and classical Islamic theology, with a strong emphasis on the Qur'an. He was also notable for defining "change," and not stability, as the essence of the created world. For more, see Ibrahim Kalin, *Knowledge in Later Islamic Philosophy: Mulla Sadra on Existence, Intellect, and Intuition* (New York: Oxford University Press, 2010).

3. Cevdet Paşa, *Tezakir*, vol. 1, 2nd ed. (Ankara: Türk Tarih Kurumu Yayınları, 1986), pp. 111, 113.

4. Ibid., p. 118.

5. 12. FO 78/3131, Zohrab to Salisbury no. 1, political and secret, Jidda, March 17, 1880; quoted in Tufan Buzpınar, "Vying for Power and Influence in the Hijaz: Ottoman Rule, the Last Emirate of Abdulmuttalib and the British (1880–1882)," *The Muslim World* 95 (January 2005), p. 2.

6. Cevdet Paşa, *Tezakir*, vol. 1, pp. 137–38.

7. Ibid., pp. 111, 113.

8. Ibid., p. 130.

9. Lewis, *The Middle East*, p. 88.

10. The Şeyh-ül İslam was Zembilli Ali Efendi. Halide Edip Adıvar, *Türkiye'de Şark-Garp ve Amerikan Tesirleri* [East-West and American Influences in Turkey] (Istanbul: Can Books, 2009 (reprint of 1955 edition), p. 58.

11. Catherwood, *Brief History of the Middle East*, p. 124; Karabell, *People of the Book*, p. 177.

12. Karabell, p. 184.

13. Bulgarian historian Maria Todorova, with reference to author Holm Sundhaussen, speaks of negative Balkan perceptions about the Ottoman Empire, such as "the 'golden' pre-Ottoman period" and the "Turkish yoke," as "myths." (Maria Nikolaeva Todorova, *Balkan Identities: Nation and Memory* [London: C. Hurst and Co., 2004, p. 7].) American historian Zachary Karabell concurs: "The reputation of the Ottomans [besides European prejudice] suffered from the nationalist movements that swept the Balkans and the Near East in the nineteenth and twentieth centuries. First the Greeks in the 1820s and then the Hungarians, Serbs, Bulgarians, Romanians, and, finally, the Arabs of the Near East defined themselves as nations that had been conquered, brutalized, and silenced by Ottoman autocrats. For the Greeks and other Balkan peoples, there was an added religious element: the Muslim Ottomans, they claimed, had oppressed Christian peoples. Even the Arabs, who caught the infectious bug of nationalism just before World War I, distanced themselves from the Ottomans, though their main bone of contention was more ethnic than religious." Karabell, *People of the Book*, p. 167.

14. Lucien Gubbay, *Sunlight and Shadow: The Jewish Experience of Islam* (New York: Other Press, 2000), p. 99.

15. http://www.jewishvirtuallibrary.org/jsource/vjw/Turkey.html.

16. Halil İnalcık, *Essays in Ottoman History* (Istanbul: Eren Publishing, 1988), pp. 231, 245.

17. Halil İnalcik and Donald Quataert, eds., *An Economic and Social History of the Ottoman Empire, 1300–1914* (Cambridge, UK: Cambridge University Press, 1997), p. 492.

18. Abdullahi Ahmed An-Na'im, *Islam and the Secular State* (Cambridge: Harvard University Press), 2008, p. 185.

19. İnalcık, *Essays in Ottoman History*, pp. 235–36.

20. Prof. Ahmet Yaman, "Osmanlı Pozitif Hukukunun Şer'iliği Tartışmalarına Eleştirel bir Katkı" [A Critical Contribution to the Debates on the Shariah-Compliance of Ottoman Positive Law], *İslamiyat* 8, no. 1 (January–March 2005): 116.

21. A statement found in some of the *fatwas* of Ottoman Şeyh-ül İslams reads: "This is not a matter of the Shariah; the decision of the [sultan] has to be followed." [*Şer'i maslahat degildir, ulu'l emr nasıl emretmişse öyle hareket lazımdır.*]

Taha Akyol, *Osmanlı'da ve İran'da Mezhep ve Devlet* [State and Religion in the Ottoman Empire and Iran] (Istanbul: Doğan Publishing, 1999), pp. 149–50.

22. Yusuf Halaçoğlu, *Osmanlılarda Devlet Teşkilatı ve Sosyal Yapı* [State Organization and Social Structure among the Ottomans] (Ankara: Türk Tarih Kurumu, 1995), pp. 188–90.

23. Berdal Aral, "The Idea of Human Rights as Perceived in the Ottoman Empire," *Human Rights Quarterly* 26, no. 2 (2004): 460.

24. Kemal H. Karpat, ed., *Ottoman Past and Today's Turkey* (Leiden/Boston: Brill, 2000), p. 142.

25. Ibid., pp. 137–40. Karpat (pp. 139, 140) criticizes the "mistaken picture" about guilds in the Ottoman Empire (that they were "invented and totally controlled by the state") and underlines the fact that the guilds were "really autonomous." These craftsmen associations were "amazingly similar to the medieval European guilds" and were governed by guild law, which "did not emanate from the government. Rather, the government had scant knowledge about it, and all parties concerned viewed it as emanating from below."

26. Niyazi Berkes, *The Development of Secularism in Turkey* (Montreal: McGill University Press, 1964), p. 34.

27. Gönül Pınar, ed., *İslam ve Modernite* [Islam and Modernity] (Istanbul: Remzi Publishing, 2007), p. 195.

28. Bernard Lewis and Benjamin Braude, eds., *Christians and Jews in the Ottoman Empire: The Functioning of a Plural Society* (New York: Holmes & Meier Publishers, 1982), p. 388.

29. Halil İnalcık, *From Empire to Republic: Essays on Ottoman and Turkish Social History* (Istanbul: Isis Press, 1995), p. 132.

30. For an evaluation of the Islamic spirit of the Tanzimat, see Butrus Abu-Manneh, "The Islamic Roots of the Gülhane Rescripts," *Die Welt des Islams* 34 (1994): 173–203.

31. See Doğan, *Origins of Liberalism and Islamism in the Ottoman Empire*, pp. 158, 194.

32. Mehmet Seyitdanlioğlu, "The Rise and Development of the Liberal Thought in Turkey," *Hacettepe Üniversitesi Edebiyat Fakültesi Dergisi* (special issue prepared for the seventy-fifth anniversary of the Turkish Republic, 1997).

33. Sadık Rıfat Paşa was "well within the framework of traditional Islamic political thought." Bernard Lewis, *The Emergence of Modern Turkey* (London: Oxford University Press, 1961). p. 130.

34. The name of the legislation is "Tabiyet-i Osmaniye Kanunnamesi." Bilal Eryılmaz, *Osmanlı Devletinde Gayrimüslim Tebaanın Yönetimi* [The Administration of Non-Muslim Subjects in the Ottoman Empire] (Istanbul: Risali Yayınları, 1996), pp. 147–50.

35. Tarık Zafer Tunaya, *Türkiye'de Siyasal Partiler*, vol. 1 [Political Parties in Turkey] (Istanbul: Hürriyet Vakfı Yayınları, 1984), pp. 586–90.

36. Carter V. Findley, "The Acid Test of Ottomanism: The Acceptance of Non-Muslims in the Late Ottoman Bureaucracy," in *Christians and Jews in the Ottoman Empire*, ed. Braude and Lewis, p. 365.

37. Roderic H. Davison, "Turkish Attitudes Concerning Christian-Muslim Equality in the Nineteenth Century," *American Historical Review* 59, no. 4 (July 1954): 854.

38. Ibid., p. 853.

39. Ibid., p. 855.

40. Ibid., p. 857.

41. Cyrus Hamlin, *Among the Turks* (New York: Carter and Brothers, 1878), pp. 80–81; quoted in Selim Deringil, "'There Is No Compulsion in Religion': On Conversion and Apostasy in the Late Ottoman Empire: 1839–1856," *Comparative Studies in Society and History* 42, no. 3 (July 2000): 551.

42. Mustafa Avcı, *Osmanlı Hukukunda Suçlar ve Cezalar* [Crimes and Punishments in Ottoman Law] (Istanbul: Gökkubbe Publishing, 2004), p. 389.

43. BBA HR. MKT 3/65; 16 Rebiyulahir 1260/5 May 1840. Foreign Ministry to Commanders of Akka and Sayda; quoted in Deringil, "'There Is No Compulsion in Religion,'" p. 560.

44. Ezel Kural Shaw, *History of the Ottoman Empire and Modern Turkey*, vol. 2 (Cambridge, UK: Cambridge University Press, 1977), p. 125.

45. Hamlin to Anderson, September 5, 1857, ABCFM, Armenian Mission, V, no. 276; quoted in Davison, "Turkish Attitudes Concerning Christian-Muslim Equality in the Nineteenth Century," p. 860.

46. Leila Fawaz, *Occasion for War: Civil Conflict in the Lebanon and Damascus in 1860* (Berkeley: University of California Press, 1994), p. 152; quoted in Deringil, "'There Is No Compulsion in Religion,'" p. 559.

47. Deringil, "'There Is No Compulsion in Religion,'" p. 559.

48. Ibid., p. 565.

49. Ibid., p. 567.

50. Mustafa Akyol, "God & Turkey: Church and State in Istanbul," *National Review Online*, March 4, 2005.

51. Doğan, *Origins of Liberalism and Islamism in the Ottoman Empire*, p. 151.

52. Karpat, *Ottoman Past and Today's Turkey*, pp. xi, xii.

53. Şerif Mardin, *The Genesis of Young Ottoman Thought: A Study in the Modernization of Turkish Political Ideas* (Princeton, NJ: Princeton University Press, 2000), p. 119.

54. *Ibret, no. 46 of 1872*, cited in Lewis, *Emergence of Modern Turkey*, p. 167.

55. Ibid., p. 149.

56. James Madison, "The Most Dreaded Enemy of Liberty," *Essays on Liberty*, vol. 1 (Irvington-on-Hudson, NY: Foundation for Economic Education, 1952), p. 88.

57. This was true for the premodern era as well. Medieval Islamic history reveals "tolerance in secure times" and "intolerance in times of threat." Kara-

bell, *People of the Book*, p. 67. In the modern era, liberal ideas and attitudes flourished in the late Ottoman Empire, but they waned with the destruction of the empire and the colonization of Muslim lands, as we will see later in this chapter.

58. Karpat, *Ottoman Past and Today's Turkey*, p. 17.

59. Yusuf Akçura, a prominent Turkish nationalist at the beginning of the twentieth century, first used the term *İslamcılık* (Islamism) in 1904 to define Abdülhamid's policies. Ismail Kara, *Türkiye'de Islamcılık Düsüncesi* [Islamist Thought in Turkey] (Istanbul: Kitabevi Publishing, 1997), p. 31.

60. All the information and quotations about Sultan Abdülhamid's role in the Philippines are from Kemal Karpat, *The Politicization of Islam: Reconstructing Identity, State, Faith, and Community in the Late Ottoman State* (New York: Oxford University Press, 2000), pp. 234–35.

61. Karpat, *Ottoman Past and Today's Turkey*, p. 16.

62. Ibid.

63. Schacht, *Introduction to Islamic Law*, p. 93.

64. Taha Akyol, *Medine'den Lozan'a: 'Çok-Hukuklu Sistem' in Tarihteki Deneyleri* [From Medina to Lausanne: The Historical Experiments with Multiple Legal Systems] (Istanbul: Milliyet Publications), p. 42.

65. Karpat, *Ottoman Past and Today's Turkey*, p. 3.

66. Two events were particularly significant. The first was the Kuleli Incident of 1859, a failed conspiracy by forty-odd participants—many of them army officers and Muslim theology professors and students—to kill the sultan for allowing equality between Muslims and Christians. The second (and more important) one was the Privates' Rebellion of April 1909, which was a reaction to the Second Constitutional Period but even more so to the growing domination of the Committee of Union and Progress (CUP), the main Young Turk organization.

67. Rossella Bottoni, "The Origins of Secularism in Turkey." Paper presented at the 28th Conference of the International Society for the Sociology of Religion, Zagreb, July 18–22, 2005. Also see Ahmet Cihan, *Reform Çağında Osmanlı İlmiye Sınıfı* [The Ottoman Religious Scholarly Class in the Reform Age] (Istanbul: Birey Publishing, 2004), pp. 275–88.

68. It was Mustafa Kemal (later Atatürk) who claimed in 1924 that the Ottoman Empire's 250-year-long delay in importing printing presses was due to "religious bigotry." But even Niyazi Berkes, a Turkish historian with secularist sympathies, notes: "Calligraphers constituted the main opposition group" to the printing press, and "leading *ulema* of the time, including the Şeyhul-Islam Abdullah, wrote favourable comments" when İbrahim Müteferrika, the first mass publisher in the Ottoman Empire, asked in 1727 for an imperial edict that "the act of printing be declared by the Şeyhul-Islam as commendable and useful for the Muslims and in accord with the glorious Şeriat."

Niyazi Berkes, *The Development of Secularism in Turkey* (New York: Routledge, 1998), p. 40.

69. Aynur Demirdek, "In Pursuit of the Ottoman Women's Movement," in *Deconstructing Images of "The Turkish Woman*," ed. Zehra F. Arat (Basingstoke, UK: Palgrave Macmillan, 2000), p. 79.

70. Bahithat al-Badiya, "A Lecture in the Club of the Umma Party," in *Modernist Islam, 1840–1940: A Sourcebook*, ed. Charles Kurzman (Oxford: Oxford University Press, 2002), p. 76.

71. In 1917, the Ottoman Empire adopted a new family law that forbade the marriage of minors and gave women the right to divorce their husbands. It also allowed women, at the time of betrothal, to write into the marriage contract that if the husband took another wife, her marriage would be immediately null and void. This effectively ended polygamy, for most women increasingly chose this option.

72. Hilmi Ziya Ülken, *Türkiye'de Çağdaş Düşünce Tarihi* [History of Modern Thought in Turkey], vol. 2 (Istanbul: Ülken Yayınları, 1966), pp. 443–93.

73. Mehmet Şener, *İzmirli İsmail Hakkı* (Ankara: Diyanet Vakfı Yayınları, 1996), pp. 22–24.

74. Ibid., pp. 98–100.

75. Qur'an 17:84. The quote is from İsmail Kara, *İslamcıların Siyasi Görüşleri* [The Political Ideas of the Islamists] (Istanbul: İz Publishing, 1994), p. 24.

76. Qur'an 53:39. The quote is from Kara, *İslamcıların Siyasi Görüşleri*, p. 24.

77. Ibid., p. 25.

78. Doktor Hazık, *Din ve Hürriyet* (Istanbul, 1916), p. 9; quoted in Kara, *İslamcıların Siyasi Görüşleri*, p. 44.

79. Ahmed Naim, *İslamiyet'in Esasları, Mazisi ve Hali* [The Principles, the Past and the Current State of Islam] (Istanbul, 1911), p. 373; quoted in Kara, *İslamcıların Siyasi Görüşleri*, p. 25.

80. Sabahattin Bey, *Türkiye Nasıl Kurtarılabilir?* [How Can Turkey Be Saved?] (Istanbul, 1918), pp. 27–28; quoted in Doğan, *Origins of Liberalism and Islamism in the Ottoman Empire*, p. 210.

81. "Doğrudan doğruya Kur'ân'dan alıp, ilhâmı, Asrın idrâkine söyletmeliyiz İslâm'ı." Mehmet Akif Ersoy, *Safahat*, 9th ed. (Istanbul: İnkılâp ve Aka Publishing, 1974), p. 478.

82. Louis de Bernières, *Birds Without Wings* (New York: Random House, 2005), p. 16. (This book is a novel, but the author refers to a historical fact with the quoted slogan.)

83. "In Fear of Greeks, Jews Plead for Aid," *New York Times*, April 3, 1913.

84. Justin McCarthy, *Death and Exile: The Ethnic Cleansing of Ottoman Muslims, 1821–1922* (Princeton, NJ: Darwin Press,1996), p. 1.

85. David Fromkin, *A Peace to End All Peace: The Fall of the Ottoman Empire and the Creation of the Modern Middle East* (New York: Henry Holt, 1989).

86. John Obert Voll, *Islam: Continuity and Change in the Modern World* (Syracuse, NY: Syracuse University Press, 1994), p. 99.

87. Ehud R. Toledano, *Slavery and Abolition in the Ottoman Middle East* (Seattle: University of Washington Press, 1998), p. 118.

88. Charles Kurzman, ed., *Liberal Islam: A Sourcebook* (Oxford: Oxford University Press, 1998), p. 41.

89. His name is spelled Khayr al-Din in most English sources. Albert Hourani summarizes his views in *Arabic Thought in the Liberal Age, 1798–1939* (Cambridge, UK: Cambridge University Press, 1962), p. 90.

90. Ibid., p. 88.

91. *The Liberal Spirit of the Qur'an* was a 1905 book by Sheikh Abdelaziz Thaalbi (1876–1944). See Mohamed Charfi, *Islam and Liberty: The Historical Misunderstanding* (London: Zed Books, 2005), p. 22.

92. Reşid Rıza, *Gerçek İslam'da Birlik* [Unity in True Islam], trans. Hayrettin Karaman (Istanbul: İz Publishing, 2003), p. 114.

93. Toby Lester, "What Is the Qur'an?," *The Atlantic*, January 1999.

94. Bernard Lewis, *Semites and Anti-Semites: An Inquiry into Conflict and Prejudice* (London: Phoenix Giant, 1997), p. 133.

95. Hourani, *Arabic Thought in the Liberal Age*.

96. Ahmed Kanlıdere, *Reform Within Islam: The Tajdid and Jadid Movement Among the Kazan Tatars (1809–1917)* (Istanbul: Eren Publishing, 1997), pp. 69, 75.

97. Armstrong, *Muhammad*, p. 41.

98. Nikki R. Keddie, "The Revolt of Islam, 1700 to 1993," in *Islam: Critical Concepts in Sociology*, vol. 2, ed. Bryan S. Turner (Oxford: Routledge, 2003), p. 89.

99. Ibid., p. 88.

100. Lothrop Stoddard, *The New World of Islam* (Chautauqua, NY: Chautauqua Press, 1922), pp. v, viii.

101. Nasim A. Jawed, *Islam's Political Culture: Religion and Politics in Predivided Pakistan* (Austin: University of Texas Press, 1999), p. 79.

102. "Muslim anti-Semitism is a modern phenomenon and it is a modern anti-Semitism which has a lot to do with the changes within the Muslim and Arab world from the 19th century onwards and with an import of anti-Semitic ideas from Europe, but not with Islam as a religion. The religion was later used to dress this modern anti-Semitism with Islamic clothes." Thomas Schmidinger, "Importing the Protocols of the Elders of Zion: Anti-Semitism in Islamic Societies." Paper presented at the 13th Summer Academy of the Institute for the History of the Jews in Austria, March 4, 2003, http://www.eisca.eu.

103. For an excellent analysis of Islamism as an outcome of the anti-imperialist wave in the Middle East—which was sparked, of course, by Western imperialism—see Fuller, *A World Without Islam*, pp. 243–66.

CHAPTER SEVEN: ROMANS, HERODIANS, AND ZEALOTS

1. Benjamin R. Barber, paper presented at the Istanbul Seminars, organized by *Reset Dialogues on Civilizations*, Istanbul, June 2–6, 2008. Reworded according to author's suggestion.

2. Gavin D. Brockett, "Collective Action and the Turkish Revolution: Towards a Framework for the Social History of the Atatürk Era, 1923–38," *Middle Eastern Studies* 34, no. 4 (October 1998): 49.

3. Ibid., p. 50.

4. Ibid., p. 53.

5. Nur Yalman, "Some Observations on Secularism in Islam: The Cultural Revolution in Turkey," *Daedalus* 102, no. 1 (Winter 1973), p. 161.

6. Lewis, *The Middle East*, p. 311.

7. In *Akl-i Selim* (Istanbul, 1929), p. 393; quoted in M. Şükrü Hanioğlu, "Garbçılar: Their Attitudes toward Religion and Their Impact on the Official Ideology of the Turkish Republic," *Studia Islamica* 86 (1997): 147.

8. Undated letter (1925) from Abdullah Cevdet to his wife, Fatma Hanım. He also provides information about his meeting with Mustafa Kemal in Abdullah Cevdet, "Gazi Paşa'nın Köşkünde," *Ictihad* 194 (December 15, 1925), pp. 3813–16; quoted in Hanioğlu, "Garbçılar," p. 147.

9. Erik Jan Zürcher, *Turkey: A Modern History* (London: I. B. Tauris, 2004), p. 168. Zürcher's book on the PRP is *Political Opposition in the Early Turkish Republic: The Progressive Republican Party, 1924–1925* (Leiden: E. J. Brill, 1991).

10. Turkish historian Zafer Toprak, during an interview given to journalist Neşe Düzel: "Atatürk Fransa'nın 3. Cumhuriyeti'ni kurdu" [Atatürk Founded France's Third Republic], *Taraf*, October 10, 2008.

11. Erik Jan Zürcher, remarks at the "Secularization and Modernization in Turkey" program held at Bilgi University, Istanbul, October 14, 2009.

12. Şerif A. Mardin, "Ideology and Religion in the Turkish Revolution," *International Journal of Middle East Studies* 2, no. 3 (July 1971): 208.

13. "Her yeri dolduran Türktür. Ve her yanı aydınlatan Türk'ün yüzüdür." *Daily Diyarbekir*, September 6, 1932; quoted in *Atatürk yılında Diyarbakır*, vol. 15 of *Kara-Amid* magazine, Diyarbakır, 1981, p. 8.

14. Moderate nationalists such as Ziya Gökalp had defined Turkishness as a cultural identity, whereas more radical individuals such as Yusuf Akçura emphasized ethnic purity. Kemalism, especially in the 1930s, accepted Akçura's version and praised "pure Turks" with Central Asian origins. Büşra Ersanlı, "Bir Aidiyet Fermanı: 'Türk Tarih Tezi'" [An Edict of Belonging: The Turkish Historical Thesis], in *Milliyetçilik* [Nationalism], ed. Tanıl Bora (Istanbul: İletişim Publishing, 2004), p. 802.

15. Martin van Bruinessen, "Race, Culture, Nation and Identity Politics in Turkey: Some Comments." Paper presented at the Mica Ertegün Annual Turkish Studies Workshop, Department of Near Eastern Studies, Princeton University, Princeton, NJ, April 24–26, 1997.

16. British journalist Grace Ellison observed as early as 1928 that Kemalism was gradually becoming "a new religion."; quoted in Mete Tunçay, *Türkiye Cumhuriyeti'nde Tek Parti Yönetiminin Kuruluşu* [The Establishment of the Single-Party Regime in Turkey] (Istanbul: Turkiye Araştırmaları Dizisi, 2005), pp. 332–38.

17. "Ey Samsun'da karaya çıkan ilâh," from a poem entitled "Bizim Mevlüt," by Behçet Kemal Çağlar.

18. "Kabe arabın olsun, Çankaya bize yeter!" from a poem entitled "Çankaya," by Kemalettin Kamu.

19. Taha Akyol, *Ama Hangi Atatürk* [But Which Atatürk] (Istanbul: Doğan Publishing, 2008), p. 179.

20. Eran Lerman, "Mawdudi's Concept of Islam," *Middle Eastern Studies* 17, no. 4 (October 1981): 493.

21. Wilfred Cantwell Smith, *Modern Islam in India: A Social Analysis* (London: Gollancz, 1946), p. 149.

22. Ibid., p. 68.

23. Pipes, *In the Path of God*, p. 122. As Pipes notes, public reactions to this April 1967 article ran so high that the Syrian regime confiscated the issue, blamed the article on American and Israeli agents, and severely punished the writer and the editor. Yet these face-saving actions probably were not enough to hide the real intentions of the regime.

24. Stephanie Cronin, ed., *The Making of Modern Iran: State and Society under Riza Shah, 1921–1941* (New York: Routledge Curzon, 2003), p. 202.

25. Ibid., pp. 202–4.

26. Ibid., p. 202.

27. Stephen Kinzer, *Reset: Iran, Turkey, and America's Future* (New York: Times Books, 2010), p. 78.

28. Cronin, ed., *Making of Modern Iran*, p. 196.

29. Ibid., p. 199.

30. Erol Güngör, *İslam'ın Bugünkü Meseleleri* [The Issues of Islam Today] (Istanbul: Ötüken Publishing, 1981), pp. 222–25. Güngör refers to Arnold Toynbee's *Civilization on Trial* (Oxford: Oxford University Press, 1948).

31. *Jewish Encyclopedia*, "Hellenism," http://www.jewishencyclopedia.com/view.jsp?letter=H&artid=567.

32. Ibid.

33. Mal Couch, ed., *A Bible Handbook to the Acts of the Apostles* (Grand Rapids, MI: Kregel Publications, 2004), p. 192.

34. Ibid.

35. James C. Vanderkam, *An Introduction to Early Judaism* (Grand Rapids, MI: Eerdmans, 2001), p. 41.

36. The longtime American policy of supporting pro-Western dictators in the Middle East was critically acknowledged by none other than Condoleezza Rice, the U.S. secretary of state under President George W. Bush. "We must

be clear," she said in 2006, "that we really believe that the people of the Middle East deserve a democratic future, something that American Presidents were not willing to say for 60 years. We were only concerned with stability, not with democracy, and we got neither." "Woman of the World," interview with Condoleezza Rice, *Reader's Digest*, September 2006.

37. Keddie, "The Revolt of Islam," p. 90.

38. Henry Munson, "Lifting the Veil: Understanding the Roots of Islamic Militancy," *Harvard International Review* 25, no. 4 (2004).

39. Thomas Hegghammer, "Jihadi Studies," *Sunday Times*, April 2, 2008.

40. From Bin Laden's 1998 *fatwa* on *jihad* against America. Quoted in Catherwood, *Brief History of the Middle East*, p. 257.

41. The sentence on collateral damage is from a cartoon by Jeff Danziger, syndicated cartoonist for the *New York Times*, August 8, 2006.

42. See Yvonne Haddad, *Islamists and the Challenge of Pluralism* (Washington, DC: Center for Contemporary Arab-Studies and Center for Muslim-Christian Understanding, Georgetown University, 1995), p. 10.

43. Lerman, "Mawdudi's Concept of Islam," p. 504.

44. Smith, *Modern Islam in India*, p. 149.

45. Charles J. Adams, "Mawdudi and the Islamic State," in John L. Esposito, ed., *Voices of Resurgent Islam* (New York: Oxford University Press, 1983), pp. 119–21.

46. Daniel Pipes, *Militant Islam Reaches America* (New York: W. W. Norton, 2003), p. 8.

47. Wilfred Cantwell Smith, *Islam in Modern History* (Princeton, NJ: Princeton University Press, 1957), pp. 94–95; Armstrong, *A History of God*, p. 367.

48. Armstrong, *A History of God*, p. 367.

49. For a connection between the experience of torture and radicalization, see Chris Zambelis, "Is There a Nexus between Torture and Radicalization?," *Terrorism Monitor* (Jamestown Foundation) 6, no. 13 (June 26, 2008).

50. See Peter L. Berger et al., eds., *The Desecularization of the World: Resurgent Religion and World Politics* (Grand Rapids, MI: Wm. B. Eerdmans Publishing, 1999).

CHAPTER EIGHT: THE TURKISH MARCH TO ISLAMIC LIBERALISM

1. Binder, *Islamic Liberalism*, p. 83.

2. http://henuzozgurolmadik.blogspot.com/.

3. Recep Peker, "Uluslaşma-Devletleşme" [Nationalization–State-Building], *Ülkü* 7, no. 40 (June 1936): I–VII, p. 3.

4. The center-periphery dichotomy was suggested as a good model for interpreting Turkish politics by Şerif Mardin in "Center-Periphery Relations: A Key to Turkish Politics?," *Daedalus* 102, no. 1 (Winter 1973): 169–90.

5. Mary F. Weld, *Bediüzzaman Said Nursi: Entellektüel Biyografisi* [His Intellectual Biography] (Istanbul: Etkileşim Publishing, 2006), p. 39.

6. Ibid., pp. 76, 77, 79.

7. Both the quote and the term *Homo kemalicus* are from M. Hakan Yavuz and John L. Esposito, eds., *Turkish Islam and the Secular State* (Syracuse, NY: Syracuse University Press, 2003), pp. 7, xxi.

8. "İslâm dünyasının bugünü" [The Islamic World Today], *Yeni Asya*, May 4, 2007.

9. Necmeddin Şahiner, *Son Şahitler Bediüzzaman Said Nursi'yi Anlatıyor* [The Last Witnesses Speak about Said Nursi] (Istanbul: Yeni Asya Publishing, 1994, p. 277.

10. Avni Özgürel, "Yassıada infazlarını unutmamak gerek" [Don't Forget the Executions of Yassıada], *Radikal*, September 20, 2009.

11. Şerif Mardin, "Turkish Islamic Exceptionalism Yesterday and Today: Continuity, Rupture and Reconstruction in Operational Codes," *Turkish Studies* 6, no. 2 (Summer 2005): 145.

12. Mehmet Şevket Eygi, *Bugün*, February 10, 1969.

13. The number of Nur followers in contemporary Turkey is estimated to be between two and six million. Yavuz and Esposito, *Turkish Islam and the Secular State*, p. 13.

14. Mehmet Metiner, *Yemyeşil Şeriat, Bembeyaz Demokrasi* [Strong Green Shariah, Snow White Democracy] (Istanbul: Doğan Publishing, 2004), p. 59.

15. Ibid., pp. 58, 59.

16. Ahmet Yaşar Ocak, *Türkler, Türkiye ve İslam* [Turks, Turkey and Islam] (Istanbul: İletişim Yayınları, 1999), p. 134.

17. Robert D. Kaplan, "At the Gates of Brussels," *The Atlantic*, December 2004.

18. Ibid.

19. Muhammed Çetin, "Business, Faith and Freedom," *Today's Zaman*, October 23, 2008.

20. In April 1998, Turkish newspapers started printing peculiar news stories linking several liberal journalists and the then-leader of the Human Rights Association (IHD) to a Kurdish terrorist group. The journalists lost their jobs and received death threats, while the leader of the IHD survived a near-fatal shooting. The two stories were proven false rather quickly, but it was not until 2000 that journalist Nazlı Ilıcak found evidence that the stories had been prepared on orders from the Turkish military. The case came to be called *Andıç*, a Turkish word unfamiliar to most, meaning "Memorandum."

21. "Tayyip'in Bitişi" [The End of Tayyip (Erdoğan)], *Hürriyet*, September 24, 1998; "Muhtar Bile Olamayacak" [He Won't Even Be a Local Governor], *Radikal*, September 24, 1998.

22. In his public speech in Siirt Province on December 6, 1997, Erdoğan recited part of a poem written in 1912 during the Ottoman Empire's endless

decade of war: "Mosques are our barracks, domes our helmets, minarets our bayonets, believers our soldiers." *Hürriyet*, September 24, 1998.

23. Ibid.

24. Nilüfer Narlı, "The Rise of the Islamist Movement in Turkey," *Middle East Review of International Affairs* 3, no. 3 (September 1999). Narlı observes this difference between Erbakan's Welfare Party and the Virtue Party that replaced it, but the factor that made the difference was the reformist movement within these two subsequent parties.

25. Sultan Tepe, "Turkey's AKP: A Model 'Muslim-Democratic' Party?," *Journal of Democracy* 16, no. 3 (July 2005): 69–82.

26. Fareed Zakaria, "A Quiet Prayer for Democracy," *Newsweek*, May 14, 2007.

27. "Turkish Armenians to Vote for Ruling AKP," *Armenian Online News*, July 13, 2007, http://www.hamovhotov.com/timeline/?p=860.

28. Mustafa Akyol, "The Protocols of the Elders of Turkey," *Washington Post*, October 7, 2007.

29. I wrote about this in Akyol, "AKP Is Not Islamist, But Somewhat Muslimist," *Hürriyet Daily News*, December 8, 2009.

30. Arınç gave this speech on April 16, 2007, at the Turgut Özal Thought and Action Society, which presented him with its annual Democracy Award.

31. According to the records of the Turkish National Library, only eighty-five books with a title mentioning "liberalism" were published in Turkey between 1923 (the beginning of the Turkish Republic) and 1980. The number rose to 507 between 1908 and 2008. Taha Akyol, "Liberalizm Açığı" [Liberalism Deficit], *Milliyet*, July 19, 2008. In academia, too, theses addressing "liberalism" or "liberal policies" are on the rise, from an average of six annually between 1989 and 1999 to an annual average of twenty-one between 2000 and 2007. Taha Akyol, "Üniversite ve Liberalizm" [The University and Liberalism], *Milliyet*, August 14, 2008.

32. A statement by former Turkish Islamist Mehmet Metiner, explaining why the Islamists in Turkey began to adopt more liberal views after the 1980s. "Fears for Turkey's Future Roil Vote on Constitution," *Wall Street Journal*, September 9, 2010.

33. Aydın's suggestion that the Islamic world needs "liberal democratic culture" to solve its ideological disputes appeared in an interview in *Zaman*, March 23, 1998.

34. Sadik Ünay, *Neoliberal Globalization and Institutional Reform: The Political Economy of Development and Planning in Turkey* (New York: Nova Publishers, 2006), p. 37.

35. The prime minister at the time, Şükrü Saraçoğlu, and his foreign minister, Numan Menemencioğlu, had good relations with and a sympathetic attitude toward Nazi Germany.

36. Reşat Kasaba, ed., *The Cambridge History of Turkey*, vol. 4 (Cambridge, UK: Cambridge University Press, 2008), pp. 182–83.

37. Orhan Pamuk, *Istanbul: Memories of a City* (New York: Vintage Books, 2006), p. 183.

38. Hüner Sencan, *İş Hayatında İslam İnsani* [Homo Islamicus in Business Life] (Istanbul: MÜSİAD, 1994).

39. Feroz Ahmad, "The Development of Capitalism in Turkey," *Journal of Third World Studies* (Fall 1998).

40. European Stability Initiative, *Islamic Calvinists: Change and Conservatism in Central Anatolia*, September 19, 2005, Berlin/Istanbul, www.esiweb.org, pp. 23–24.

41. Ibid., p. 24.

42. Ibid.

43. Zafer Özcan, "Akla ve Paraya İhtiyacı Olmayan Şehir Kayseri" [Kayseri, the City that Needs Neither Wisdom nor Money], *Aksiyon* 571 (November 14, 2005).

44. See Ziya Öniş, "Conservative Globalists Versus Defensive Nationalists: Political Parties and Paradoxes of Europeanization in Turkey," *Journal of Balkan and Near Eastern Studies*, vol. 9, no. 3 (December 2007).

45. "Türkiye'nin gerçek burjuva sınıfı biziz" [We Are the Real Bourgeois Class of Turkey], *Star*, July 20, 2009.

46. Ibid.

47. Ali Çarkoğlu and Binnaz Toprak, *Religion, Society and Politics in a Changing Turkey* (Istanbul: TESEV [Turkish Economic and Social Studies Foundation] Publications, 2007), pp. 101, 33.

48. The comparison to the Taliban comes from ex-Islamist Mehmet Metiner, who says, "We were thinking like the Taliban in the 70s," in *Yemyeşil Şeriat, Bembeyaz Demokrasi*, p. 17.

49. Mehmet Şevket Eygi, "Yanlış Kıraatler" [Wrong Readings], *Milli Gazete*, January 14, 2009. In this case, the term *mujahid* does not imply a violent movement. The term has been used often in Turkey to refer to committed Islamists who want to serve the cause by political, social, and intellectual action.

50. Kenan Çayır, *Türkiye'de İslamcılık ve İslami Edebiyat: Toplu Hidayet Söyleminden Yeni Bireysel Müslümanlıklara* [Islamism and Islamic Literature in Turkey: From the Rhetoric of Collective Salvation to New Individualistic Muslimhoods] (Istanbul: Bilgi University Press, 2007), p. 128.

51. Ibid.

52. Ibid., p. 118.

53. Ali Bardakoğlu, "Dindarlığımızın Güncelleştirilmesi" [The Updating of Our Religiosity], interview in *Hürriyet*, September 10, 2004.

54. "'Kadının en makbulü koyun' diyen hadis olmaz" [No Hadith Can Say, "The Best Woman Is like a Sheep"], *Vatan*, June 17, 2006.

55. For more, see Mustafa Akyol, "[Sexism Deleted] in Turkey," *Washington Post*, July 16, 2006.

56. Personal interview with Dr. Mehmet Görmez, Istanbul, May 14, 2009.

57. All quotes are from Mehmet Şevki Aydın's articles in the *Diyanet* magazine: October 2008, pp. 20–23; December 2008, pp. 24–27; November 2008, pp. 20–23.

58. "Dinlerini anlatmak en doğal hakları," *Hürriyet*, April 21, 2009.

59. "Top Turkish Religious Official Says Saint Paul Church Should Be Reopened," *Hürriyet Daily News*, August 23, 2010.

60. Ali Bulaç, "Azınlık, Zımmi, Muahid!" [Minority, Dhimmi, Contractee], *Zaman*, January 6, 2010.

61. All quotes are from Hayrettin Karaman's articles in *Yeni Şafak*: "Necat Konusu," August 29, 2008; "Dinden Dönen Öldürülür mü?," September 11, 2009; "İslam Ülkelerinde Demokrasi," August 4, 2006; "Dine Zorlamak," September 24, 2006.

62. Hayrettin Karaman, "Kadınlarla Tokalaşmak," *Yeni Şafak*, September 9, 2009.

63. "Dayak yiyen kadın karete öğrensin," *Radikal*, October 26, 2008.

64. Sami Hocaoğlu, "Kur'an kitaplığına yeni katkılar" [New Contributions to Qur'an Library], *Yeni Şafak*, June 28, 2004.

65. Dücane Cündioğlu, "Düşünürken modern, inanırken geleneksel" [Modern While Thinking, Traditional While Believing], *Yeni Şafak*, December 13, 2009. Cündioğlu, a conservative who is highly critical of Islamic capitalism, says this disapprovingly.

66. Zakaria, *Future of Freedom*, p. 73.

67. Vali Nasr, *Forces of Fortune: The Rise of the New Muslim Middle Class and What It Will Mean for Our World* (New York: Free Press, 2009).

68. Graham E. Fuller, *The New Turkish Republic: Turkey as a Pivotal State in the Muslim World* (Washington, DC: U.S. Institute of Peace Press, 2008).

69. Ibid., p. 49.

70. See Kinzer, *Reset*, p. 198. This new Turkey can actually be more helpful to America, argues Kinzer, formerly the *New York Times* bureau chief in Turkey. Now, he asserts, "Turkey can go places, engage partners, and make deals that America cannot."

71. Nazanine Moshiri, "Interview with Rachid Ghannouchi," Al Jazeera English website, February 3, 2011.

72. Soner Çağaptay, "Arab Revolt Makes Turkey a Regional Power," *Hürriyet Daily News*, February 16, 2011.

73. Olivier Roy, "This Is Not an Islamic Revolution," *New Statesman*, February 15, 2011.

74. Olivier Roy, "Where Were the Tunisian Islamists?," *International Herald Tribune*, January 21, 2011.

75. Walter Russell Mead, *God and Gold: Britain, America, and the Making of the Modern World* (New York: Alfred A. Knopf, 2007), p. 372.

CHAPTER NINE: FREEDOM FROM THE STATE

1. Vincent Cornell, "Islam: Theological Hostility and the Problem of Difference," King Fahd Center for the Middle East and Islamic Studies, University of Arkansas, http://www.worde.org/articles/Cornell_Islam-TheologicalHostility.php.

2. Tariq Ramadan, *In the Footsteps of the Prophet* (New York: Oxford University Press, 2007), p. 103.

3. Afsaruddin, *First Muslims*, p. 17.

4. Qur'an 8:1, Bewley translation, with Arabic words anglicized.

5. Seyyed Hossein Nasr, *The Heart of Islam: Enduring Values of Humanity* (New York: HarperOne, 2002), p. 147. Nasr argues that the Shiite ideal is nomocracy, too—and that theocracy was established in the Shiite world only with the 1979 Iranian Revolution.

6. The most dramatic example of this was the late-nineteenth-century "Mahdi" in Sudan, Muhammad Ahmad bin Abd Allah. He, like the Wahhabis, rebelled against the Ottomans and declared, "Let everyone who finds a Turk kill him, for the Turks are infidels." He ultimately lost to the British. P. M. Holt, *The Mahdist State in Sudan* (Oxford: Clarendon Press, 1958), p. 51.

7. Qur'an 4:59, Shakir translation.

8. Qur'an 42:38, Bewley translation.

9. Afsaruddin, *First Muslims*, p. 26.

10. Ibid., p. 190.

11. Esposito, ed., *Oxford History of Islam*, p. 146.

12. See Michelangelo Guida, "Seyyid Bey and the Abolition of the Caliphate," *Middle Eastern Studies* 44, no. 2 (March 2008); Abdelwahab El-Affendi, *Who Needs an Islamic State?* (London: Malaysia Think Tank, 2008), pp. 85–88.

13. Kemalettin Nomer, *Şeriat, Hilafet, Laiklik* [Shariah, Caliphate, Secularity] (Istanbul: Boğaziçi Publishing, 1996), p. 380.

14. El-Affendi, *Who Needs an Islamic State?*, p. 83.

15. Ibid., p. 69.

16. http://www.hizb-ut-tahrir.org/english/books/hizb-ut-Tahrir/chapter_09.html.

17. El-Affendi, *Who Needs an Islamic State?*, p. 33.

18. See chapter 3.

19. This occurred in Pakistan in the late 1970s and 1980s, when General Zia ul-Haqq initiated his policy of "the Islamization of laws." Soon it turned out that each of Pakistan's diverse groups wanted implementation of its own version of the Shariah, and, in the end, Zia could handle the escalating tension only by adopting martial law, which was secular. Taha Akyol,

Medine'den Lozan'a, pp. 203–9; Mohammad Amin, *Islamization of Laws in Paki-stan* (Lahore: Sang e Meel Publications, 1989).

20. Abdullahi Ahmed An-Na'im, "Thomas Jefferson, Islam and the State, *Huffington Post*, March 20, 2008.

21. An-Na'im, *Islam and the Secular State*, p. 1.

22. For an interesting analysis of the matter, see Ahmet T. Kuru, *Secularism and State Policies toward Religion: The United States, France, and Turkey* (New York: Cambridge University Press, 2009).

23. Here An-Na'im only argues (*Islam and the Secular State*, p. 139) that the way to practice Islamic politics must be through "civic reason, which means that reasons can be debated among all citizens without reference to religious beliefs." Muslims can promote policies that derive from their beliefs, in other words, but they should use the voice of reason to bring them to the public square, which would include secular or non-Muslim people, or simply Mus-lims with different political views.

24. Caliph Umar banned some practices that were allowed in the Qur'an— such as marriage to non-Muslim women and "timed marriage"—and sus-pended the implementation of others, such as cutting off the hands of thieves and distributing conquered lands among the soldiers. In each case, he showed the possible negative implications as his justification. Mehmet Erdoğan, *İslam Hukukunda Ahkamın Değişmesi* [The Change of Verdicts in Islamic Law] (Istan-bul: M. Ü. İlahiyat Fakültesi Vakfı Yayınları, 1990), pp. 51, 161.

25. All statements come from http://www.islam4uk.com.

26. Muhammad Bin Ahmed al-Sarakhsi, *Sharh Kitab al-Siyar al-Kabir* (Paki-stan: Nusrullah Mansour, 1405 AH/1985 AD, 4:1530; cited in Safi, "Over-coming the Religious-Secular Divide," p. 19.

27. El-Affendi, *Who Needs an Islamic State?*, p. 19.

28. Olivier Roy, "Islam in Europe: The Exception to the Rule?," Eurotopics. net, May 2, 2007. In the same article, Roy also observes: "Salafism, the type of Islam to which many born-again Muslims in Europe adhere, explicitly opposes all national cultures, including Islamic ones, and demands a religion purified of all cultural influences and local flavor. That also explains why Salafism attracts culturally uprooted young people like second-generation Muslims in Europe . . . . In contrast, one finds that the Turkish expatriate population throughout the rest of Europe continues to be closely connected to Turkey (by means of its language, television, and various organizations) and is rarely involved in acts of Islamic terrorism. This shows that practiced Islam is less radical the stronger the ties to the country of origin are."

29. Ian Buruma and Avishai Margalit, *Occidentalism: The West in the Eyes of Its Enemies* (New York: Penguin Press, 2004), p. 43.

30. These are the words of Umar Farouk Abdulmutallab, the twenty-three-year-old Nigerian who tried to blow up a passenger airliner near Detroit

on Christmas Day 2009. "I imagine how the great *jihad* will take place," he reportedly wrote in a February 2005 Internet post, "how the Muslims will win, God willing, and rule the whole world, and establish the greatest empire once again!!!" Margaret Wente, "The Global Internet Jihad: Web of Terror," *Globe and Mail*, January 8, 2010.

31. Qur'an 109:6, M. Pickthall translation, http://www.islam101.com/quran/QTP/index.htm.

32. As discussed in chapter 1.

33. In classical Islam, there is no concept of an "Islamic economy." The idea emerged in the twentieth century, crystallizing in the 1960s as part of Islamist thinking. Timur Kuran, "On the Notion of Economic Justice in Contemporary Islamic Thought," in Haleh Esfandiari and A. L. Udovitch, eds., *The Economic Dimensions of Middle Eastern History* (Princeton, NJ: Darwin Press, Princeton, 1990), p. 94.

CHAPTER TEN: FREEDOM TO SIN

1. Alexis de Tocqueville, "Letter to Beaumont," quoted in Jack Lively, *The Social and Political Thought of Alexis de Tocqueville* (Oxford: Clarendon Press, 1962), p. 13.

2. Qur'an 107:4, 6, Bewley translation, with Arabic words anglicized.

3. Qur'an 2:256, Shakir translation.

4. Qur'an 10:99, Shakir translation.

5. Qur'an 3:104, Shakir translation.

6. Cook, *Commanding Right and Forbidding Wrong in Islamic Thought*, p. 22.

7. Ibid., p. 23.

8. Ibid., p. 24 (emphases by Cook).

9. Ibid., p. 24.

10. Ibid., pp. 427–59.

11. Qur'an 2:256.

12. Van Ess, *Flowering of Muslim Theology*, p. 30.

13. Mead, *God and Gold*, p. 370.

14. Ibid., p. 371.

15. The Qur'an (24:27–28, Shakir translation) states: "O you who believe! Do not enter houses other than your own houses until you have asked permission and saluted their inmates; this is better for you, that you may be mindful. But if you do not find any one therein, then do not enter them until permission is given to you; and if it is said to you: Go back, then go back; this is purer for you; and Allah is Cognizant of what you do."

16. Cook, *Commanding Right and Forbidding Wrong in Islamic Thought*, p. 542.

17. Ali Kurani, *Amr Bah Ma'ruf wa Nahy Az Munkar*, Tehran 1373 sh., 3.9, 7.12; quoted in Cook, *Commanding Right and Forbidding Wrong in Islamic Thought*, p. 556.

18. Robert Lacey, "The Secret Behind the Veil: Saudi Women Find Solace in 'Safe Love,'" *Sunday Times*, October 18, 2009.

19. Muhammad Sa'id Al-'Ashmawi, "Shari'a: The Codification of Islamic Law," in *Liberal Islam*, ed. Kurzman, p. 52.

20. Even traditional scholars made a distinction between extramarital and premarital sex; they prescribed stoning for the former (which doesn't exist in the Qur'an) and lashes for the latter (which is the real punishment dictated by the Qur'an for adultery and the calumnious accusation of it). Meanwhile, the beginning of the Sura Noor (chapter 24 of the Qur'an), which specifies the punishment for adultery, speaks about the married woman and her husband, which might suggest that adultery happens only when there is a married couple and the bond of marriage between them is violated.

21. For a defense of this argument, see Charfi, *Islam and Liberty*, p. 58. Charfi is a law professor in Tunis.

22. For those who might be horrified by the idea that extramarital sex can be penalized, it might be worthwhile to note that laws in twenty-four of America's fifty states still regard adultery as a crime. Jonathan Turley, "Of Lust and the Law," *Washington Post*, September 5, 2004.

23. "Diyanet'ten Van kriterleri: İslam dünyasında bir 'ilk'" [A First in the Muslim World: The Van Criteria from the Diyanet], *Hürriyet*, June 5, 2008.

24. Şükrü Küçükşahin, "Koç: İnsanın günah işleme özgürlüğü var," *Hürriyet*, July 20, 2006. Minister of Culture and Tourism Atilla Koç, quoted in this story, also said, "It is against the spirit of religion to try to create heaven on Earth" and "Herkesin günah işleme özgürlüğü var" [Everyone has the freedom to sin], *Vatan*, January 10, 2009; Fatma K. Barbarosoğlu, "Günah işleme özgürlüğü" [Freedom to Sin], *Yeni Şafak*, October 1, 2004. I, too, have written about the freedom to sin: Mustafa Akyol, "Bırakınız İçsinler" [Let Them Drink], *Star*, June 20, 2009.

25. Qur'an 16:61, Shakir translation.

26. Qur'an 103:3, Shakir translation.

27. Qur'an 5:94, Bewley translation, with Arabic words anglicized.

CHAPTER ELEVEN: FREEDOM FROM ISLAM

1. "U.S. Cautiously Backs Afghan Christian," WorldNetDaily (www.wnd .com), March 22, 2006.

2. *No Place to Call Home: Experiences of Apostates from Islam, Failures of the International Community* (New Malden, Surrey, UK: Christian Solidarity Worldwide, 2008), p. 4.

3. Ibid.

4. *Sahih Bukhari*, vol. 4, bk. 52, no. 260.

5. *No Place to Call Home*, p. 8.

6. A. E. Mayer, *Islam and Human Rights: Tradition and Politics* (Boulder, CO: Westview Press, 1999), p. 27.

7. Qur'an 18:29.

8. Qur'an 4:137, Shakir translation.

9. Avcı, *Osmanlı Hukukunda Suçlar ve Cezalar*, pp. 388, 389.

10. Friedmann, *Tolerance and Coercion in Islam*, p. 126.

11. Afsaruddin, *First Muslims*, p. 27.

12. El-Affendi, *Who Needs an Islamic State?*, pp. 61–62.

13. Friedmann, *Tolerance and Coercion in Islam*, p. 126.

14. David Forte, "Islam's Trajectory," http://www.realclearpolitics.com/articles/2006/08/islams_trajectory.html, accessed October 23, 2006.

15. Friedmann, *Tolerance and Coercion in Islam*, p. 101.

16. Kamali, *Freedom of Expression in Islam*, p. 93.

17. Ibid.

18. Avcı, *Osmanlı Hukukunda Suçlar ve Cezalar*, p. 383.

19. Kamali, *Freedom of Expression in Islam*, p. 97.

20. Ibid., p. 96.

21. Hourani, *Arabic Thought in the Liberal Age*, p. 237.

22. "Grand Ayatollah Hossein-Ali Montazeri: 'Not Every Conversion Is Apostasy'" (in Persian). *BBC Persia* Service, October 14, 2009.

23. For a list, see Mohammad Omar Farooq, "On Apostasy and Islam: 100+ Notable Islamic Voices Affirming the Freedom of Faith," http://apostasyandislam.blogspot.com/.

24. Friedmann, *Tolerance and Coercion in Islam*, p. 5.

25. Qur'an 6:108, Bewley translation, with Arabic words anglicized.

26. That slogan and others, such as "Butcher those who mock Islam" and "Slay those who insult Islam," were carried on placards during a London rally held to protest Danish cartoons satirizing the Prophet Muhammad. "Arrest Extremist Marchers, Police Told," *The Guardian*, February 6, 2006.

27. Leviticus 24:16.

28. Thomas Aquinas, *Summa Theologica* 2:2, q. 13.

29. Kamali, *Freedom of Expression in Islam*, p. 249.

30. Ibid., p. 249.

31. Qur'an 4:140, Shakir translation.

32. Qur'an 6:67, Shakir translation.

33. Qur'an 28:55, Shakir translation.

34. Qur'an 4:152, Shakir translation, with Arabic words anglicized.

35. Orhan Pamuk got into trouble with the "insulting Turkishness" laws during an interview with a Swiss journal, *Das Magazin*, in February 2005, when he said: "Thirty thousand Kurds have been killed here [in Turkey], and a million Armenians. And almost nobody dares to mention that. So I do." After prosecution, and an international outcry, charges were dropped in 2006.

36. One tragic case was the 2007 assassination of Hrant Dink, a Turkish Armenian journalist, by a young ultranationalist who believed that some of Dink's criticisms of Turkish nationalism constituted "insulting Turkishness."

37. Ecumenical Patriarch Bartholomew I of Constantinople paid tribute to this Muslim sensitivity for the Virgin Mary during a speech on August 15, 2010, at the ancient Sümela Monastery, in northeastern Turkey, which was then reopened for Christian worship after eighty-eight years. "Bartholomew I celebrates first Mass at Our Lady of Sumela after 88 years," *AsiaNews.it*, August 16, 2010.

38. Qur'an 13:1, Bewley translation, with Arabic words anglicized.

39. Qur'an 5:48, Bewley translation, with Arabic words anglicized.

40. There are other verses that herald "victory" against the unbelievers— those are the ones that the champions of the Islam-will-conquer-the-world argument love to quote. But those verses refer to the specific war—an existential one—between the early Muslim community and the Meccan pagans who tried to annihilate them. Instead of a theory of "abrogation," which implies a contradiction in the Qur'an, the better way of understanding these various verses is to regard the pluralism verses as the norm and the victory verses as relevant to cases of war.

41. Qur'an 3:20, Bewley translation, with Arabic words anglicized.

Epilogue

1. Reuel Marc Gerecht, *The Wave: Man, God, and the Ballot Box in the Middle East* (Stanford: Hoover Institution Press, 2011), p. 6.

2. The term *liberal* should be used with some caution, because a common mistake in the West is to envision all anti-Islamist forces in the Middle East as "liberals." This is wildly inaccurate, for there is a decades-long history of secular dictatorship in the region, with elements that are still active—in Arabic they are called *feloul*, or "the remnants." These forces are certainly secular, but they also are illiberal, antidemocratic, and often corrupt. Hence they have no moral high ground to claim against the Islamists. A second mistake that is common in Western media is a more nuanced one: disregard of the fact that even some of the genuine liberals in the Middle East have an elitist prejudice against the Islamists, who often represent the less affluent segments of their societies.

3. See my article: "How Tahrir Square Betrayed Itself," *Hürriyet Daily News*, July 6, 2013.

4. In the wake of Egypt's military coup, a spokesman for deposed President Morsi indeed said, "Democracy is not for Muslims." See Behzad Yaghmaian, "The Price of Terminating Democracy in Egypt," *Wall Street Journal*, July 7, 2013.

5. For a more detailed version of this argument, see Noah Feldman, "Democracy Loses in Struggle for Egypt's Presidency," *Bloomberg View*, July 6, 2013.

6. Olivier Roy, "The Myth of the Islamist Winter," *New Statesman*, December 13, 2012.

7. See my article: "AKP Is Too Turkish—Not Too Islamic," *Hürriyet Daily News*, February 1, 2012. Thomas Carothers and Nathan J. Brown also argue: "Turkey's democratic troubles are not due to Islamist illiberalism on the part of the AKP, but rather the habits of political overreach and arrogance common to dominant parties everywhere, no matter what their ideological or religious stripes," in "The Real Danger for Egyptian Democracy," Carnegieendowment.org, November 12, 2012, http://carnegieendowment.org/2012/11/12/real-danger-for-egyptian-democracy/eg5z.

8. Ihsan Dagı, "Pursuing Islamism with Democracy," *Today's Zaman*, December 9, 2012.

9. Ibid.

10. A hard-core Islamist website condemns the Muslim Brotherhood for being too soft on alcohol: "Muslim Brotherhood Reassures Tourists: Alcohol and Women Will Be There," Kavkazcenter.com, December 28, 2011, http://kavkazcenter.com/eng/content/2011/12/28/15563.shtml.

11. The term *illiberal moderates* was coined by Amitai Etzioni, professor of international relations at George Washington University, Washington, DC, to define the mainstream Muslim political attitude in the contemporary world. See Amitai Etzioni, "Illiberal Moderates: The Global Swing Vote," *Huffington Post*, June 12, 2007, http://www.huffingtonpost.com/amitai-etzioni/illiberal-moderates-the-g_b_51761.html.

12. See Abdullah Saeed, "Rethinking Citizenship Rights of Non-Muslims in an Islamic State: Rashid Al-Ghannushi's Contribution to the Evolving Debate," *Islam and Christian-Muslim Relations*, vol. 10. no. 3 (1999).

13. Caryle Murphy, "Saudi Youth Question Traditional Approach to Islam," *Al-Monitor*, February 4, 2013, http://www.al-monitor.com/pulse/originals/2013/02/saudi-youth-question-mohammed-al-ari-tom-cruise-of-wahhabism.html.

14. Ibid.

15. Ibid.

16. Leonard Binder, *Islamic Liberalism* (Chicago: University of Chicago Press, 1988), p. 19.

Index

Page numbers in *italics* refer to maps.